Christmas 2022.

    Dear Krissy and James.

As you had expressed an
interest in travelling to the
Highlands at same point,
This book gives a great
    introduction — enjoy!

    Lots of love,
        Kathryn xoxo.

THE HIGHLANDS

THE HIGHLANDS

PAUL MURTON

BIRLINN

Previous spread. Loch Tay

First published in 2021 by
Birlinn Limited
West Newington House
10 Newington Road
Edinburgh
EH9 1QS

www.birlinn.co.uk

Maps drawn by Helen Stirling
Contains Ordnance Survey Data
© Crown copyright and Database copyright 2021

The maps in this book are for the purposes of general
orientation only and serve as a guide to the location of
many of the key places mentioned in the text

ISBN: 978 1 78027 721 9

British Library Cataloguing-in-Publication Data
A catalogue record for this book is available
from the British Library

Designed and typeset by Mark Blackadder

Printed and Bound by Bell & Bain Ltd, Glasgow

CONTENTS

INTRODUCTION

The Scottish Highlands cover a vast area of northern Scotland. This book concentrates on the 'classic' Highlands – the Grampians. The region is bounded by the Highland Boundary Fault in the south, the western limit is largely formed by the Trossachs and the A82 as the road heads across Rannoch Moor towards Glencoe. The lochs of the Great Glen and the Caledonian Canal mark the northern border, and the eastern edge roughly follows the eastern boundary of the Cairngorms National Park as it meanders over high tops towards the Angus Glens.

For most of my life I have lived on the edge of the Scottish Highlands – first on the shores of Loch Long in Argyll – historically the 'ship loch' of galleys, birlinns and Viking longships. Backing onto Beinn Ruadh where my father's ashes were scattered by the Atlantic winds, my childhood home looked south and west towards the Firth of Clyde and the Lowlands, while to the north, craggy hills rose in steep waves towards the mountains of the Arrochar Alps and Breadalbane. As a student at the University of Aberdeen, I was continually drawn west to the mountains of the Mounth and the Cairngorms, spending weekends and holidays hitch-hiking to find the freedom of the high places, clearing my mind of the clutter of study and essay writing by climbing Lochnagar or following Jock's Road across the purple scented moors. After more than a decade of absence, I returned before the millennium to live in the lee of the mountains in a house that sits just yards from the Highland Boundary Fault. To the south lie Flanders Moss and the Carse of Stirling. To the north lie the woods and forest-clad Menteith Hills. Beyond them, the land rises to meet the peaks of Ben Venue, Ben Ledi, Ben Vorlich and Stuc a' Chroin, mountains lying on the edge of the southern Highlands.

The novelist Sir Walter Scott, the 'Wizard of the North' was impelled by the romantic notion that human character is shaped by the landscape. In his celebrated novels, Highland protagonists reflect the rugged environment that bears down on them. This is a world where a heroic landscape creates heroic people – men and women whose spirits are Highland – wild, untamed, and true to nature. While I don't buy into the idea that Highland living confers a degree of moral and existential authenticity that's unavailable to less fortunate mortals, I think it's true that the Highlands, as a physical entity, can have a profound effect on most people, visitors and natives alike. They certainly have had on me. The ancient landscape of the Highlands has helped shape my view of the world and has influenced the person I have become. My heart, you could say, is in the Highlands.

But what are the Highlands? The obvious answer is a geological one, I suppose. As my brother, The Professor of Geology, likes to point out, the Highlands are separated from the rest of Scotland by the geological fault line that runs from Arran and the Cowal peninsula in the south-west to Stonehaven in the north-east: the Highlands are everything lying to the north of the Highland Boundary Fault. But I argue that there is much more to the Highlands than this fixed geological reality. The Highlands are also a concept: mountains of the mind, peaks and rock spires of the imagination, a landscape of myth and legend. The Highlands we experience have a set of unique qualities that have nothing to do with rocks and fault lines, and everything to do with our response to the landscape, which has changed over time as 'ways of seeing' have evolved.

Early travellers regarded mountain environments as harsh, alien and hostile, a view that was informed by notions of natural beauty that derived from scripture. For generations the ideal landscape was epitomised by the Garden of Eden: a sacred, fertile world of abundance where humanity could flourish. The countryside of the English shires, with its well-tended fields and bucolic scenes, seemed closer to this concept of natural beauty than anything north of the Highland fault line. Having learned to admire tamer landscapes, southern visitors to the Highlands considered themselves a long way from Eden when confronted by wild weather, barren hillsides and windswept moors.

The author, soldier and government spy Daniel Defoe, who toured the whole length of Britain in 1724–26, described the Highlands as a 'barren and frightful country . . . full of hideous desert mountains and unpassable, except to the Highlanders who possess the precipices'. For Defoe, and many others like him, this was a land of robbers and murderous clans whose principal occupation seemed to be cattle rustling and fighting – a land where the natives spoke with a foreign tongue and whose manners, customs and dress were from a completely different world.

The existence of this other world was well known to all Scots who lived on the other side of the Highland fault line. For centuries, Scotland was a kingdom divided into Highlands and Lowlands. Scottish monarchs fought bloodily for control over their northern neighbours, whom they regarded as an uncivilised rabble and who frequently plundered the fertile Lowlands for livestock, goods and even women. Preyed-upon Lowland farmers and smallholders came to hate everything about the wild men of the north, their culture and their mountainous homeland.

It is also true that Highlanders regarded the Lowlands and southern society as an equally alien and threatening culture, whose destructive influence was spreading year by year into their domain – into the *Gàidhealtachd* – a land where an ancient Celtic society was still dominated by warrior clan traditions. Seeing the inexorable material and social rise of the Lowlands, Highlanders feared for the future of their culture and independence and did whatever they could to resist change. They felt isolated and surrounded by southerners – *Sassunach* – the Gaelic word for Saxon, was a term that was applied to most foreigners.

In the 18th century, two Jacobite rebellions – or risings as their supporters called them – further exacerbated the Highland–Lowland divide. In 1745, Charles Edward Stuart, Bonnie Prince Charlie, arrived in the Highlands with high hopes of reclaiming the crowns of the United Kingdom, no money and only a handful of supporters. His presence in the *Gàidhealtachd* aroused ancient feelings of loyalty, and the dream of a Gaelic cultural renaissance. Several naturally conservative clans answered the call and rallied to the Royal Stuart standard. The army eventually assembled by Bonnie Prince Charlie comprised in large part Gaelic-speaking Highlanders. The Presbyterian, Protestant Lowlands mostly ignored the prince's

On the shores of Loch Lomond, at the start of the Highlands.

call, and looked on warily as the Jacobites marched south, scattering government troops in their wake.

The eventual defeat of the Jacobite cause in 1746 pierced the heart of the old *Gàidhealtachd*. Bonnie Prince Charlie spent five months on the run in the Highlands – a fugitive protected by devoted Highlanders. The prince and many of his key Jacobite supporters then fled to continental Europe, but the fate of the Highlands was sealed. The *Gàidhealtachd* became a militarised zone under an army of occupation. Jacobites were hunted down, imprisoned, transported to the colonies, or executed in large numbers. Tartan was banned and so was wearing the plaid as the victorious government clamped down on Highland culture. In fact, just about everything that people today identify as Highland was then seen in a negative light, representing all things uncivilised, rebellious, primitive, impoverished, wild, inhospitable and alien.

Glencoe – the heart of the Highlands.

But once the Highlands and its inhabitants had been safely subdued, attitudes changed and outsiders began to make journeys of discovery into this unknown land. They began to see the people and the landscape through different eyes. A generation after the Jacobite defeat at the Battle of Culloden, the story of Bonnie Prince Charlie and his failed rebellion chimed with a new artistic and cultural movement – Romanticism – which drew from a deep well of emotion, unrequited love and heroic failure, where reason was the slave of the passions. The Highlands – its people and decaying culture – had these attributes in abundance. These were the elements that inspired Sir Walter Scott to weave narratives set in the Highlands. Scott drew the Highlands as a place of magic, mystery and adventure, where the natives were brave, noble human beings. Scott's tremendous popular success created a new phenomenon – the tourist seeking a taste of Highland adventure.

Among the first tourists was Sarah Murray, who came to the Highlands on a quest to discover the picturesque and the sublime. Sarah found both in spades – usually in the guise of raging torrents and waterfalls – and wrote gushingly about her experiences in her hugely enjoyable book *A Companion and Useful Guide to the Beauties of Scotland*, first published in 1799. I quote liberally from its pages, partly for its insights into the Highlands of the 18th century, and partly because it is very entertaining.

Sarah Murray was a 52-year-old widow from Kensington when she embarked on her travels. She had married late in life. Her husband was a Scotsman, Captain William Murray, the third son of the Earl of Dunmore in Perthshire. Sadly, after just three years of wedlock Captain Murray died. In her grief, Sarah's desire to know the land of her husband's birth more intimately grew. In May 1796, she left London with her maid by her side while her manservant took the outside seat of her horse-drawn carriage. In her book she offers instruction to the would-be traveller: 'Provide yourself with a strong, roomy carriage, and have the springs well corded; have also a stop-pole and a strong chain to the chaise. Take with you linchpins, and four shackles, which hold up the braces of the body of the carriage; a turn-screw, fit for fastening the nuts belonging to the shackles; a hammer and some straps.'

Practical advice. In Sarah's day, the roads in Scotland were little more than rough cart tracks, full of potholes and steep inclines (what's changed?) – so the tourist had to be prepared for all challenges – especially having sufficient food to get him or her through an uncertain day. Sarah considered it essential to have a good quantity of wine on board – in case of emergencies – and worthwhile to pay extra for a reliable and sober driver. To keep her man Allan sweet, she gave him an extra half-crown a week – an enormous sum in those days. Probably worth it if you didn't want to spill your wine!

After Sarah Murray, other tourists arrived on the scene. Many were following Scott's literary trail and keen to visit the scenes described in his epic poems and novels. *Black's Picturesque Guide to Scotland* was on hand to help. Full of literary quotes, *Black's* was among the best-known early guidebooks available. I frequently quote from its pages too, to demonstrate how little or how much things have changed in the Highlands and how ways of seeing the landscape have altered over time. First published in 1840 in Edinburgh, *Black's Guide* remained in print for nearly a century. My father always kept a copy in the glove compartment of his car when we went on holiday. With its elegant engravings of Highland views and beautifully produced maps, the battered old green book became an early inspiration for my own travels across Scotland, first as a teenage hitch-hiker and later as a film-maker.

Another early inspiration was W. H. Murray's incomparable *Mountaineering in Scotland*. Murray wrote his book in a German prisoner of war camp during the Second World War. His pioneering account of Scottish climbing during the 1930s had me spellbound. The quality of his prose and his instinctive rapport with the natural world encouraged me to look more intently at the landscape of the Highlands.

So, with a backward glance and a nod to my illustrious predecessors, I offer you my own guide to the central Highlands.

PART ONE

**EXPLORING THE LOCHS OF THE TROSSACHS, THEN ON TO
BALQUHIDDER, GLEN OGLE AND CRIANLARICH**

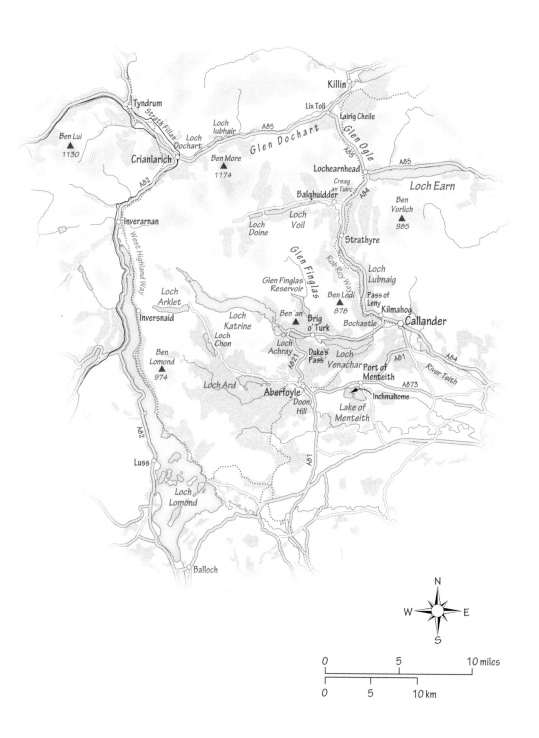

CALLANDER TO LOCH ACHRAY

The Highlands in miniature – Romans and the last witch – *The Lady of the Lake*

Lying on the Highland Boundary Fault to the north of the big cities of central Scotland is an area of astonishing beauty that has attracted and inspired visitors for the last 200 years. The scenic charms of the Trossachs include lochs, waterfalls, ancient woods and craggy mountains, all bound together by an atmosphere of romance, mystery and legend. Because of its relative accessibility, the Trossachs became a destination for southern writers and artists in the late 18th and early 19th centuries, creative souls who were the vanguard of the Romantic movement. Their interpretation of the dramatic scenery triggered a flood of visitors wanting to experience for themselves the picturesque and the sublime in the melancholy perfection of the views and the thrilling sensations provided by wild nature. The area would later be described as 'the Highlands in miniature'.

Callander is the largest village in the Trossachs, straddling the A84 a couple of kilometres south of where the road enters the Pass of Leny and continues on into the Highlands. Because of Callander's strategic position on the River Teith, which flows south through the mountains, it bills itself as a Highland gateway. Among its many claims to fame is a starring role in the BBC medical

Previous spread. Loch Katrine, from the summit of Ben A'an.

Above. Callander, the gateway to the Highlands.

drama *Dr Finlay's Casebook*. Doubling as the fictional village of Tannochbrae, views of Callander graced the screens of millions of television sets in the 1960s. As the opening titles began, good folk across the country settled down to a Sunday evening with Dr Finlay, Dr Cameron and their housekeeper Janet, enfolded in the bosom of the Callander hills. Ah, the joys of a simpler age!

There is a darker side to this Highland idyll, however. Helen Duncan (née MacFarlane) was born in Callander in 1897. She became widely known as a spiritualist and a medium. 'Hellish Nell' travelled up and down the country, holding seances and invoking the spirits of the dead from a nebulous substance known to mediums as ectoplasm.

Helen's occult performances attracted the attention of the police because they were obviously fraudulent, but in wartime Britain they also represented a threat to national security: at a public seance in 1941, she claimed to be speaking to the spirit of a dead sailor who had drowned after his ship HMS *Barham* was sunk by a German U-boat in the Mediterranean. The sinking of HMS *Barham* had been kept secret by the British government. How had Helen known about it? Had security been compromised?

Police later raided a seance Helen was holding in Portsmouth, home to the Royal Navy's Home Fleet, and arrested her. The authorities thought that Helen's spiritual powers had given her access to top-secret information about the D-Day operation. Brought to trial at the Old Bailey in London, she became the last person in Britain to be tried under the 18th-century Witchcraft Act. She was found guilty and spent nine months in Holloway Prison. The 'last witch' died in 1956.

Towering above Callander is Ben Ledi, the first real mountain on the Highland side of the Boundary Fault. High above the slated rooftops, the Callander Crags also mark the physical change from Lowland to Highland. The early traveller Sarah Murray noticed the geology, and in particular the unusual type of stone that is peculiar to the fault line. Visiting in 1796, she wrote, 'These crags are entirely composed of small stones cemented in a socket of clay, and to be so hardened as to be as firm as solid rock. It is called the plumpudding stone: the towns are entirely built of it.'

Puddingstone is a type of conglomerate rock that is thought to have been formed in hot semidesert environments between 50 million and 60 million years ago. Although Sarah Murray saw many Callander buildings made of this stone, there are now only a few examples left; after Sarah's time Callander was redeveloped as a tourist hub, complete with a railway station, hotels and boarding houses to accommodate the influx of visitors.

Just north of the village is a hamlet called Kilmahog. Fortunately, the name has nothing to do with porcine slaughter but comes instead from the Gaelic Cille MoChùig, meaning 'the church of St Chug', whose Celtic origins are obscure to say the least. Today, Kilmahog is notable for its two touristorientated woollen mills: the Trossachs Woollen Mill and the Kilmahog Woollen Mill. Although they are now purely retail outlets, the mills once produced tweed on looms powered by water taken by means of a lade from the Garbh Uisge – the 'rough waters' before it joins the Eas Gobhain and becomes the River Teith. Today, the Lade Inn stands close to where the original water intake was located and is a favourite watering hole and a venue for live music. Ironically, it started life in the 1930s as the alcohol-free Wayside Tearooms, run by two teetotal sisters Alie and Sheana Maclaurin. Now it's a pub. Whatever would they have thought, I wonder?

On the west bank of the Garbh Uisge, and reached by a bridge close to the Lade Inn, is the old Callander to Oban railway line. It closed in 1965, but has found new life as part of the long-distance cycle path Route 7. In a field just a stone's throw away from the old track bed is a surprising relic from the era of marching imperial legions – the Roman fort at Bochastle. The fort is thought to date from AD 85, and was built after the Romans had defeated the native Highlanders in AD 83 at a place they called Mons Graupius. The Empire was struggling to suppress the wild Caledonians of the north and began instead to build a line of forts to control the passes into the Highlands. The Bochastle fort was one of these. Little remains of the original structure today; a few low mounds and ditches serve as a reminder of this northern outpost of the Roman Empire.

Just to the west of the fort at Bochastle is an even older relic: the 2,500-year-old Iron Age Dunmore fort. Like its Roman counterpart, it once occupied a strategically important location, guarding the same major route from the Lowlands to the Highlands. In certain lights, especially when the sun is low, the fort is quite conspicuous, with broad defensive terraces contouring around its north-western flank. The terraces would probably each have had the protection of a wooden palisade. Because of its relative height above the surrounding countryside, lookouts inside the fort would have been able to keep watch on approaching friend or foe.

The road west heads towards the Trossachs proper and passes below the Dunmore fort. I often come this way when heading to my home in Aberfoyle. Over 200 years ago, Sarah Murray took the same route to experience the scenic splendour of the Trossachs. The first loch she came to was Loch Venachar – or 'Loch Van-a-choir' as she spelt it – a body of water, she tells us, whose Gaelic name means the 'lake of the fair valley'. This is because of the appearance of the corn, which 'when ripe, and waving, gives a fair look to the vale in contrast to the black craggy mountains that surround it'.

One of these dark summits is Ben Ledi – a name that is thought to derive from the Gaelic, meaning the 'mountain of God'. Although not high (at 879 metres it's a good bit below Munro height), Ben Ledi commands attention. It can be seen as far away as Edinburgh.

You might think Loch Venachar, whose waters reflect God's very own mountain, would be a heavenly place, but beneath its often glassy surface lurks a malevolent shape-shifting spirit known as a kelpie, one of the most dangerous creatures in Highland folklore. And on the northern shore of the loch is a wood called Coille a' Bhròin – 'the wood of weeping'. To understand why it earned the name, we have to go back over 200 years to an event which, according to local legend, took the lives of 15 children.

In 1800 John Leyden – a scholarly young man – was touring the Highlands and collecting folk tales. When he arrived on the shores of Loch Venachar, he wrote that the people were 'alarmed at the appearance of that unaccountable being – the water horse which hadn't been seen since the days of the great catastrophe'. The catastrophe in question had occurred some 15 years earlier, on the Sabbath. On that fateful Sunday, a group of 15 children were playing by the loch in the woods of Coille a' Bhròin when the water horse appeared and carried every one of them off to its lair beneath the waves. In his journal, Leyden wrote: 'I made

Loch Venachar, according to legend the home to a shape-shifting kelpie.

enquiries concerning the habits of the animal, and was only able to learn that its colour was brown, and that its motion agitated the lake with prodigious waves, and that it only emerged in the hottest midday to be on the bank. And that it could speak.'

The Kelpie could speak! Unfortunately, Leyden doesn't tell us what it said – or what sort of conversation you could possibly strike up with a water horse – but I'm guessing its language of choice would have been Gaelic!

Scottish folklore is full of stories about kelpies. They are generally feared and best avoided. If you are ever alone, in a wood perhaps or beside the shores of a lonely loch, and heard the sound of galloping hooves approaching, the only way to save yourself from the kelpie's wicked intent is to cross running water by jumping a burn – if you can find one in time.

Heading west through the oak woods that line the banks of Loch Venachar, the landscape becomes increasingly wild and rugged. In the early 19th century, the whole area was reimagined by Sir Walter Scott in his epic narrative poem, *The Lady of the Lake* – a highly romanticised fantasy about a beautiful girl, rival lovers and a king in disguise, all caught up in an age of chivalry and violence. The poem was a publishing sensation.

Loch Achray. Sarah Murray found 'the solemnity and the sublimity of the scene beyond description'.

Within a matter of months, it had sold more than 20,000 copies.

The Lady of the Lake was very precise in its descriptions of the landscape and name-checked actual places in and around the Trossachs. This lent a degree of authenticity to Scott's historical fiction. Perhaps it was only natural that readers of the poem should want to visit the scene of the action. A modern parallel would be movie fans turning filming locations into sites of pilgrimage. To help the new literary tourists find the places they were looking for – and to capitalise on Scott's popularity – *Black's Picturesque Guide to Scotland* quoted liberally from the poem:

The stag at eve had drunk his fill,
Where danced the moon on Monan's rill,
And deep his midnight lair had made
In lone Glenartney's hazel shade;
. . .
In the deep Trossachs' wildest nook
His solitary refuge took.

I first became aware of *The Lady of the Lake* when I lived for a short time with a group of literary-minded students in 'the deep Trossachs' wildest nook'. We had rented the Victorian Old Manse on the shores of Loch Achray – without doubt a jewel among the lochs in the area.

There were nine of us renting rooms at the Old Manse. We were a mixture of undergraduate and postgraduate students mostly studying the arts, and we were given to a certain degree of hormonal melodrama. I can't say that I was inspired by Scott's *The Lady of the Lake,* a copy of which had been left for us to read by the owner. To me, the prose was old-fashioned and the story ludicrously improbable, but the feelings engendered by Scott's romantic fantasy seemed to chime with our individual, and increasingly turbulent, emotional lives. As autumn nights drew in and the weather deteriorated, bitterness and sexual jealousy erupted – classic hallmarks of tragic romanticism – something that readers of *The Lady of the Lake* would have recognised.

Travelling to Loch Achray in 1796, more than a decade before the publication of Scott's poem, Sarah Murray arrived in her horse-drawn chaise from Callander after a hair-raising drive that had jolted every bone and fibre of her being. Despite her alarm at the dangerous road she had travelled, Sarah was highly attuned to the romantic atmosphere that hung over Loch Achray, or 'Loch-a-chravy' as she called it: "'the lake of the field of devotion': The awfulness, the solemnity and the sublimity of the scene is beyond, far beyond description, either of the pen or pencil. Nothing but the eye can convey to the mind such scenery!'

BRIG O' TURK TO LOCH KATRINE

Loveless Ruskin and Effie Gray – SS *Sir Walter Scott* – the Glasgow water supply

A few years after Sarah Murray's 'sublime' experience of Loch Achray, the poets Wordsworth and Coleridge turned up. They, too, were looking for inspiration in nature. A generation later, the composer Mendelssohn arrived. His visit, after his reading of Scott's *The Lady of the Lake,* inspired him to write a piece of music that later became the setting for his famous 'Ave Maria'. When artists like Knox and McCulloch brought paint and canvas, the hills of the Trossachs became Alpine peaks and the lochs became Italian lakes. Such artists believed that there was a moral and artistic truth to be discovered in the landscape they came to represent.

In 1853, two friends and a young bride followed the Romantic trail to the Trossachs. They were the Pre-Raphaelite artist John Millais, his friend, the great art critic John Ruskin, and his young bride, Effie Grey. What happened when they rented a cottage in the village of Brig o' Turk caused a scandal and a flood of speculation.

They had come on a mission to paint Ruskin's portrait. Ruskin was a great defender of the bold, revolutionary approach to painting exemplified by Millais and other members of the Pre-Raphaelite Brotherhood, whose avowed aim was to paint truthfully to nature – 'with a singleness of heart, rejecting nothing and selecting nothing'.

After a long search, Millais found the perfect location beside the burn in Glen Finglas above Brig o' Turk (a place name which incidentally has nothing to do with the inhabitants of Asia Minor – the name is probably derived from the Gaelic *tuirc*, a wild boar). Ruskin described the inspirational location in a letter to his father: 'Millais has fixed on his place – a lovely piece of worn rock, with foaming water, and weeds and moss, and a noble overhanging bank of dark crag and I am to be standing looking quietly down the stream.'

More than a century and a half later, when I was a resident of the Old Manse, I decided to go in search of Millais' piece of 'worn rock'. Taking a postcard of the original portrait of Ruskin for reference, I found the exact spot after scrambling down the side of a steep gorge. Although the burn at the bottom is now tamed by the Glen Finglas dam further upstream, the stone where Ruskin stood is clearly visible. This was where he posed for his portrait, with a gaze that was calculated to express the ideas he shared with Millais about painting from nature. But the act of painting did more than just embody these values. It helped end Ruskin's marriage to Effie Gray.

When he painted Ruskin's portrait, Millais was at the top of his game and was considered to be one of the most talented and imaginative artists of his generation. His celebrated *Ophelia* had wowed the crowds and secured his reputation. He was an artistic celebrity. Ruskin's young wife Effie Gray was drawn to Millais. Unlike her socially awkward husband, who was ten years her senior, she was outgoing and playful. Effie and Ruskin had met when she was just nine years old. He had courted her for many years, seeing off younger rivals, on one occasion narrowly avoiding a duel. But their marriage was a disaster from the moment of their wedding night. Feeling rejected, Effie soon fell in love with the charismatic Millais who was happy to take her in his paint-spattered arms. Effie asked Ruskin for an annulment of their marriage on the grounds that their union had never been consummated. In the hearing that followed, Effie remarked that on their wedding night, Ruskin had 'imagined women were quite different to what he saw I was, and that the reason he did not make me his wife was because he was disgusted with my person the first evening'.

Standing on the stone where Ruskin had posed for Millais, I wondered if he had known that his wife was already in love with Millais? Had he somehow encouraged the affair to let him off the hook and end his unhappy marriage? Whatever the truth behind this love triangle, Effie seems to have found happiness. She bore Millais eight children. Ruskin, on the other hand, never married again and never found love.

From the western end of Loch Achray, a single-track road leads through the Pass of Trossachs, an area which gave its name to the entire region. The origins of the word are obscure and several experts have tried over the years to define the meaning of 'Trossachs'. Some say it's Brythonic, others say it's a corruption of an old Gaelic word *trasdaichean*, meaning a 'glen connecting two others'. Dorothy Wordsworth, when visiting with her brother William in 1803, thought it meant 'many hills'. The minister of nearby Aberfoyle suggested it meant 'a bristly place' but gave no evidence for his translation. Experts have recently argued that Trossachs simply means a crossing point – in this case the pass between Loch Achray and the much bigger Loch Katrine. Having said that, since there are many such crossing points throughout Scotland, you'd expect there to be many more Trossachs – but there is only one.

In *The Lady of the Lake*, Sir Walter Scott describes the path from Loch Achray to the much bigger Loch Katrine in fantastical language. Loch Katrine, he says, is an enchanted never-never land, far from the realities of the modern world. Hidden away in the mountains, it was only possible to reach the loch by means of a sort of ladder made of heather roots and the branches of trees. Of course, there never was such a ladder. That was merely poetic licence used by Scott to heighten the sense of drama and mystique surrounding the lake where the heroine of his epic poem lived.

SS *Walter Scott* on Loch Katrine.

Nevertheless, the magic of Loch Katrine was strongly felt by Sarah Murray when she finally reached its eastern end, having negotiated a tortuously bumpy track in her carriage. In front of her were the enchanting, island-studded waters of Loch Katrine as they narrow beneath the heights of Ben Venue and Ben A'an: 'When I first caught sight of Loch Catherine, I was astonished. I was delighted! A faint ray of the sun was just then penetrating through the mist still resting on the tops of the surrounding mountains and crags, tinging the woods on their sides, and gleaming on the beautiful islands in the loch.'

Seeing a group of fishermen working near the shore, Sarah hailed them and spent the next couple of hours being rowed around in their boat while they cast their nets after fish. She was in her own watery version of heaven. Meanwhile, her man, who believed the place to be the haunt of the Devil, spent his time digging out the horses, which had sunk up to their shoulders in a bog.

Sailing among the islands is still the most popular way to explore Loch Katrine. It extends for some 12 kilometres or so in a north-westerly direction from Trossachs Pier, where tourists and visitors can be seen queuing eagerly in the summer months to board the old steamship SS *Sir Walter Scott*, named after the man who did so much to popularise this part of Scotland. The little ship sails daily up the loch to the pier and tearoom at Stronachlachar – a trip which makes for one of my favourite local excursions whenever I have friends and family to entertain. The company that runs the SS *Sir Walter Scott* allows bicycles on board. This makes it possible to cycle from Stronachlachar back to Trossachs Pier along the old single-track, and traffic-free, waterside road – a wonderful round trip, and an excellent way to see the glories of Loch Katrine from both the water and from the land.

The last time I was on board the SS *Sir Walter Scott*, I was a guest of the captain – a young woman in her late twenties called Debbie White. Up on the bridge, she steered the ship past the wooded islands that Sarah Murray had found so attractive.

What, I wanted to know, had led Debbie to her chosen career?

'Well, I love the scenery. Loch Katrine has to be one of Scotland's most beautiful lochs. I had been working as a crew member for a couple of years and happened to mention to one of the other skippers how much I fancied his job. He said, "Why not go for it?" and so I did. Now I have a lot to think of: what might go wrong? The weather! So my head is very busy!'

We were passing one of the islands to port. 'That's called Ellen's Isle,' said Debbie. 'It gets its name from Sir Walter Scott's poem *The Lady of the Lake*. Ellen was the heroine and that's where she lived with her family.'

Amazing the power of the imagination, I thought. Even features in the landscape have been named after characters in Scott's fantasy.

As the wooded island dropped astern, Debbie told me that the SS *Sir Walter Scott* had first sailed the waters of Loch Katrine in 1899. She was built on the Clyde at Dumbarton. Half the cost of the purchase was taken up with the delivery charge. Moving the boat to its elevated, landlocked location was a major undertaking. She was sailed up the River Leven from Dumbarton, into Loch Lomond and up as far as Inversnaid, then broken down into moveable sections and dragged 150 metres uphill by horses to Stronachlachar where she was put back together again and launched into Loch Katrine. She has been in service ever since.

Keeping an eye on the weather, Debbie signalled from the bridge to the engine room using a brass telegraph. Curious to find out if her message for more power had been delivered, I went in search of engineer Derek Dunn whose domain was deep in the bowels of the ship. There I found him standing beside a somewhat small, perhaps, but perfectly formed steam engine. Derek told me that, like the ship it powers, the engine was built in Dumbarton. 'A lot of the best engines were,' he said. 'This is a Matthew and Paul triple expansion steam engine from 1899 – and it's pretty much original.'

Derek had started his working life as an engineer in the merchant navy. 'It's a pleasure now at the end of my career to be responsible for this wonderful piece of machinery. It's an honour really to give a couple of years of my life to maintain her and keep her running. When I go, someone else will take on the mantle.'

It was obvious that Derek had a lot of affection for his engine, and I was struck by the fact that he referred to it as 'she'.

'Engines are like the ships they power. Each has a personality of its own, and you end up being married to them. That's why I call her *she*!' he explained.

When we berthed at Stronachlachar, I was met by Archie Stevenson from Scottish Water. Climbing into his Land Rover, we made our way along a private road following the southern shore of

Loch Katrine. Archie was taking me to see the entrance to one of Scotland's most impressive feats of Victorian civil engineering – the Glasgow Corporation Water Works.

As we rattled along the single-track road, Archie told me about the history of the project. By the early years of the 19th century, Glasgow's burgeoning population was in desperate need of fresh water. In 1801, 100,000 Glaswegians depended on the polluted river Clyde and drew water from just 30 wells. That's one well per 3,000 people. Cholera, typhus and typhoid struck in lethal waves and with depressing regularity. Piped water was introduced for the wealthy, but the majority of the population was forced to continue using filthy, sewerage-contaminated water. In 1832 and 1848, two major cholera outbreaks killed thousands.

The Corporation of Glasgow took control of the city's failing water companies and set about finding a clean and healthy supply. In 1856 work began to bring the crystal-clear waters of Loch Katrine to the heart of industrial Glasgow. It was a monumental task.

Archie led me through a security gate to a raised area beside the loch. The inlet pool captures the water in an artificial amphitheatre built of great blocks of stone. The entrance to the tunnel, which carries the water on its journey to Glasgow 41 kilometres away, recalls the great feats of engineering of Ancient Rome, and was designed to look like a triumphal arch of one of the Roman emperors. On the portico are inscribed the words 'Glasgow Corporation Water Works'.

As I gazed at the swirling water below us, Archie listed some statistics: 'The water flows 26 miles from this point to Glasgow, with a drop of just ten inches every mile. Over the course of three years, 80 tunnels (some over a mile long) were dug through the hills – 22 aqueducts carry the water high over river valleys. Over 3,000 navvies were employed to build it. They only had candles, pick-axes and explosive. All done without mechanical digging aides. Just blood, sweat and tears. And yet it's a very precise piece of engineering. The original scheme took 40 million gallons each day from the loch. It has been upgraded since then to a capacity of 90 million gallons a day.'

'Somebody obviously likes the water!' I said.

'We all do. It's the best in the world – but then I'm biased!' Archie grinned.

The opening ceremony of the Loch Katrine water supply took place in 1859, with Queen Victoria as guest of honour. Perhaps predictably, given the queen's record for attracting inclement weather, the day was a very wet one. The *Scotsman* newspaper reported how meteorology had little regard for the comfort of the monarch and the rest of the royal party: 'the rain poured down, in incessant torrents, soaking everyone to the skin'.

Fortunately, the queen was later able to shelter from the worst of the weather. She availed herself of all the mod cons of the Victorian world in a purpose-built cottage nearby – just in case she was caught short. Royal Cottage, as it's now known, was a very expensive umbrella with royal loos attached. Before seeking its comforts, the queen first turned a ceremonial handle to open the sluice gates, letting Loch Katrine's water begin its slow progress to Glasgow. In the pouring rain, a military band played the national anthem, and several cannons fired a royal salute. According to popular myth, the explosive shockwave produced by the cannonade was so great that it shattered the windows of Royal Cottage. The organisers of the event had obviously got more bang for their buck than they'd bargained for.

Back at Trossachs Pier, passengers disembarked from the SS *Sir Walter Scott*. The little steamship cast a broken reflection on the still waters where she was moored. A buzzard climbed a thermal above the trees higher and higher until it disappeared behind the pyramid peak of Ben A'an.

Ben A'an is another landscape feature touched by the pen and imagination of Sir Walter Scott. Until he reinvented the Trossachs, early maps called it Am Binnean, 'small pointed peak'. Sir Walter, not being a Gaelic speaker, probably misheard *binnean* for Ben A'an. To add to the confusion, this rocky outcrop is also referred to in print as Ben An. But whichever way you want to say it or write it, Ben A'an is a superb viewpoint with sweeping panoramas of Loch Katrine and the mountains beyond – a scenic reward that amply repays the effort expended to stand on its summit. Like a trip on the SS *Sir Walter Scott*, the climb up Ben A'an is on my list of things to do whenever friends come to stay or if I'm wanting to escape from the world for an afternoon. From the car park on Loch Achray a path leads steeply uphill for a distance of about 2 kilometres and a height gain of about 350 metres. It's certainly a grand way of spending two or three hours of the day if you've got them to spare.

THE DUKE'S PASS TO LOCH ARKLET

Doon Hill – Rob Roy at Ledard – the Garrison of Inversnaid

From the car park at the bottom of Ben A'an, the road to Aberfoyle sweeps around Loch Achray and climbs over the Duke's Pass at 240 metres above sea level. This scenic road was originally built by the Duke of Montrose in the 1880s to allow access

to the lands of his estate. It also enabled the duke to capitalise on the increasing number of tourists who wanted to visit the places that Sir Walter Scott had fictionalised. Anyone intending to use the road had to pay a fee at the Toll House at the Aberfoyle end. When I lived in the Old Manse on Loch Achray, my friends and I would often drive over the Duke's Pass to enjoy a pint in Aberfoyle. One night, coming back from an evening of hilarity and a few beers, my friend John, who was driving his Morris Traveller, misjudged one of the hairpin bends and smashed through the crash barrier, bringing us to an uncomfortable stop. With two wheels dangling precariously over a small cliff, we extricated ourselves through the car's half-timbered rear door. John encouraged us with these words: 'It's fine! I'm holding her on the handbrake!' For many years afterwards, John was known by the sobriquet 'Johnny Handbrake'.

For the last 20 years or so, I have lived in Aberfoyle. The village mainly developed in the 19th century after the railway – now sadly dismantled – arrived in 1882, bringing tourists and day-trippers to the self-styled 'Gateway to the Trossachs'. The railway also made it easier to export slate, which had been quarried in the hills above the village since the 18th century.

The now almost-forgotten Aberfoyle quarry was at one time the third most important in the country, and was renowned for the high-quality slate it produced. The quarry was dug at a remote location, but was still accessible from the road over the Duke's Pass. A village, known as the Aberfoyle Cottaries, was built there in the late 1800s to house the workers and their families. There was even a school to provide the children with a rudimentary education. Today, the village has gone, although extensive workings, spoil tips and

Aberfoyle, which sits on the Highland Boundary fault, has been my home village for more than 25 years.

ruined buildings remain. As for the slate itself, it is still being used in considerable quantities by the Forestry Commission to build and repair the extensive network of forest access roads.

Geologically, Aberfoyle sits on the Highland Boundary Fault. The fault line, which runs just a couple of hundred metres from my house, is a very real feature. To the south are the flat peatlands of Flanders Moss; to the north the Highlands rise in a wave of ridges and high peaks. The Boundary Fault that lies between them isn't entirely inactive. In the years that I've lived in the area there have been at least two seismic events – a low crashing

noise followed by a deep rumbling that was enough to rattle windows and shake the house. Thanks to these experiences, I now know what is meant when someone asks, 'And did the earth move for you?'

So Aberfoyle is a place where things can go bump in the night – physically, and perhaps also spiritually having acquired a name for itself as the haunt of fairies and other-worldly phenomena. This supernatural connection carries so much weight that recently an attempt was made to rebrand Aberfoyle as 'Fairyland'. Fortunately, this proposal never became a reality.

In Highland folklore, fairies are not the diaphanous flower sprites imagined by Victorian illustrators. Instead, they are dangerous, shape-shifting spirits living in a parallel world alongside the one we humans know with our five senses. However, special souls who have the gift of a sixth sense can penetrate the veil and see into the fairy world. One such 'gifted' person was the Reverend Robert Kirk – minister of Aberfoyle in the latter years of the 17th century.

The reverend was a local man who immersed himself in Gaelic folklore. He also claimed to have second sight, which gave him privileged access to the invisible world of the fairy folk. To get to know them better, he took to walking on the wooded slopes of Doon Hill, which overlooks the village and was known locally as a gateway to fairyland.

From his extensive research, Kirk wrote his famous, and wonderfully titled, treatise: *The Secret Commonwealth of Elves, Fauns and Fairies*, published in 1691. The subjects of *Secret Commonwealth* were the spiritual beings known in Gaelic as the *sidh*, the fairies of Celtic folklore. Kirk explained how they lived unseen among us, and how many human beings have a spectral fairy double.

Within a year of his book's publication, Kirk was dead. His body – or what appeared to be his body – was found on Doon Hill. But local people didn't believe that it was Kirk, claiming instead that the body was his fairy double and that Kirk had been taken prisoner by the *sidh* whose trust he had betrayed by writing his book. As a punishment, his soul is said to be trapped beneath the roots of an ancient pine tree on the summit of Doon Hill. Spookily, it is the only pine in a forest of oaks.

A path leads from the old ruined kirk (and the grave that purports to be the last resting place of the reverend) to Doon Hill, where an air of enchantment hangs among the trees, amplified by the eerie sight of hundreds of scraps of cloth, ribbons and other trinkets that adorn branches and bushes around the lone pine on the summit. Most are messages of hope and wishes for healing, written by modern pilgrims to the 'other world'. It's a contemporary version of an ancient Highland custom that the Reverend Kirk would have understood.

Heading west out of Aberfoyle, a single-track road signposted to Stronachlachar and Inversnaid terminates after 24 kilometres on the banks of Loch Lomond. Five kilometres from the village, it skirts the shores of picturesque Loch Ard – the 'high loch of the headlands' – where the shapely peak of Ben Lomond constantly draws the eye. When the young Glaswegian bookseller Thomas Atkinson first beheld Loch Ard, he wrote ecstatically about the effect it had on his senses: 'The whole expanse of Loch Ard burst upon our enraptured gaze. Imagine for yourself a sheet of pellucid water, precipitous rocks fringed with mountain ash, a shelving bay of purist sand sparkling beneath the golden ray of sunset. Imagine an unclouded sky; for the vista a conical mountain, now thrown into shade of the deepest and most ethereal purple. Imagine all this and you have but an imperfect idea of the mingled magnificence and beauty of Loch Ard at sunset.'

Atkinson was on his way to spend three nights at a lochside farm called Ledard. He wanted to experience life in a Highland community and found himself immersed in an entirely foreign society where the 'romantic' customs and language were quite alien to his Lowland ways. Atkinson's visit took place 11 years after the publication of Scott's *The Lady of the Lake* and just four

years after the novel *Rob Roy* appeared. Perhaps this is why he refers to the area as 'that romantic district'.

I recently visited Ledard farm, which is about a half-hour cycle ride from home. Many of the buildings mentioned in Atkinson's account still exist. Taking me on a tour of his property was Fergus Wood. An avuncular, talkative sheep farmer, musician and all-round entrepreneur, Fergus was keen to show me the historic and literary sites. First on the whistle-stop tour was a grey-slated old barn. It was decked out in tartan with reproduction swords hanging on the walls. Trestle tables were laid out as if Fergus were expecting the arrival of a feasting clan. In reality, he caters for 'top-end tourists' who are looking for an authentic slice of Highland life.

Fergus made a grand, sweeping gesture to indicate the passage of time. 'I want you to go back to the 17th century. In this very building the folk of Ledard, whatever their station in life, would celebrate the Hairst Kirn – the harvest festival. And it was right here that the famous – indeed notorious – Rob Roy MacGregor had his coming of age. He stood right there and entertained his neighbours with an eyewitness account of the Battle of Killiecrankie.'

Fergus continued: 'Behind the farm is a water-fall – you'll see it when you go up the hill. That's where Rob Roy courted his wife-to-be Helen MacGregor. They married at the edge of the pool, which now bears her name.'

'That's very romantic,' I said.

Fergus and I walked to a long stone building with an ancient, buckled roof. This was the byre

Modern pilgrims have left their messages of hope and healing on Doon Hill.

Loch Ard, 'the high loch of the headlands'.

– the oldest building in the area by far. 'After Scott had written *The Lady of the Lake*, he wrote a follow-up – his novel *Rob Roy*. For inspiration he came right here to Ledard. He used to sit by the waterfall and Helen's pool to write. When it rained he went into the byre to continue. He said he needed to hear the waterfall to keep the words flowing!'

West of Loch Ard, the narrow road heads into the old MacGregor country, winding past the Teapot, where illicit whisky was once distilled and consumed, and on to Loch Chon – 'the dog loch' – which is barely visible though the tangled branches of oak woods lining the shore. This is a favourite haunt for wild goats, which can be seen sometimes gathering in a hairy flock, sporting hairstyles that look more Rastafarian than Highland. Three hundred years ago, the woods were also the haunt of Rob Roy and his band of cattle-thieving MacGregors.

Rob Roy, the Laird of Inversnaid, was based close to the banks of Loch Arklet, which is much bigger now having been dammed in the 19th century as part of the Glasgow Water Supply scheme. From here, Rob Roy MacGregor combined cattle 'lifting' with his support for the Jacobite cause. But defeat in 1715 brought government reprisals. Troops burned houses and drove off livestock. Rob Roy fled and the army built a garrison to crush future lawlessness.

The troops who occupied the area were billeted close to where Rob Roy and his wife Helen had their home at Corrie Arklet. Surprisingly, the Garrison of Inversnaid is still marked on the modern Ordnance Survey map. It obviously ceased its military role long ago, and for over 200 years the buildings on the site served as a hill farm. Today, the garrison is run as a bed and breakfast. Surprisingly, there is plenty of evidence of its original function – if you know where to look for it.

The owner Kelly Bray met me in the farmyard, which she explained was once the parade ground. 'It was originally built by the Duke of Montrose in 1718 after the first Jacobite rebellion of 1715. That barn, which we use as a tractor shed, was once a three-storey barrack block. The farmhouse itself was once a two-storey guardhouse.'

Kelly led me across the old parade ground to the doorway of a semi-derelict building – another barrack block. Incised into the sandstone of the old doorway were distinct grooves. 'This is where the men sharpened their bayonets on the stonework by the door,' she said.

'It's amazing isn't it?' I said. 'These marks are almost like signatures.'

Kelly traced the outline of one of the bayonet grooves with her finger. 'Yes. Three-hundred-year-old signatures of the men who were chasing after Rob Roy. And they never got him!'

THE LAKE OF MENTEITH

Priors and canons – Mary Queen of Scots – curling and the Bon Spiel

About 5 kilometres from Aberfoyle, following the line of the Highland Boundary Fault east, is a beautiful body of water. This is the Lake of Menteith. It's unusual in name, being the only 'lake' north of the River Tweed, but also in nature, being one of the very few lochs in Scotland that doesn't give birth to a river. Instead, water flows into the lake. None seems to flow out.

The lake was created during the last ice age when a huge lump of ice from a glacier was buried in the rocky rubbish left as the glacier retreated. The ice then melted and left a shallow depression called a kettlehole. This filled with water to become a loch: in this case, Loch Menteith, or Loch Inchmahome, as it used to be known.

Instead of water flowing out of the loch in a river, it seeps into the surrounding flat, boggy ground – an area once known as the Laich of Menteith – *laich* meaning a low-lying area. This old name may account for how the loch became known as a lake. The story goes that a 16th-century Dutch map-maker was enchanted by the loch when he arrived to survey the area. When he asked local folk what it was called, they thought he was referring to the whole district – the Laich of Menteith. The map-maker misheard and thought

The priory on the island of Inchmahome, Lake of Menteith.

Thick ice is rare these days on the Lake of Menteith.

they had just called the loch a lake. And the name, the Lake of Menteith, has stuck ever since.

Although the lake is small, covering just 2.5 square kilometres, it has three islands: Inch Talla, where the ruins of a Comyn Castle can be seen through the trees (this fortified island later became a base for the earls of Menteith and the dukes of Albany before they built their castle at Doune); the tiny Dog Isle, where the earls are said to have kept their hounds; and Inchmahome, which is big enough to have supported a 13th-century Augustinian priory, whose canons were devoted to pastoral work, teaching the word of Christ to the people of the district.

In the summer months, a ferry run by Historic Environment Scotland carries passengers to Inchmahome. For such a small island it packs a lot of history. Robert the Bruce came here, and so did his Stuart descendant Robert II. But the most famous of all Scottish royals to grace the island was Mary, Queen of Scots. When she arrived, Mary was only four years old. This was no holiday. She and her mother, Marie de Guise, were hiding from an invading English Army. King Henry VIII wanted the child queen as a bride for his sickly son Edward – a marriage that would have united the crowns of England and Scotland. Henry wouldn't take no for an answer.

During this episode, Scottish forces were soundly beaten and the country ravaged in what history remembers as 'the Rough Wooing'. Desperate to avoid capture, Marie de Guise escaped with her daughter to the sanctuary of Inchmahome, where they spent three weeks before fleeing again, this time to France.

Although their stay on the island was a short one, it was long enough for a number of legends to develop. Mary is supposed to have played queen with a make-believe court attended by four Marys, an episode remembered in the old song of the same name: 'Mary Beaton, Mary Seaton, Mary Carmichael and me'. Not content with bossing her playmates around, Mary Stuart is supposed to have used her time wisely. She learned languages, employed herself at needlework and even planted a boxwood bower which, according to legend, survives to this day. I've seen it myself on many occasions. It's highly unlikely that four-year-old Mary could have planted the bower, but I'm told that it is old enough to have been around when she hid on this sequestered isle.

In the 20 years or so that I have lived close to the lake, the most memorable days have been those when it has frozen over and the ice has been thick enough to allow people to walk across to Inchmahome. This has happened on just three occasions in two decades. The last time was during the harsh winter of 2010/11. After days of arctic low temperatures, the ice was iron hard and covered with exquisitely beautiful frost blooms. Bubbles trapped in the ice made strange patterns beneath the surface, and deep scores in the ice ran across the surface, where cracks had opened and then refrozen. The whole massive ice sheet shifted imperceptibly, making eerie groaning noises as it settled under its own weight.

Realising the potential of the frozen lake, local people began to venture across it. Some brushed dust and cobwebs from half-forgotten skates and took to the ice, gliding far out towards the islands. Others played ice hockey. The more traditionally minded shoved heavy granite curling stones across the frozen water in the spirit of friendly competition. In Victorian times bitter frosts regularly transformed the lake into a huge ice rink, making it the venue for Scotland's great annual curling match called the Bon Spiel. A splendid spectacle also known as 'the roaring game', the Bon Spiel attracted thousands to watch and thrill at the clash of stone on ice.

One Victorian tourist found the excitement of a Highland curling match infectious: 'There was the true "ring" of a national pastime about the whole affair. "Tss-s-s-s," hissed the stone, as it was sent skimming over the ice. Loud and ceaseless were the cries of "Soup it up, soup it up, mun" from the excited bystanders.'

Sadly no longer. After a century of increasingly warm winters, ice seldom forms on the lake, or on any of the other traditional curling locations across the country. The last outdoor Bon Spiel took place on the Lake of Menteith in 1979 when the north of Scotland played the south of Scotland. It was a fantastic occasion and attracted over 5,000 spectators. Then in February 2011, after a gap lasting a generation, hopes were high for a repeat of the old excitement. For the first time in over three decades, the ice was thick enough for the Bon Spiel to be played again. But, at the last moment, the match was called off. The local authority closed it down before it had started. The reason? Health and safety, i.e. where to put the portaloos and the parking problems that would arise from an influx of spectators. This was a tragic outcome in my view. Can you imagine the Spanish authorities in Pamplona banning the festival of the Running of the Bulls for reasons of health and safety? I think not!

Curling is considered by those in the know to have originated in Scotland, although a similar game has also traditionally been played in the Netherlands. The earliest evidence for the Scottish game comes from a curling stone inscribed with the date 1511 but the sport is likely to be a lot older. Curling has always been a grassroots activity. At one time, every village in the Highlands had its own curling pond. You can still see them today – usually overgrown with weeds and seldom, if ever, used except for those rare occasions when the frost and ice return.

THE PASS OF LENY TO CRIANLARICH

Rob Roy again – the Braes of Balquhidder – the Legion of the Ninth

The A84 road north of Callander enters the Highlands proper when it crosses the Highland Boundary Fault at the Pass of Leny. Here the Garbh Uisge cascades through a narrow, rocky defile. Sarah Murray caught the mood in 1796 when she wrote: 'It was a gloomy morning; the waters roared, and the mountains looked black, particularly Ben Lidi, or Ben-le-Dia, the hill of God, scowling over the pass of Lennie.'

Black's Guide is equally romantic in its description: 'At the bottom of the glen the river makes

The Falls of Leny.

the "falls of Lenny" breaking in harsh thunders, tumbling from ledge to ledge, sweeping round rocks and eddying in dark inky pools.'

On the right bank of the Garbh Uisge is the route of the old Callander to Oban railway line, described by *Black's* as 'one of the most beautiful in Scotland'. There are no steam trains on the track these days. Instead, it doubles as a cycle path and a section of the long-distance Rob Roy Way, providing people with a scenic alternative to the busy main road on the other side of the river.

Emerging from the dramatic scenery of the Pass of Leny, the old railway line climbs towards Loch Lubnaig – which translates from the Gaelic as the 'crooked loch', although I have to say I've seen crookeder lochs in the Highlands. Nevertheless, on a clear, still day the reflections in the water are simply amazing, especially in autumn, when the colours of the birch and larch high on the steep face of Creag na h-Airigh are mirrored on the loch's serene and glassy surface. Without a telltale ripple in the water, it's difficult to tell up from down.

On the shore opposite Creag na h-Airigh is a large white house called Ardchullarie Lodge. In the past, I knew it as the home of singer/songwriter Jim Kerr from the Scottish band Simple Minds. I have since learned that it was previously the country retreat of James Bruce – an 18th-century explorer who claimed to have discovered the source of the Blue Nile. When Bruce returned to

The still waters of Loch Lubnaig.

Ardchullarie from his African adventure, he wrote an account of his discovery. Unfortunately his book wasn't very well received – it was belittled by several leading intellects of the day. Bruce's detractors included the famous Dr Johnson who dismissed his account as a fabrication. As a consequence, Bruce became known as the 'travel liar'. Wounded, with his reputation destroyed, he retired to his home on the shores of Loch Lubnaig where he hid from the world until his death in 1794. On a happier note, James Bruce has since been recognised as an early and significant European explorer of the African continent.

The route of the old railway line eventually reaches the northern end of Loch Lubnaig and the attractive village of Strathyre. In the days of steam, there was a station here which allowed tourists and visitors relatively swift access to this part of the southern Highlands.

On a day out walking, a friend of mine – the author Carl MacDougall – once told me that his parents spent their honeymoon at the Ben Sheann Hotel, in a room with a view of Beinn an t-Sithein (like Doon, another 'fairy hill') opposite.

'The strange thing,' said Carl, as he parked his car in the village, 'was that when my mother woke up the following morning she found herself in bed alone. My father had got up at dawn and left the hotel to climb Beinn an t-Sithein.'

'Why did he do that?' I asked, gazing up at the ben.

'I don't know, but my mother said that after that dad always seemed "away with the fairies".'

Apart from this Highland fairy connection, Strathyre's only other notable association is with the Gaelic poet and evangelist Dugald Buchanan. Carl showed me a memorial dedicated to Buchanan, who was born near the village in 1716.

In life, he was revered as the pre-eminent composer of sacred Gaelic lyrics. His poem 'The Dream' was translated by one of his admirers:

As I reclined in sleep's embrace,
And idly dreamed as others do,
I seemed to grasp sweet pleasure's cup,
But, ah! it vanished from my view!
Methinks that one beside me stood,
Who to me said, 'Oh fool thou art
To think that thou canst hold the wind,
Or that the world can fill thy heart.'

'A rather Presbyterian critique of the folly of idle dreaming – when only God should "fill thy heart",' remarked Carl.

North of Strathyre, the village of Balquhidder is a place I often visit on day trips from home with friends and relatives. In the picturesque old graveyard that surrounds the ancient ruined kirk we encounter once again Scotland's best-known outlaw – Rob Roy MacGregor – in what purports to be his final resting place.

Rob Roy, so called because of his flowing red locks (Roy is an anglicisation of the Gaelic word *ruadh*, 'red'), was born in 1671 at Glengyle on the shores of Loch Katrine. During the first Jacobite rebellion of 1689, Rob and his father led a band of MacGregors to the Battle of Killiecrankie. After he came of age, Rob took his mother's name of Campbell, and began trading as a cattle dealer. He did this because it was wise not to use the MacGregor name. Since 1603, the entire MacGregor clan had been proscribed for their involvement in a murderous attack on the Colquhouns at Glen Fruin, a battle that left 200 Colquhoun clansmen dead – along with a group of young boys who had come to watch the fight. In the aftermath of this

The last resting place of the outlaw Rob Roy in Balquhidder.

bloodshed, the MacGregor name was abolished by King James I and VI. Anyone using it or wearing the MacGregor tartan faced death as a punishment.

As Robert Campbell, respected cattle dealer, Rob Roy did well and used his wealth to become the Laird of Inversnaid near Loch Arklet. But his fortunes reversed after he borrowed £1,000 from the Duke of Montrose. Unable to repay the debt, Rob Roy quickly found himself bankrupted and outlawed by the duke. In revenge, Rob Roy went to war against Montrose, lifting cattle and extorting the duke's tenants to pay protection money.

If they paid Rob Roy, their property and livestock were safe from his marauding band of MacGregor clansmen. If not . . .

In this grubby quarrel, Rob Roy sought his own protection and found a willing patron in the Campbell Duke of Argyll – a fierce rival of Montrose. Because of his Campbell allegiance, both Rob Roy's later involvement in Jacobite risings and his loyalty to the Stuart cause have been questioned. The Duke of Argyll was no Jacobite. He was a strong supporter of the Hanoverian government in Westminster. It has even been suggested that Rob Roy was a spy. He may have passed on important information about Jacobite sympathisers and Jacobite plans to Argyll.

During his lifetime, the exploits of Rob Roy became known to the wider British public after the novelist and government spy Daniel Defoe wrote a fictional biography called *The Highland Rogue*. This rollicking account so captivated the German-speaking King George I that he issued a full pardon for Rob's nefarious activities.

Rob Roy died not far from Balquhidder in 1726 at the age of 63. According to some accounts, it was a land dispute with Clan MacLaren that ultimately led to Rob Roy's death a few weeks after he was wounded in a duel to settle the matter.

As the old outlaw's fame spread, Rob Roy's grave in the kirkyard at Balquhidder became a place of pilgrimage. People from all over the world continue to pay their respects to the man who has often been depicted as a sort of Highland Robin Hood, a characterisation that was further mythologised by Sir Water Scott in his eponymous novel of 1817.

I recently met up with local historian Donald MacLaren, who also happens to be the chief of Clan MacLaren. Perhaps because of the traditional MacGregor and MacLaren rivalries, Donald is not a supporter of the Highland Robin Hood version of events.

'To put it bluntly,' said Donald, 'Rob Roy was only ever concerned with saving his own skin and looking after number one. But to give him his due, he was a cunning operator. He used his wits to double-cross and play his enemies against each other. Above all, he was a great survivor. He was imprisoned several times and always managed to escape. The thing that annoys us MacLarens is that the MacGregors were imposters here at Balquhidder. They were trying to take over. Tradi-

tionally, these have always been MacLaren lands, and yet in popular imagination, they are now associated with Rob Roy and the MacGregors.'

The grave that is popularly thought to be Rob Roy's lies among three others – his wife Helen's and two of their four sons. A metal rail surrounds them all. But it's inscribed with the wrong date, falsely making Rob 70 when he died. There is also an interesting plaque which proclaims, 'MacGregor Despite Them' – a reference to the proscription of the clan and Rob's apparent heroic defiance of it. But according to Donald MacLaren, all is not as it seems.

'It's all fake. It's for the tourists. They put coins on the grave slab and leave flowers. We don't know for sure that he lies here. Some people have claimed he's buried on an island in Loch Lomond. True, the grave slabs themselves are authentic. In fact, they are ancient. They are medieval and therefore much too old to be contemporary – they were carved centuries before Rob Roy's time. The railing is Victorian, and the name plates are all 20th century! And the biggest flaw in this story is this: why would the MacLaren clan allow a man who was their enemy to be buried in their traditional and sacred burial place, here in the ruins of the old kirk?'

'If what you say is true, the latter-day myth-makers who reinvented Highland history have a lot to answer for,' I said. 'But if Rob Roy isn't beneath the grave slab, perhaps that's not inappropriate. Given his past record for escaping, it's at least consistent with his character!'

Leaving the old graveyard, I set off up a path behind the kirk. I was heading to the summit of Creag an Tuirc – the 'crag of the boar' – renowned as the traditional gathering place for Clan MacLaren, and marked today by a cairn erected

The Braes of Balquihidder, 'Where the blaeberries grow' / mang the Highland heather'.

by the Clan MacLaren Society. This makes an ideal place to admire the views of the Braes of Balquhidder, with Loch Voil and Loch Doine nestling below.

Just over 200 years ago, Robert Tannahill, a weaver from Paisley, was inspired by this same view. He wrote a song to an old tune and called it 'The Braes o' Balquhither':

> Let us go, lassie, go,
> To the Braes of Balquhither,
> Where the blaeberries grow
> 'mang the Highland heather;
> Where the deer and the rae,

> Lightly bounding together,
> Sport the lang Simmer day
> On the braes o' Balquhither.
>
> I will twine thee a bower
> By the clear siller fountain,
> An' I'll cover it o'er
> Wi' the flowers o' the mountain;
> I will range through the wilds,
> An' the deep glens sae dreary,
> An' return wi' their spoils
> To the bower o' my dearie.
> [. . .]

The viaduct on the Oban–Callander railway line at Glen Ogle, once described by Queen Victoria as Britain's answer to the Kyhber Pass.

Now the simmer is in prime,
Wi' the flowers richly bloomin'
An' the wild mountain thyme
A' the moorlands perfumin',
To our dear native scenes
Let us journey together,
Where glad innocence reigns
Mang the braes o' Balquhither.

The song became very popular in Scotland, and travelled to Ireland, where it acquired new lyrics and spread around the world, becoming known as 'Wild Mountain Thyme', a favourite with folk singers everywhere.

I remember seeing the Corries folk duo playing in Dunoon when I was a teenager. They played an unforgettable rendition of 'Wild Mountain

Thyme'. It brought tears to my eyes and a vision of the famous view stretching all the way down to Loch Voil and Loch Doine where William Wordsworth and his sister Dorothy saw a young girl in a field, singing as she worked with a scythe:

> Behold her, single in the field,
> Yon solitary Highland Lass!
> Reaping and singing by herself;
> Stop here, or gently pass!
> Alone she cuts and binds the grain,
> And sings a melancholy strain;
> O listen! for the vale profound
> Is overflowing with the sound.

The young lassie was singing in Gaelic, which was

a language that neither William nor his sister could speak, so exactly what she was singing about is a mystery. But the vision inspired William to verse, interpreting the scene through the prism of his own imagination.

From the Braes of Balquhidder the A84 road north passes through a gap in the hills and down towards Lochearnhead, which has been an important Highland crossroads for centuries. Here roads divide: a single track takes the southern shores of Loch Earn, while the main A85 road to Crieff and Perth takes the northern shore. Lochearnhead was also an important railway junction in the heyday of steam locomotion. Just south of the village at Balquhidder station, the Lochearnhead, St Fillans and Comrie railway joined the Oban to Callander line, connecting the district to the wider national rail network. The line to Comrie opened in 1904, and was closed in 1951. The Oban to Callander line survived for longer. Heading north, it climbed steeply along the western flanks of dramatic Glen Ogle, a name which comes from the Gaelic *gleann-eagal*, meaning the 'glen of dread'. Queen Victoria once said it was Britain's answer to the Khyber Pass.

Black's Guide gives a vivid description of the railway line and the scenery it passed through: 'We are struck by the evident traces of some extraordinary convulsions of nature. The brow and face of the mountain are contorted – large boulders and masses of rock having been, as it were, forcibly thrust from the bosom of the hill in all directions, accompanied by steep clefts, precipitous ridges, and overhanging shelves.'

The old railway line cut through this unstable-looking avalanche of rock and was carried elegantly over the worst by a dramatic 12-arch viaduct to reach the pass at Lairig Cheile where there is a lochan hidden in the trees. But in 1965 the inherent instability of the hillside resulted in a landslide that closed the line for good. Today, the viaduct remains, standing proud on the bare hillside. It's a grand monument to Victorian engineering and a significant landmark when seen from the main road opposite. It also carries the long-distance cycle path Route 7 and the Rob Roy Way.

On the other side of the Lairig Cheile pass, the road descends to the junction at Lix Toll. In former times travellers paid for the privilege of using the road at the white toll house which still stands at the crossroads near the garage and filling station. For some strange reason, latter-day conspiracy theorists have connected Lix Toll with the Roman occupation of Britain. Lix, some argue, should be written LIX, the Roman numerals for 59, recalling the 59th legion. Others have an even more esoteric explanation. LIX stands for L IX, referring to the Legion of the Ninth, which is said to have disappeared under mysterious circumstances somewhere in the Highlands. I remember as a child reading a novel by Rosemary Sutcliffe called *The Eagle of the Ninth*, but I seem to recall that the standard bearer on the front cover held aloft an eagle clutching the Roman numerals VIIII – the old way of writing the number nine, a convention that was used by the legion. Not LIX Toll then, but LVIIII Toll. I have to say, this makes no sense to me! However, a more likely explanation for the derivation of Lix traces the word to the Gaelic *leac*, meaning a slab or a gravestone.

From Lix Toll, the route west sweeps up the broad expanse of Glen Dochart, which Sarah Murray found a little underwhelming compared to the 'sublime scenery' she had already passed through. However, when she came to Loch

The ruined castle at Loch Dochart was once a stronghold of Clan Campbell.

Dochart she encountered 'a view of the sublime and the beautiful united'.

Today, Loch Dochart and the adjoining Loch Iubhair are easily missed. Traffic tends to speed past their tranquil waters, which for the most part are screened by the trees of a conifer plantation. But if you know where to look, glimpses can be had of the ruined fortifications on the isle mentioned by Sarah Murray. The three-storey castle was built in the 16th century and was once a stronghold of Clan Campbell. One winter, the castle was attacked by a band of MacGregors, who

The memorial cross to Sergeant Harry Laurie on the summit of Ben Ledi.

crossed over on the frozen waters of the loch. In 1646, during the Wars of the Three Kingdoms, Clan Macnab, who supported the Royalist side against the Covenanters, burned the castle to the ground.

About a kilometre further west, and just outside the village of Crianlarich, is the farm of Inverardran which sits in the shadow of Ben More.

Whenever I pass by I'm reminded of the tragic fate of a friend of mine who was killed in a climbing accident one winter. Sarah and her boyfriend had reached the icy summit of Ben More and were descending a steep snow slope when she slipped. Unable to break her fall, she careered down the mountain and crashed into a rock several hundred feet below. In a state of shock, her boyfriend hurried to help. When he reached her, Sarah was unconscious and bleeding from a deep head wound. Sarah's boyfriend continued down the mountain to seek help and was able to raise the alarm when he reached the farm at Inverardran.

The Killin Mountain Rescue team were called out in response. As night began to fall an RAF Westland Wessex helicopter joined the search for Sarah, but when it approached the mountain, a sudden gust of wind threw it off course, causing the tips of the main rotor blade to strike an overhanging rock. The pilot tried to gain height, but the flailing blades cut through the tail section of the Wessex, which spun out of control, crashing onto the side of the mountain. The wrecked helicopter then slid downhill for 80 metres and caught fire. The three RAF crew members escaped, but the two members of the mountain rescue team were thrown out. Sergeant Harry Laurie, the team leader, received fatal injuries. The rescue had become a disaster.

The following morning Sarah's body was recovered. She was 27 years old and had died as a result of her fall. My friend Gus, who was on his way north a couple of days later, saw the wreckage of the helicopter being loaded onto a trailer by air accident investigators. Although I wasn't there to see it, the image has stuck with me ever since. And whenever I climb nearby Ben Ledi, the memorial cross on the summit to Sergeant Laurie is another reminder of this tragedy.

Ben More overshadows Crianlarich – a name that derives from the Gaelic for 'the low pass'. Being on a major route through the Highlands, Crianlarich has been a significant destination and crossroads for centuries. This is where the A85 from Perth in the east, meets the A82 from Glasgow to Fort William. In the past, two military roads also met here, but the village didn't really develop until the coming of the railways, when it grew as an important junction. Today, Crianlarich is where the Glasgow to Oban line splits off to the west, while the West Highland Line continues north to Fort William. Before its closure in 1965, the old Callander to Edinburgh line also came into the village. Crianlarich is still served by a railway station that boasts a busy tearoom – mostly because it's able to take advantage of a captive clientele. Passengers travelling north to Fort William have to leave the Glasgow to Oban train and wait while some of the carriages are repurposed for their onward journey. Grabbing a quick cup of tea and a scone seems a good way of passing the time while chatting, perhaps, to trainspotters. They're often looking out for rare sightings of steam locomotives that occasionally grace the West Highland Line with special excursions. A sight not to be missed!

When I was a teenager, train travel was beyond my means. Hitch-hiking was how I generally got around the Highlands, and Crianlarich was a name I frequently scrawled in felt-tip pen on a piece of cardboard. I have memories of standing outside the village hotel on a winter's night, waiting to meet up with my fellow hitch-hiker Gus. As the minutes turned to hours, I began to feel as cold as the giant icicle that hung from the gutter above my head. It must have been six feet long. I stamped my feet in the frosty air. Then, glancing up at the icicle, I warily moved aside.

Gus eventually turned up in a lorry. Sitting beside the driver, he hailed me from the cab. Climbing aboard, we rumbled off into the night, heading north to a chilly campsite beneath the mountains of Glencoe.

PART TWO

A ROUND OF OLD PERTHSHIRE FROM LOCH EARN, COMRIE
AND ABERFELDY TO GLEN LYON, LOCH TAY AND KILLIN

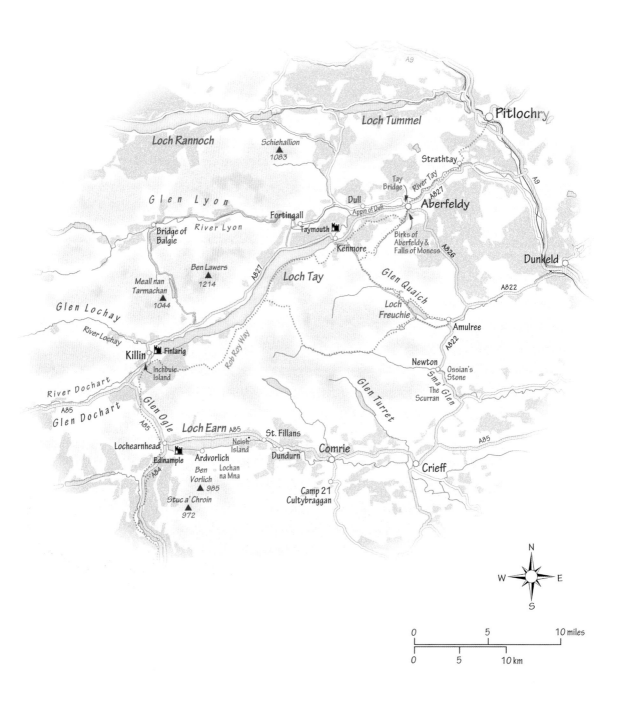

Black Duncan – a sack full of heads – a cure for rheumatism

The old county of Perthshire has been in and out of existence as political boundaries have changed. Sometimes it's there, sometimes it's not – twice in my own lifetime. From the mid 1970s, Perthshire disappeared from the map entirely and was replaced by the drearily bureaucratic Central Region. Latterly, when the old name was revived, its borders shifted. Now, parts of what had been western Perthshire are administered by Stirling District Council. The land is still the same whoever draws the political map. This tour around old Perthshire explores the Highland heart of Scotland and ignores recent local government boundaries, recalling a simpler time when Perthshire was Perthshire.

Loch Earn, which is just off the A84 road north of Callander, stretches east for 10.5 kilometres. The loch is said to take its name from the Gaelic Loch Éireann, which in English means the Loch of Ireland. This is odd because Loch Earn lies close to the heart of an ancient Pictish kingdom, and a long way from the influence of the west coast Gaels who claimed descent from Irish dynasties. Perhaps, as the influence of the Gaels spread east, names were changed, including that of Loch Earn.

Black's Picturesque Guide to Scotland claims that '[t]here are many to whom Loch Earn presents the perfection of Lake Scenery'.

Sarah Murray, who visited some 60 years before *Black's* published its first guide, would have enthusiastically agreed. Riding along the southern shores of the loch, she admired the views from in her carriage while her man Allan urged the horses on. 'Loch Earn is beautifully surrounded by hills and crags, the outline of which is truly picturesque. In short, the whole scene is delightful.'

What Sarah couldn't have known is that Loch Earn boasts a surprising feature, and one that occurs in very few inland bodies of water: it is tidal. But these tides are not like maritime tides, which are caused by the waxing and waning of the moon. The freshwater tides of Loch Earn are wind-blown. Because the loch lies east to west, the prevailing westerly winds can exert pressure on the surface of the loch. This pushes the water mass from one end of the loch to the other and results in a measurable oscillation in depth – a phenomenon known as a seiche. When the wind blows on the surface of the water, it forms an uphill slope. When the wind drops, the water levels out again, creating a tidal fluctuation.

Overlooking the southern end of the loch, just outside the village of Lochearnhead, is Edinample Castle. Now a private home, Edinample was formerly a stronghold of Clan Campbell. The castle was built by Sir Donald Campbell, the 7th Laird of Glenorchy – a power-hungry and ruthless man who is known to history as 'Black Duncan'. During his long career, he plotted with murderous intent to take over the leadership of Clan Campbell and in the course of his lifetime he either built or took possession of seven castles from which he projected his power and authority. Edinample was one of these castles. It was built in the late 1500s (probably around a pre-existing structure) on land that he had previously taken from Clan MacGregor.

A local legend gives an insight into Black Duncan's propensity for violence and malevolent behaviour. During the construction of Edinample

Edinample Castle, on the shores of Loch Earn, was built by 'Black Duncan' and is reputedly haunted by the ghost of the castle's chief builder.

Castle, he ordered his chief builder to create a parapet along the roofline so he could survey his surrounding estates. Black Duncan was enraged when he discovered that the builder had forgotten to do this. Grabbing the man by the scruff of the neck he threw him off the roof and killed him. The ghost of the poor fellow can be seen, it's said, pacing the roof where the parapet should have been.

Close to Edinample Castle is Glen Ample where a well-trodden right of way leads through the hills to Loch Lubnaig. The footpath begins close to an attractive humpbacked bridge carrying the single-track road over the Ample Burn. A few years ago, after a tremendous summer thunderstorm, a sudden torrent swept the bridge away. Whole trees

were torn up by their roots and were heaped up like felled giants along the riverbank.

The majestic Ben Vorlich (985 metres) and its craggy counterpart Stuc a' Chroin (975 metres) rise to the east of Glen Ample, commanding the views of the western end of Loch Earn. Being on the edge of the Highland fault line, these exposed hills catch the wind ahead of others, and are infamous for the gales that frequently rip across their summits.

The first time I climbed Ben Vorlich, which means the 'hill of the bay' in Gaelic, I was in the company of an old friend Colin and my two eldest children, Calum, who was 14 at the time, and Erin, who was 11. It was an overcast, blustery day in early autumn. We set out from the car park in a swirl of wind-blown leaves. As we climbed the

Ben Vorlich, due to its position, is one of the windiest mountains in the region.

path through the glen, the wind began to increase significantly. Ahead of us rose the pyramid of Ben Vorlich. Clouds were dramatically tearing over its summit. It looked windy up there – a thought that was later confirmed by a walker coming down the track. I asked if he'd been to the top.

'Just about got blown off!' he said, glancing at Calum and Erin. 'It's not the best place for young-sters. They'll be flattened by the gusts.'

With this unwelcome advice, he continued down the mountain. I looked warily at the scud-ding clouds and then at my children. 'What do you think kids? Shall we keep going and take it step by step? If it gets too rough, we'll simply turn around and come down.'

Calum looked eager to press on. Erin appeared

less enthusiastic, but fell in behind me when I led the way. When we left the relative shelter of the glen and reached the broad and exposed shoulder of Ben Vorlich's northern ridge, the wind began to fight our every step. With my encouragement, we struggled on. Then a particularly strong gust caught us. It pushed Erin off the path and off her feet. She picked herself up, and was less than impressed with my lame attempt to make light of it all: 'Put some stones in your pockets. That will stop you being blown around like thistle down!'

The ridge ahead of us levelled out before it merged with the steep rocks and scree of the summit pyramid. Here the wind was ferocious. We took shelter behind a boulder as a violent gust tore across the mountain, preceded by a noise that sounded like a runaway express train. Small stones and clumps of grass were picked up as it passed by, leaving an unexpected moment of calm.

'Come on kids!' I shouted, grabbing Erin by the hand and rushing like a soldier into battle. I was making for the next large boulder a few metres away, hoping to reach its shelter before the wind struck again. We made it just in time. When the gust arrived, it was like being caught in a vortex. A few seconds later, it died away to nothing.

'I want to go back down,' pleaded Erin. She definitely wasn't enjoying this day out with her dad.

I thought for a second.

'Erin,' I said, 'I think we'll soon be in the shelter of the summit cone. If I'm right, we should go on.'

I paused and listened. 'It's quiet now. Let's go for it!'

My prediction proved correct. The path up the final section of the mountain was indeed sheltered, but we could still hear the wind howling like a banshee among the black rocks of the corrie, where the screes dropped steeply into a dark abyss below.

At the summit, it was perfectly calm, like being in the eye of the hurricane where the air is miraculously still. I wanted to take a quick photograph to commemorate our conquest. I was just about to press the shutter when another violent gust caught us. Calum clung onto the concrete pillar of the trigpoint. Erin flattened herself into the ground. Recovering my balance as it passed, I reframed my camera and took the shot. When I had the film developed, I saw for the first time that Erin had tears in her eyes. Perhaps this is why Ben Vorlich remains her first – and last – Munro. I still feel slightly guilty.

Ardvorlich House lies at the foot of Ben Vorlich overlooking Loch Earn. The present structure dates from 1760, but Ardvorlich has been home to the Stewarts since the 16th century. Despite its sunny outlook, it's a place steeped in bloody legend, with tales of murder and clan warfare that belie many romantic and poetic notions of Highland history.

Close to the road, and just outside the grounds, is a solitary headstone. It's a memorial to a bloody skirmish between the Stewarts of Ardvorlich and the MacDonalds of Glencoe and serves as a reminder of the days when the writ of law did not extend far in the Highlands – where murder and blood feuds were the brutal reality of daily life. The stone bears a weather-worn inscription: 'Near this spot were interred the bodies of 7 Mcdonalds of Glencoe killed when attempting to harry Ardvorlich Anno Domini 1620.'

The deaths were the last act in a feud that had started with the murder of John Stewart of Strathgarry in Atholl by a group of MacDonalds. In revenge, a band of Highland Stewarts, including James Stewart of Ardvorlich, followed the murderers home to Glencoe, where they attacked them, killing the chief and his son.

Bloodied and furious, the MacDonalds regrouped and organised a retaliatory raid on the Stewarts of Ardvorlich. They were led to their objective by a MacGregor man from Glen Dochart, who went by the name of McClerich.

James Stewart, the Laird of Ardvorlich, was not at home when the MacDonalds descended. In his absence, his wife bravely held off the attackers. When James returned, he discovered his home surrounded, and a MacDonald about to set fire to the thatch of his byre. James Stewart shot the man dead. Shortly afterwards, his own men turned up and slaughtered the remaining MacDonalds to a man. Only McClerich got away, but he was later hunted down and killed in a nearby wood,

The headstone near Ardvorlich commemorates a bloody skirmish between the Stewarts and MacDonalds.

which ever since has borne his name: Coille Chleirich. The victorious Stewarts dragged the bodies of the slain MacDonald clansmen down to the shores of Loch Earn and buried them.

According to a local source, their remains were discovered a century later when work was being undertaken to build the southern road along the shoreline. Inside a shallow grave, labourers unearthed seven skeletons, 'complete with decaying rags and metal buttons'. The bodies were reburied and the headstone with its inscription

erected. Most walkers and climbers heading up the path to Ben Vorlich pass the memorial as it lies close to their route up the mountain.

Although the Stewarts of Ardvorlich survived the attack, they were no strangers to violence. In 1580, their ancestor Alexander Stewart married a woman called Margaret Drummond. Her brother John Drummond had the job of protecting the king's deer from poachers. When Drummond caught a band of MacGregors hunting deer in the royal forest, he clipped their ears. Quite literally, he cut them off. But this primitive act of summary justice had terrible repercussions.

Wounded and humiliated, the MacGregors slunk home, only to return some time later, bent on revenge. They eventually caught up with John Drummond, killed him and cut off his head. Wrapping the gory trophy in a piece of tartan, they made their way to Ardvorlich where John Drummond's heavily pregnant sister Margaret was home alone. When the MacGregor men arrived, Margaret innocently offered them food and shelter, according to the traditional Highland custom. She brought them bread and cheese and then went off to cut slices of cold lamb shoulder for her unexpected guests. While she was out of the room, the murderous MacGregors took the severed head of Margaret's brother, placed it in the centre of the table, and stuffed its gaping mouth with the bread and cheese. When Margaret returned and saw her brother's bloody and desecrated head staring up at her from the centre of the table, she became hysterical and ran from the room.

Traumatised, Margaret disappeared from the house for several days. When her husband, Alexander Stewart, returned home, he tried in vain to find her. Eventually, Margaret returned – but she was not alone. In her arms she carried her newborn baby son. She'd given birth high in the hills beside a lochan that is today known as Lochan na Mna, 'the lochan of the woman'. The child survived and was christened James Stewart. When he grew to manhood, he spent his life hunting down and killing MacGregors. His story inspired Sir Walter Scott to write a fictionalised and romanticised account of his life, appearing as Major Allan M'Aulay in the novel *A Legend of Montrose*.

The road along the southern shores of Loch Earn leads eventually to the pretty village of St Fillans, which was renamed and redeveloped as an estate village during the 19th century. Before that time St Fillans was known as Portmore. Sarah Murray, passing through Portmore, found her eye drawn to an 'island of beautiful shape, covered in wood' which lies close to the village.

The island, known as Neish Island, is artificial and was originally a crannog. It later formed the foundations of a fort that became the last refuge of Clan McNeish when they'd been almost wiped out after a series of bungled raids on their neighbours. For a while the McNeishes kept the peace, but just before Christmas 1612, a feud with their old enemies the Macnabs of Loch Tay came to a head – or several heads to be precise.

To celebrate the forthcoming festive season, Macnab sent his servant to procure supplies. As the man was returning from market in Crieff, he was attacked and robbed by the McNeish clan, who made a feast of what rightly belonged to Macnab.

In revenge, the chief sent his 12 sons to attack Neish Island. The brothers are said to have carried their boat over the snowbound hills from Loch Tay to Loch Earn, where they launched it and rowed to Neish Island. Inside the fortress, the clansmen were lying in a drunken stupor. Taking advantage of their inebriated state, the 12 Macnab brothers broke in and slew every McNeish they could find, except for a small boy who had hidden under a table to escape the slaughter. Tradition has it that all modern McNeishes are this boy's descendants. When the bloodletting was over, the Macnab brothers returned home in triumph, carrying a sack full of heads, which they presented to their father. He was well pleased with his Christmas present. To this day, the bloody episode is commemorated by the Macnab coat of arms, which includes a severed head and the boat that carried them to victory.

A short distance east of the village, rising dramatically from the flat meadowlands of the River Earn, is Dundurn or St Fillan's Hill. Dundurn – 'the fort of the fist' – almost certainly dates from the Iron Age and is mentioned in 7th century Annals of Ulster as the location of a siege. This took place when the Gaels of Dalriada were expanding eastwards against the Picts who occupied Dundurn. The strategic position of the fort allowed the Picts to hold up the advance of the Gaels into their heartland. Archaeologists believe there have been at least two forts on the rocky outcrop – one made of wood, and a later one of stone. Contouring around the hill below the summit are a series of ruined walls that form defences and courtyards. On the summit is a slab of rock, known locally as either St Fillan's Chair, or St Fillan's Bed.

St Fillan was a legendary Celtic Christian missionary from Ireland who established a base at Dundurn in the 6th century. He's said to have preached from his elevated 'chair', blessing the country and all those who lived within its compass. For many centuries afterwards, various healing properties were associated with this ancient and once sacred site. Writing in the *Statistical Account of Scotland* in 1791, the minister of the parish reported: 'The rock on the summit of the hill, formed, of itself, a chair for the saint, which still remains. Those who complain of rheumatism in the back must ascend the hill, sit in this chair, then lie down on their back, and be pulled by the legs to the bottom of the hill. This operation is still performed, and reckoned very efficacious.'

A painful way to find a cure. Personally, I think you're better off with an osteopath.

FROM COMRIE TO KENMORE

Earthquakes and POWs – the Sma' Glen – the mighty Lords of Breadalbane

From St Fillans a cycle path makes use of the old railway line that ran from Lochearnhead to Perth. When trains plied the track, they provided a wonderfully scenic way of travelling through this part of the Highlands. Although steam trains might have been slow, they allowed people to travel in a vastly more civilised and relaxed fashion than we do today, locked away inside cars, swerving to avoid potholes, or stuck behind caravans and missing the views of the lochs and hills. Sadly, of course, the trains have gone, but a project to reopen the line as a footpath is underway, restoring the lochside views to cyclists and walkers.

The village of Comrie, known as 'The Shaky Toun', used to be on the old railway line. A clue to its nickname lies in what is apparently the smallest listed building in Britain, and which sits on a hill just outside the village – Earthquake House. Having followed the cycle route from St Fillans, I was keen to take a breather and discover more about the intriguingly named little house. Chris Palmer, the custodian of Earthquake House, gave me a tour.

Chris told me that Comrie lies on the Highland Boundary Fault, which is why the area is seismically active. Seemingly, some periods are more volatile than others. The 19th century was a very shaky century by all accounts. 'Back then, Comrie was the earthquake capital of Scotland and earned the name "The Shaky Toun",' said Chris. 'In the 1830s, over 7,000 shaky moments were recorded – at first in the town – and then at Earthquake House, which was specially built as a recording station.'

Chris explained that the principal 'movers and shakers' behind the recording scheme were two local men, a shoemaker and a postmaster. They were thrown into action – quite literally – by the 'great earthquake' of 1839 when people were hurled from their beds by the force of underground shock waves.

I was intrigued to learn about the inventiveness of Comrie's Victorian amateur seismologists and how they developed a primitive instrument to measure the earthquakes. It was made of wooden blocks, like skittles, each with a different weight, and set to fall into a sandpit. The stronger the quake, the heavier the block that fell. Simple but effective.

Or simply ineffective? Chris admitted that the instrument never really worked properly. But the pioneers, who later included a couple of church ministers, came up with the word 'seismometer' for their inaccurate device. This makes the men of Comrie the world's very first seismologists, even if they weren't very successful ones.

Lying to the south of Comrie is a fascinating relic from the Second World War: nearly a hundred red-roofed Nissen huts are lined up in neat rows on flat ground near the River Earn. These once made up Camp 21 – one of two maximum security prisoner-of-war camps in Britain. At full capacity, it held 4,000 German prisoners of war – many of them amongst the most hard-line, fanatical Nazis ever captured by the British. In 1944, prisoner Sergeant Wolfgang Rostberg was beaten to death behind the camp wire by a group of ardent Nazis. They believed he was an informer and had him condemned to death at a kangaroo court. Five

Earthquake House at Comrie – known as the earthquake capital of Scotland.

Camp 21, near Comrie, housed 4,000 German POWs during the Second World War.

men from the camp were later convicted and hanged at Pentonville Prison for his murder.

Camp 21 was also known as Cultybraggan, named after the farmland it was built on in 1941. Prisoners were housed according to their perceived level of threat: A, B, C or D. They were also given colour-coded patches to wear: white for the relatively harmless, black for the most dangerous Nazi party members. The unthreatening 'whites' were allowed to work locally on farms and on building sites. Most of the prisoners settled down to a relatively comfortable life. Games were organised. There was a choir, an orchestra and classes for learning English. Strong friendships were also made with civilians living in the local community.

After the war, some of these relationships continued. In a letter written by Wolfgang Ruckert in 1948, the former prisoner expressed his thanks for the kindness shown to him: 'I feel pretty bad because I have not yet written to you . . . I hope you are well and Maryline too. How is the garden and the peas and the beans I was sowing? I wanted to thank you so very much for all your kindness you showed me, so that sometimes I could forget that I was a prisoner.'

Gratitude was also expressed in more than just words. In 2016, another former inmate, and member of the SS, Heinrich Steinmeyer, left a small fortune in his will to the residents of Comrie, bequeathing his home and life savings. This was an extraordinary act of generosity to people who must at one time have seen him as an enemy.

Today, Camp 21 at Cultybraggan is run by a community trust, which hopes to keep wartime memories alive by refurbishing and repurposing the old Nissen huts that are now open to the public for viewing.

The town of Crieff, like Comrie, lies on the Highland Boundary Fault, and is described by Sarah Murray as 'one of the barrier Highland towns, sweetly situated, just as it were, without the jaws of the Highlands; I say jaws, for I observed that in most grand passes there are castle-like hills at the entrance, as sturdy guards to chop off and obstruct the way of obtruders'.

A somewhat overblown description, which makes Crieff seem more like a town on an Alpine pass than it does in reality. But then, Sarah was driven to see the dramatic, the romantic and the picturesque in everything she encountered, however unlikely. Perhaps William McGonagall, Scotland's 'worst poet' is nearer the truth in his ode, 'Beautiful Crieff', which includes this couplet:

> Ye lovers of the picturesque, if ye wish to
>   drown your grief,
> Take my advice, and visit the ancient town
>   of Crieff.

Crieff in Sarah Murray's day was the second biggest town in Perthshire, after the Fair City itself. It still is. The town's position at a crossroads between the Highlands and the Lowlands allowed it to flourish from the 18th century onwards, first as a cattle town, and then as a Victorian health resort. During the 18th century, the Crieff *trysts*, cattle markets, drew vast herds of cattle from the mountains of the north. Each year, up to 30,000 of these beasts arrived for sale, driven by Highland drovers who had a reputation for drinking, merrymaking and fighting. As a deterrent, the town displayed the dangling corpses of hanged miscreants – murderers and thieves – from gallows on the thoroughfare: a warning to other Highlanders arriving with their cattle not to misbehave. It's hard to imagine today, but Crieff was like the American Wild West, especially with every Jacobite rising when more violence would erupt. Rob Roy MacGregor came with his men, despite the presence of government troops, and rang the town bell. His clansmen sang lusty Jacobite songs and toasted their 'king across the water'. In 1716, following the military muddle that was the Battle of Sheriffmuir, a violent mob of Highlanders burned Crieff to the ground.

After the rebellions had been crushed and the town rebuilt, the cattle trade moved further south to Falkirk, forcing Crieff to reinvent itself. This is when it found favour with rich people possessed of literary and romantic sensibilities – people like Sarah Murray who passed though on her way to locate the graves of two tragic young women.

Celebrated in folk song, Bessy Bell and Mary Gray were childhood friends. In the 17th century they sought refuge from the plague by escaping to the country. But their lover followed, carrying the disease with him.

> Betsy Bell and Mary Gray
> They were bonny lasses
> They bigget a bower on yon burnside
> And theekit it o'er wi' rashes.
> But the plague came from the burrows-town
> And it slew them baith thegither.

Sarah Murray found the graves of the two 'bonny

Crieff Hydro originally opened in 1868 and offered a huge range of water-based treatments for physical complaints.

lasses' downstream from Crieff above the River Almond, in the hanging wood of Lyndoch. She describes a walled enclosure with the simple inscription, 'The Tomb of Bessy Bell and Mary Gray' and saw evidence of the graves 'by the rising of the sod'. However, when I visited recently, I found no stone wall and no headstone – just a tree and a railing enclosing a piece of ground.

Thoughts of the plague would have been far from the minds of Victorian entrepreneurs who wanted to develop the town as a health resort by promoting its 'serene air and dry healthy situation'. The jewel in this particular crown was – and still is – the Crieff Hydropathic Establishment, other-wise known as the Crieff Hydro, which was built by an enterprising doctor and opened in 1868,

offering cures for a variety of symptoms. The treatments, which were something of a craze for fashionable and wealthy people across Europe, were mostly water-based, and involved elaborate rituals: bathing, showering, soaking, sweating and being wrapped in hot and cold wet towels. This punishing and uncomfortable regime, combined with wholesome food and fresh air, cured almost any disease, or so it was claimed. Illness could simply be 'washed away' at the Hydro. Of course, there was little or no evidence to support such boasts, but that didn't stop people heading for Crieff in the hope of a cure. Today, the Hydro is still standing, having been transformed into a modern spa resort with its own golf course. The traditional watery theme is maintained with an indoor pool, steam room, sauna and spa bath. There is a gym and a beauty salon for those in need of some remedial work. I'm sure guests feel so much better when they leave. I'm also certain their wallets will be considerably lighter too.

The A822 road north from Crieff climbs over high moorland, passing through the Sma' Glen where the River Almond flows close to the road. Sarah Murray took this route in 1796 and was delighted with what she found: 'Prodigious craggy mountains rising to the clouds bending their rough heads to each other over the glen through which the water rolls. I entered this silent, solemn pass (where no trace of human habitation can be seen, no sound heard, save the bleating of the sheep and the rushing of the waters) with awful pleasure.'

This is a road I know well – its sweeping curves and dramatic scenery making it a thrilling ride on motorbike (I confess, I have one). However, it's also worth slowing down to look at Ossian's Stone, which sits in a field close to the road beneath the steep slopes of The Scurran, a kilometre south of Newton Bridge.

This massive, cuboid monolith is said to be the burial place of legendary blind bard Ossian. His poems glorified the deeds of the hero Cuchulain who lived in the twilight of a pre-Christian Celtic world. The stone, which measures 2.2 metres tall by 1.5 metres across, looks like an erratic deposited by a retreating glacier (it may well be one), however, early written accounts suggest there's more to the boulder than geology.

When the old military road through the Sma' Glen was under construction in the early 18th century, the boulder blocked the way ahead. An engineer commanding the soldiers described how it was moved 'by vast labour, with their levers and jacks or hand screws'. When it was finally shifted, the troops discovered a recess in the ground directly beneath the stone. Inside were 'some ashes, scraps of bones, and half-burnt stalks of heath, which last we concluded to be a small remnant of a funeral pile'.

These remains have long since disappeared. According to the engineer's own account, local people took them away: 'The Highlanders carefully gathered up the relics and marched with them, in solemn procession, to a new place of burial, and there discharged their fire-arms over the grave.'

To this day, the location of the new grave remains a mystery, although another 18th-century traveller to Scotland was told by local people that they were 'deposited with much solemnity on the lofty summit of a rock where they might never more be disturbed by mortal feet or hands'. To me, this suggests a nearby peak – possibly The Scurran where an ancient cairn is marked on the OS map. I must have a look sometime.

Speeding on from the grave of Ossian and the mystery of the disappearing relics, my motorbike route takes me over General Wade's Newton Bridge and on to Amulree, where I usually take the single-track road up Glen Quaich, passing Loch Freuchie to reach the *bealach* at over 500 metres above sea level. This is a place of big skies, wide horizons and the call of summer skylarks. The heather-clad moors stretch away to the blue haze of the Grampian mountains with glimpses of the higher peaks to the north: Ben Lawers, Schiehallion and Beinn a' Ghlo.

The descent from the *bealach* is steep with some very tight hairpins, and takes me to Loch Tay, the sixth largest freshwater loch by area in Scotland. It measures about 23.5 kilometres from east to west, and at its widest is about 2.5 kilometres

The magnificent Taymouth Castle, once the home of the powerful Breadalbane Campbells.

with a depth greater than 150 metres. The road from Amulree eventually leads to the lochside village of Kenmore, which is equivalent to Inveraray in this part of the Highlands. Like its western counterpart, it too was a capital of Clan Campbell. While Inveraray has its chateau-style castle, home to the Duke of Argyll, Kenmore has Taymouth Castle – formerly the ostentatious palace of the Campbell Lord Breadalbane, whose family was once considered to be the most powerful branch of the Campbell clan. Descended from Sir Colin Campbell of Glenorchy, the Breadalbane Campbells spread from their original base eastwards to Loch Tay and beyond, displacing other clans which had previously held sway in the area. By the 19th century, the Marquis of Breadalbane was one of the wealthiest landowners in Scotland, with an estate that covered thousands of square miles of the country.

While they were enjoying life at the zenith of their power and influence, the Breadalbane Campbells entertained the young Queen Victoria and her husband Prince Albert. Victoria was greatly impressed. She felt as if she were in a Highland romance and wrote about her visit in *Leaves from the Journal of Our Life in the Highlands*: 'There were a number of Lord Breadalbane's Highlanders, all in the Campbell tartan, drawn up in front of the house, with Lord Breadalbane himself in a Highland dress at their head, a few of Sir Neil Menzies' men (in the Menzies red-and-white tartan), a number of pipers playing, and a company of the 92nd Highlanders, also in kilts. The firing of the guns, the cheering of the great crowd, the

One of General Wade's finest bridges, at Aberfeldy, forms part of the 18th-century military road from Crieff to Inverness.

picturesqueness of the dresses, the beauty of the surrounding country, with its rich background of wooded hills, altogether formed one of the finest scenes imaginable. It seemed as if a great chieftain in olden feudal times was receiving his sovereign. It was princely and romantic.'

This display of clan pomp and wealth was one of the last the family would ever present. The great Breadalbane empire died a slow death, finally expiring in the 1920s when the childless marquis breathed his last. The fabulously luxurious Taymouth Castle became a hotel, and later a hospital for wounded Polish troops during the Second World War. In the 1980s it served as a boarding school for American children in Europe. For some years now, Taymouth has been earmarked to become an exclusive hotel, catering for those who want to enjoy the delights of a reimagined, aristocratic Highland past.

FROM ABERFELDY TO FORTINGALL

The Black Watch – the Birks of Aberfeldy – Pontius Pilate and the Fortingall Yew

The River Tay, which winds along a bright and cheerful valley confusingly called the Appin of Dull, passes through the small town of Aberfeldy. Here the river is spanned by one of General Wade's finest bridges, which at one time carried the military road from Crieff to Inverness. The bridge is a surprisingly ornate affair. With decorative obelisks above the parapet, it might have been better positioned in the grounds of an aristocratic country house. Designed by William Adam, the father of the very famous Robert Adam (whose grand designs were much sought after by wealthy 18th-century landowners looking to build impressive mansions), the Tay Bridge at Aberfeldy was opened in 1735.

The Black Watch memorial commemorates the first muster of the Black Watch regiment.

A few years later, General Wade organised the recruitment of local men into a Highland militia to help maintain law and order. These irregular troops eventually became *Am Freiceadan Dubh*, the Black Watch regiment. The first muster took place in 1739 close to the Tay Bridge at a place marked today by a massive stone monument. On top is a Highland figure representing a member of the original Black Watch; it's claimed locally that the armed Highlander is a representation of the regiment's Private Farquhar Shaw.

In the spring of that year, the regiment received orders to leave the Highlands and march to London. As they headed south, a rumour spread that when they got to London they'd be transported to the West Indies – a method the government had previously used to 'disappear' troublesome Highlanders and enemies of the state.

As distrust of their senior officers grew, 120 men of the Black Watch, including Farquhar Shaw, decided to desert and head for home. The mutineers were intercepted a few days later in Northamptonshire. With a promise of a free pardon, the men laid down their arms and surrendered. But instead of the fair treatment they'd been promised, they were marched to the Tower of London. While the bulk of the regiment, who had remained loyally at their posts, were sent to fight in Europe, the rest were found guilty of desertion and faced the death penalty. The sentence was commuted, but to reinforce army discipline and to set an example, three men were selected to face the firing squad. Farquhar Shaw was among them. The surviving deserters were sent – as they had feared all along – to the Americas where many died of disease. The treatment of the regiment – just two years before the Jacobite rebellion of 1745, did little to encourage feelings of trust and loyalty towards the Hanoverian government in Westminster.

One of Aberfeldy's many proud boasts is to be at the geographic centre of Scotland. There isn't a monument to mark where this might be. However, I've heard that this claim can be demonstrated by a simple experiment using a cardboard cut-out map of Scotland, and a pin. The idea is to balance the map on the pinhead. The point where the map balances is the true centre of Scotland, which apparently turns out to be Aberfeldy.

Aberfeldy's fame doesn't merely rest on this highly dubious proof to be the most perfectly balanced town in Scotland (although I have to say, there is a sedate calm and equilibrium to be found in its quiet streets). In the 18th century, it was celebrated in verse by Robert Burns. Burns was captivated, not as he usually was by the charms of a young Highland lassie, but by the woods and the waterfalls above the town. These he immortalised in the poem 'The Birks of Aberfeldy'. Ever since, tourists have been making the pilgrimage to see the source of his poetic inspiration.

> The braes ascend like lofty wa's
> The foaming stream deep roaring fa's
> O'wer hung wi' fragrant spreading shaws
> The birks of Aberfeldy.

When I went in search of this beauty spot I saw that the birks – or birches – of the poem had entirely vanished – as they had by the time *Black's* published my guidebook. It remarks that the birch trees of the poem have 'entirely died out and have been superseded by rowans whose clusters of red berries in autumn are no unworthy substitute'.

Proof, if any were needed, that even back then,

the environment was changing. But after all, the natural world is a dynamic system; nothing stays the same, including the Birks of Aberfeldy.

A path through the trees leads to the fabled Falls of Moness, which actually consists of three separate falls, the highest making a splendid sight: a flash of white water streaming down a mossy rock face among the fresh green of the damp woods. The Falls of Moness is just one of literally dozens of cascades mentioned by *Black's Guide*, and it's a striking feature of early tourism that waterfalls generally exercised a powerful influence over the Victorian imagination – people simply couldn't get enough of them. The bigger and more powerful or violent they were, the better. Perhaps there was an irresistible appeal in the unrestrained onrush of water when a river was in spate, a visceral thrill that was a welcome antidote to the douceness of Victorian life.

When I visited the Falls of Moness, I was on a long-distance cycling trip. Leaving Aberfeldy, I crossed Wade's bridge and pedalled to the picturesque village of Fortingall, which sits on the banks of the River Lyon, a tributary of the Tay. I was surprised by the architecture. It was charming, but seemed somehow out of touch with its surroundings.

Most of the village dates from the 1880s and was inspired by the local landowner, Sir Donald Currie – a wealthy shipping magnate from Greenock. When he bought the Glen Lyon estate, he commissioned the architect James MacLaren to redesign the original village according to the principles of the Arts and Crafts movement. What can be seen today is largely a result of this collaboration. The sight of reed-thatched roofs strikes an odd note of bucolic Englishness in the heart of the Scottish Highlands.

The Falls of Moness, much admired by Victorian travellers, who had a passion for waterfalls.

The thatched cottages of Fortingall were built in the 1880s in the Arts and Crafts style.

The Fortingall Yew, at 5,000 years old, is possibly the oldest tree in Europe.

The name Fortingall is derived from an old Gaelic word meaning the 'fort of the strangers'. The strangers alluded to were soldiers from the legions of Rome and, unlikely as it seems, there's living proof to back up the story. Parking my bike outside the old kirk, I walked through the graveyard to an ancient wall and a locked iron gate. Behind it I saw the gnarled and weary-looking boughs of the Fortingall Yew – possibly the oldest living organism in Europe. Forester Mike Strachan, who has studied the history and legends associated with this venerable tree, was standing in the shade beneath its dark green foliage. Together, we gazed up into the knotted tangle of limbs.

Mike told me that the yew is somewhere between 2,500 and 8,000 years old. 'At a conservative estimate, it's probably somewhere in the region of 5,000 years old,' he said. 'There is also archaeological evidence, so the claim to its being the oldest living tree in the whole of Europe might well be true.'

'So, it would have been here when the Romans came to Britain,' I said.

'It was definitely here when the Romans arrived. There is even a legend that connects the Fortingall Yew with Pontius Pilate and the crucifixion of Christ. Pontius Pilate was the son of a Roman soldier stationed here at Fortingall. Pilate is said to have played in the yew's branches when he was a wee lad. When he grew up, he became the Roman governor of Jerusalem and infamously tried Jesus before his crucifixion.'

I looked sceptical.

Mike continued, 'Well, you are right not to take the story at face value. Jesus was killed 13 years before the Romans governed Britain. So the dates don't match up. But it doesn't detract from the significance of this tree, which was a sacred site long before the Romans invaded.'

Mike went on to explain how the yew symbolised eternity and regeneration for the ancient Celts. The places where yew trees grow were often venerated – which is probably why the Fortingall tree has survived. With the arrival of Christianity, the new religion recognised the sacred significance of yew trees and early Christians often built churches next to them. This happened at Fortingall, giving the site continuity as a sacred place for thousands of years. But the tree's later celebrity had serious consequences. From the 18th century onwards, there were reports of fires being lit in the hollow of the tree to commemorate festivals like Beltane. The yew later became a very popular tourist attraction. Local people cut off branches and fashioned the wood into souvenirs to sell to visiting tourists – ornamental boxes and spoons – even pieces of furniture.

'What you see now are the green shoots of recovery,' said Mike. 'It's pretty much a shadow of what it used to be. In the 18th century it was much more substantial. It measured 52 feet in circumference then.'

Thankfully, modern tourists are more respectful and the tree is protected from would-be souvenir hunters by the wall. But the story of the Fortingall Yew is an example of how the allure of a place can potentially be the cause of its destruction.

FROM GLEN LYON TO KILLIN

Ben Lawers – the Falls of Dochart – the *coin dubh*

I left the awe-inspiring Fortingall Yew, with much of the timeline of human history ringed within its trunk, and cycled up Glen Lyon, where the River Lyon cuts a deep gorge. *Black's Guide* of 1886 extols the virtues of the road, which at that time had just been built: 'The new road opens up the beauties of the ravine. As we proceed up the glen we catch glimpses through the tree-clad banks of the stream below, "now leaping sportfully from crag to crag, / Now smoothed in clear black pools."'

As the glen opened out, I struggled with tired legs, pedalling uphill to the grand old Bridge of Balgie. Here the road divides. To continue west leads to the dam at the head of Glen Lyon. The other route heads south over a shoulder of Ben Lawers and down to Loch Tay. This is the road I took, embracing the challenge of the steep, single-track road that climbs relentlessly to a height of 544 metres at the *bealach* between the Ben Lawers massif and the Ptarmigan Ridge. Here the waters of Lochan na Lairige are held back by an impressive dam built in the 1950s to supply water for a hydro-electric scheme. The *bealach* is also where most hillwalkers drive to start their day, gaining lots of height before setting off to scale one of the eight surrounding Munro summits.

Ben Lawers is really a range of seven mountains with Ben Lawers being the principal peak. For many years, the summit was believed to be above the magical 4,000-foot mark, but when a more accurate survey was conducted in Victorian times, lofty Ben Lawers fell short, measuring just 3,983 feet.

Disappointed that their beloved Ben Lawers

On Ben Lawers. A 20-foot cairn once stood on the summit – an attempt to push the mountain's height above the 4,000-foot mark. Without it, the mountain's official height is 3,983 feet.

had been downgraded, a group of heroic mountaineers took extreme measures to push the ben back into the 4,000-foot club. In 1878, they toiled for a day to build a gigantic 20-foot cairn, topped off with a boulder of white quartz. Disappointingly, the Ordnance Survey considered this to be cheating and refused to change the height on their maps. Today, there is nothing left of the huge

cairn. I'm not sure whether it became a victim of the wild mountain weather or whether it was demolished by human hands.

Since the Victorian period, botanists have been attracted to Ben Lawers. From the mid 19th century onwards, bewhiskered, tweed-wearing gentlemen with magnifying glasses could be seen crawling all over the slopes of the mountain looking at plants. These men quickly established Ben Lawers as 'the place to go' for flowering alpines in the UK. The mountain's height, combined with a geology of limestone and calcareous schist, creates a rich fertile soil perfect for rare arctic and subarctic plant species that are seldom found elsewhere in the UK. The extremely rare snow pearlwort, the mountain mouse-ear, the mountain forget-me-not, the thyme-leaved speedwell, and the alpine fleabane are among the botanical treasures to be found. I'm told they are beautiful when in bloom, and almost invisible when they're not. For sheer display, you can't beat the mountain gentian, which carpets the hillside in early summer.

The soils that give rise to rare plant species also enabled early humans to flourish on the grassy slopes of Ben Lawers. Summer grazing is a tradition that archaeologists believe extends back in time for about 9,000 years. Evidence for this lost way of life can be seen from the paths up the mountain. Scattered in small groups across the hillside are the remains of many shielings, the seasonal dwelling places of shepherds and herders. There isn't much left of these simple, temporary structures. They were built on a stone base with turf walls, topped off with a low thatched roof.

Taking cows, goats and sheep from the low ground to graze on the mountains in the summer time was a tradition practised in many mountain areas across Europe, such as in the Alps, in Norway and in the Pyrenees. The task of looking after the animals often fell to children and older folk who spent much of their time making cheese from the animals' milk. What's more, the weeks spent in the shielings were an important time in the Highland social calendar. It was 'at the shielings' that boy met girl and love blossomed.

Killin lies at the western end of Loch Tay and straddles either side of the swiftly flowing River Dochart. As it tumbles over boulders and swirls around pine-clad rocky islands, the river forms a cascade known as the Falls of Dochart, and flows dramatically through the middle of the village. Visiting in 1796, the waterfall-loving Sarah Murray wrote: 'The Lin at Killin is very striking and uncommon. The scene around is prodigiously grand, awful, and striking, with loud, white reeking cascades and torrents, dashing in every direction: altogether forming a picture not to be imagined, unseen. I wonder that the inhabitants are not all deaf from the thundering noise of the rushing waters.'

Today, the spectacle described by Sarah is much photographed. Images of the Linn, the white cottages on either side, and the bridge that crosses the river, adorn many calendars and boxes of shortbread. Killin has become an icon of the Highland picturesque.

The stone arch bridge spanning the Dochart was built in 1760 and crosses the river by way of an island called Inchbuie, a name that comes from the Gaelic Innis Bhuidhe, meaning the 'yellow island.' It was once a significant stronghold, and there are traces of at least two fortifications, which are believed to date from the Iron Age. Access to the island is usually barred by a locked iron gate, beyond which lies the ancient burial ground of Clan Macnab, whose fortunes in the area, like many other smaller clans, declined with the rise of the mighty Clan Campbell.

The name Macnab is said to come from *Mac an Aba* – 'the son of the abbot'. The abbot in question may well have been connected with the religious sites of St Fillan further up Glen Dochart, so perhaps the first Macnab's mother had a dalliance with the abbot. For centuries, their

The ancient Macnab burial ground lies on an island in the River Dochart.

offspring occupied Eilean Ran Castle on an island in the nearby River Lochay, but the chiefs of Clan Macnab ended up losing all their land, along with their traditional clan seat. In 1825, 500 Macnabs emigrated to Canada with their chief, Archibald. Of the lands they once held by the sword, only Inchbuie remains – the last resting place of the clan.

Down the road from the Falls of Dochart, through the village and over a bridge crossing the River Lochay, is a track that leads to a thickly wooded mound close to Loch Tay. On a day of torrential rain I walked among tall trees and dripping undergrowth to the shattered ruin of Finlarig Castle, which stands on top of the mound. Built in the 16th century by Donald Campbell the 7th Laird of Glenorchy, Finlarig is a place of infamy and horror – its grey walls exude a brooding and

Finlarig Castle. According to local legend, the castle courtyard features a gruesome beheading pit.

oppressive atmosphere. Within the old courtyard is a shallow, stone-lined pit. According to local stories, this hole in the ground is the notorious 'beheading pit' where many MacGregors were executed while their Campbell captors watched from a banqueting hall above.

The hatred Clan Campbell had for Clan MacGregor was fierce and deep. Legend has it that the Campbell laird bred a pack of hounds to hunt down his enemies. These great beasts – the *coin dubh* – 'black dogs' – were supposed to have been suckled by MacGregor women. The taste of MacGregor milk allowed the dogs to better know their victims. These were not happy times. The brutal reality of life in the Highlands is often forgotten by visitors who have a more romantic agenda, or who just like to enjoy the fine views.

PART THREE

**FROM DUNKELD OVER THE RIVER TAY TO
LOCH TUMMEL AND LOCH RANNOCH, THEN THROUGH
DRUMOCHTER AND ON TO DALWHINNIE**

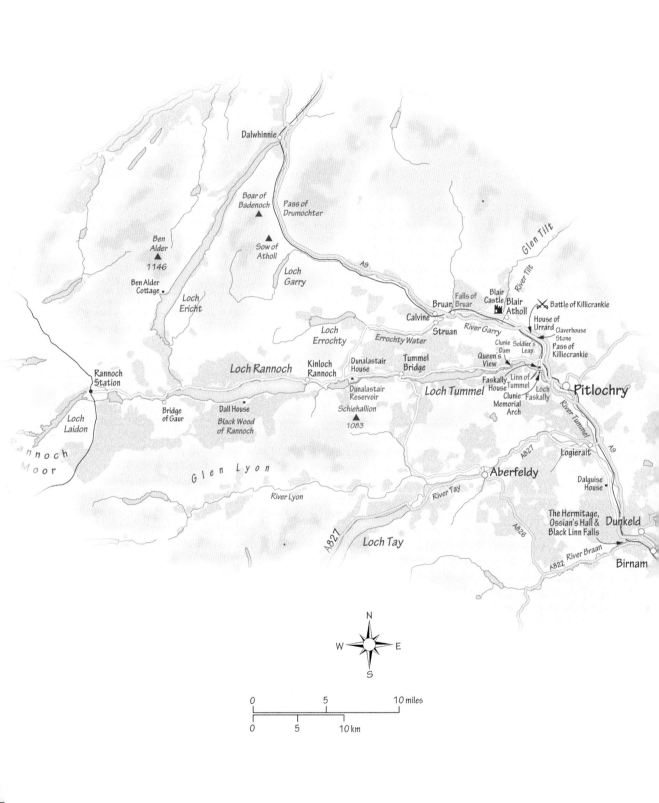

DUNKELD TO PITLOCHRY

Birnam Wood – an independent wheel man – Peter Rabbit and Mrs Tiggywinkle

The picturesque town of Dunkeld is another Highland gateway. It sits on the north bank of the Tay where the river narrows to a pinch point beneath high crags before flowing eastwards towards the Lowlands and the city of Perth.

The first time I explored Dunkeld properly was several years ago when I arrived in town on a Victorian tricycle. This was during the filming of the very first series of *Grand Tours of Scotland*. To fully immerse myself in the project, I'd enthusiastically embraced the idea of travelling through the Highlands as early tourists had done, and I was keen to use various forms of period transport to experience the country from an authentic, historical perspective. When I was presented with an original Rudge Lever Tricycle, manufactured in Coventry in the 1870s, I didn't realise just how difficult and painful Victorian locomotion could be. I soon found out.

Pumping hard on the pedals, every bone in my

Previous spread. Blair Castle

Above. With my Victorian Rudge Lever Tricycle – not the easiest form of transport.

Dunkeld Cathedral.

body rattling, I bumped and swayed dangerously towards Dunkeld wondering what I would find. My 1886 copy of *Black's Guide* was effusive: 'There are few places of which the first sight is so striking as Dunkeld; its finely wooded mountains, its noble river, its magnificent bridge, and its ancient cathedral, combine to form a picture of rare beauty.'

I hoped so. All the effort I was expending demanded a substantial reward.

Avoiding cars and pedestrians without mishap, I negotiated the narrow streets of the old town centre, rattled over the Cross where once markets were held, and made for the cathedral – the most striking and historic part of Dunkeld. Leaving my tricycle outside the iron gates of the cathedral grounds I was struck by the sight of a building made of two distinct halves: one ruined and the other a functioning place of worship.

There has been a Christian centre on the banks of the River Tay at Dunkeld for close to 13 centuries. The original church is said to have been founded around AD 730 by Celtic monks. A century later, after the kingdoms of the Picts and the Gaels were united, the church was rebuilt. Shortly afterwards, the holy relics of St Columba were brought from Iona to Dunkeld in order to protect them from marauding Vikings. With Columba's relics in safekeeping, the religious community beside the Tay flourished, becoming the centre of Scottish Christianity.

The cathedral was built, rebuilt and modified over the centuries. Most of what can be seen today dates from the 13th century. But the work of generations was destroyed twice – first during the Protestant Reformation of the 1560s, and then in August 1689 during the first Jacobite rising.

After the Battle of Killiekrankie defeated government forces fell back on Dunkeld, where they took up defensive positions around the cathedral. Outnumbered four to one, they waited for the pursuing host of 4,000 Jacobite clansmen to attack. The battle, when it came, lasted for 16 hours, with fierce house-to-house fighting. During the onslaught, much of the town was burnt to the ground, including the cathedral. With Dunkeld a smouldering ruin, the Jacobites retired and disappeared into the hills. The eastern half of the cathedral nave was eventually roofed over and became a place of worship again. The rest of the building was left open to the heavens.

In a dark corner of the cathedral was the tomb I wanted to see. It dates from the 1390s and is one of the oldest royal monuments to have survived in Scotland from the Middle Ages. On an elaborately carved stone platform lies the effigy of a knight in armour, arms crossed over his breastplate, his mailed hands pressed together as if in prayer. This pious figure represents none other than Alexander Stewart, the notorious Wolf of Badenoch – one of the wickedest characters in Scottish history.

Alexander was born in 1343. He was one of the illegitimate sons of King Robert II, who had fathered a large brood of children to various women. When Alexander's father married his mother, the bastard son of the king was retrospectively legitimised. He was then sent to the wilds of Badenoch to rule the north of Scotland on behalf of the crown. Instead of playing the king's ambassador, Alexander terrorised and pillaged much of the Highlands, earning him the sobriquet 'the Wolf'. How ironic then, that the godless Wolf of Badenoch now lies beside the High Altar in Dunkeld Cathedral in a tomb that bears the inscription: 'Here lies a good man'.

Perched precariously on the uncomfortable seat of my Rudge Lever Tricycle, I set off across the bridge that spans the Tay at Dunkeld. The present bridge was built by the Scottish civil engineer Thomas Telford and opened in 1808. Previously, there had been at least one medieval bridge over the Tay, but like its predecessor it was

The tomb of the notorious Wolf of Badenoch in Dunkeld Cathedral.

destroyed by various 'great floods' over the years. For several decades, until Telford's bridge was built, travellers wishing to cross the river had to take one of two ferries, which by all accounts was a journey that was sometimes fraught with danger. In 1766, the East Ferry was carrying 13 passengers and four horses when an oar broke. The ferrymen momentarily lost control. The craft was swept downstream in the strong current, until it hit a pier and filled with water. In the chaos, the horses jumped overboard. Some passengers survived by holding onto them, the others were carried away by the river. Six were drowned.

Telford's bridge connects Dunkeld with the village of Birnam on the south side of the Tay. Birnam, a name that resonates with historical and literary associations, is famously mentioned by Shakespeare in *Macbeth*. In the play the witches meet Macbeth on the 'blasted heath' and call out to him: 'Macbeth shall never vanquish'd be until Great Birnam Wood to high Dunsinane Hill shall come against him.' Macbeth is reassured by this

The Birnam Oak, one of the surviving trees of the Great Wood which once covered large tracts of the Highlands.

Ossian's Hall, built by the Duke of Atholl as a summerhouse.

prophesy – and in the invincibility it suggests – until Birnam Wood does indeed come to his castle at Dunsinane. The wood isn't a supernatural army of tree-like Ents from the *Lord of the Rings*, it's a host of warriors hiding behind branches cut from the great wood of Birnam.

The village of Birnam today boasts an ancient tree – the Birnam Oak – which is said to be one of the last survivors of the Great Wood. To find it, I steered my tricycle through quiet streets, following signs to a location close to the south bank of the River Tay. The tree is unmissable – an ancient, venerable specimen, its lower boughs propped up with wooden stakes, and its heart hollowed out and blackened by fire. With a circumference of 24 feet, no one knows how old the oak really is, but it's unlikely to date from the time of the real Macbeth, who lived over a thousand years ago. It also stretches credulity to think that any army would have cut branches to conceal them-

selves before marching to Dunsinane. What's more, the real Dunsinane lies in the Sidlaw Hills 30 kilometres to the south-east. That's quite a hike with a tree on your back. Of course, it has to be remembered the real Macbeth is not the Macbeth we know from the eponymous play. That's the creation of Shakespeare's imagination, which may have been fuelled by his own theatrical tour of Perthshire in 1589. Perhaps Shakespeare saw the oak then, when Birnam Wood stretched into the hills on both sides of the Tay?

Not wishing to dice with death by crossing the busy A9 on my trike, I proceeded on foot to the Hermitage, which is just outside Birnam, on the River Braan. Sarah Murray was a visitor in 1796. She had come from staying with kindly hosts who had laden her with gifts so that, 'My chaise was crammed with provisions, wine and other good things for my use.' Sarah was on her way to experience the delights of one of Scotland's very first tourist attractions: Ossian's Hall, which stood, as it does today, above the 'foaming rage' of the River Braan where 'lofty projecting rocks were striving to kiss each other'.

Ossian's Hall was built in 1782 by the Duke of Atholl to replace a summerhouse that was known as the Hermitage. The building was designed to appear like a small temple, and was decorated inside with plasterwork, a large painting of the blind, mythological poet Ossian and several mirrors. These were set to increase the impact of the scene outside, where the river passes through a narrow gorge over the Black Linn Falls. It certainly had the desired effect on Sarah Murray: 'On entering, I was astonished. The contrast between the room, the beautiful cataract and its scenery, is beyond description striking!'

Retrieving my tricycle, I made my way north, shadowing the busy A9 by following quieter roads close to the River Tay. I had been inspired to take to three wheels by an adventurous early tourist to Scotland. In 1881, Commander Reid propelled himself through the Highlands on a tricycle. Having endured 2,462 miles in the saddle, he sat down, somewhat gingerly I imagine, and produced a beautifully illustrated account of his travels. Called *Nautilus in Scotland*, it's a genuine 'ripping yarn' with some top tips for those who want to emulate his achievement. 'For the first mile or so, go easy until the muscles are fairly in tune. This allows the independent wheel man to select his pace and thus take in the beauties of nature according to his individual taste.'

The rain started to come down in torrents as I made my way beside the river to a rendezvous further upstream. In the spirit of Commander Reid, I wondered what sporting gent, when seeing a river on its tumbling course to the sea, could

Fishing on the Tay with Jock Monteith.

resist his fancy turning to thoughts of fishing. Of all the rivers in Scotland to get a man 'fumbling for his flies', the River Tay must surely excite the most.

Under a dripping oak tree, I met Jock Monteith who was going to initiate me into the art of angling. Together, we crunched our way across a gravel bank, heading to the river. The rain was even heavier now, but Jock was unperturbed. 'The best conditions to catch salmon are when they are in the right frame of mind to take a fly,' he said enigmatically.

'Whether it's raining or not?' I ventured.

'Raining or not. They are wet already!'

The idea of fly-fishing has always puzzled me. When salmon return from the sea to breed, they stop feeding. Why, in that case, would they be interested in taking a fly?

Jock told me there are various theories. The one that seemed most plausible to him suggests that a fisherman's fly annoys and provokes the salmon to lash out and get hooked.

I wasn't convinced but continued to cast hopefully downstream.

'This is a very significant river in the history of angling,' said Jock as he scrutinised my rod-handling technique. 'It has a huge catchment area: 2,500 square miles of Scotland drain into the Tay from the Grampian mountains. There's always enough water for fish to move – even in the height of summer. This makes it a place of superlatives to many anglers.'

In 1922, the British record for a freshwater rod-caught fish was set by the diminutive Miss Georgina Ballantyne when she landed a whopping 64-pound salmon. Jock showed me a photograph of the proud young woman standing triumphantly beside her landed catch. The salmon looked almost as big as she did.

Georgina's enormous salmon made me feel inadequate. I'd lost heart and faith in catching anything. I was soaked, and there hadn't been the slightest hint of a bite. I wasn't sure that angling was for me. 'The last time I went fly-fishing,' I said to Jock, 'I was eight years old. The only thing I caught then was the seat of my pants.'

Jock chuckled. 'Who landed you?'

'I think I must have landed myself,' I said. 'I was that surprised!'

Leaving Jock to spend the rest of the day immersed in both the rain and the River Tay, I continued north, following the road to Logierait and keeping on the opposite bank to the busy A9. About 8 kilometres from Dunkeld I passed a large white house with a slightly grim fortified tower. Screened from the road by a thicket of firs and rhododendrons, it had something of an institutional air. Dalguise House is now run as an adven-ture centre for primary school children. I was surprised to learn that the house was once the favoured Highland holiday destination of Beatrix Potter's family, when the writer and illustrator was a child. Every summer, for 15 years, the wealthy Potters arrived from London to take up residence so that Beatrix's father could enjoy the sporting pursuits on offer – hunting, shooting and fish-ing.

Beatrix was a rather lonely child. She spent her summers at Dalguise observing wildlife and producing animal stories, which she sent as illus-trated letters to children she knew. *The Tale of Peter Rabbit* first appeared in this way.

In my family, we have long cherished a child's breakfast bowl, illustrated with a scene and a quote from the book Peter Rabbit: 'Around the end of the cucumber frame, whom should he meet but Mr MacGregor!' I have always wondered if Mr MacGregor was based on a real Highland character. Other figures from the pen of Beatrix Potter can be traced to her time at Dalguise. Mr Jeremy Fisher, the angling frog, is said to be based on memories of her father and long days spent beside the Tay; Mrs Tiggywinkle the hedgehog was drawn from affectionate recollections of the laundry maid at Dalguise. I wonder who Squirrel Nutkin was based on?

Logierait on the River Tay was once an impor-tant village. It lies just upstream from where the Tay meets the River Tummel and was for many years an important ferry crossing. Travellers would often break their journey here before heading north to Inverness, or south to Perth. Sarah Murray took this route in 1796 with her sketchbook and pen, but perhaps the most prestigious guest to visit Logierait was Queen Victoria. Her royal tour of 1842 was interrupted when the great monarch was forced to answer the call of nature. Caught short, the royal personage popped into the loos of the Logierait Hotel for some relief. History does not record what she left by way of a tip.

When I arrived at Logierait, having crossed the Tay using the old railway bridge, I was bemused to see a large Bollywood film crew camped out on the banks of the river. A helicopter buzzed overhead. It was filming the female star of the scene as she watched some action going on midstream. Cameras recorded her wild gesticulations and a look of horror on her face. Then it started to rain. The film crew ran for cover. The star was rushed inside the Logierait Hotel where I was enjoying a spot of light refreshment. She was surrounded by an anxious entourage, who wrapped her in a silver foil survival blanket and plied her with brandy and hot chocolate.

When the rain stopped, the filming restarted, and I remounted my trike and made for Pitlochry, which *Black's Guide* says 'occupies an agreeable situation on the left bank of the river Tummel'. When Sarah Murray came through the district she was heading to Faskally House where she had friends, but she made no mention of the town.

Back then, Pitlochry was a small settlement, but after Queen Victoria wrote enthusiastically about her visit to nearby Blair Castle, tourists followed in the royal wake and Pitlochry began to prosper and grow. When the railway was built from the south to Inverness, Pitlochry's destiny as a Victorian resort was sealed. Just as in Crieff, a hydropathic establishment was founded which *Black's* describes as 'an imposing building on rising ground, surrounded by extensive pleasure grounds laid out in the most agreeable manner'. Here, Victorians could take spa water treatments and enjoy the invigorating Highland air. The old Hydro is

still there, now trading as the Atholl Palace Hotel where spa treatments continue to be offered. After cycling my Rudge Lever Tricycle for miles, my battered body could have done with some remedial work, but unfortunately, I had no time for such luxuries.

A visitor to Pitlochry today can't fail to notice the large number of retail outlets offering various versions of Highland dress, from kilts and tweeds to tartan plaids and shawls. What is true today was also true in Victorian times, and *Black's* was aware of the potential 'wardrobe malfunctions' that could ensue if the unwary tourist went unrestrained. *Black's* notes: 'It is evident that many of our southern brethren consider the plaid to be a passport through the Highlands; and while it is a fact that the Scottish Lowlander is seldom seen in such a costume, the English all too frequently adopt this dress.'

Southerners, it seems, couldn't resist the sheer theatricality of swinging kilts 'aboon their knees'!

The scenery that Sarah Murray admired as she travelled to Faskally House has been completely altered by a dam across the River Tummel at Pitlochry. Where the River Tummel meets the Garry there were once 'furious falls'. This is where Sarah watched salmon leap as they tried to reach their spawning grounds. She noted a large net bag fastened to a long pole. It was used by fishermen to catch salmon falling back into the river having failed in their leap against gravity and the rushing torrent. Today, the 'foaming, roaring' falls that excited Sarah have been tamed. The dam has since increased the level of the Garry and the Tummel to create Loch Faskally and the pretty Linn of Tummel (from the Gaelic *linne*, a deep pool). The Linn is owned by the National Trust for Scotland and offers quiet woodland walks.

The spectacular Queen's View, named after Queen Isabella, the wife of Robert the Bruce.

LOCH TUMMEL TO RANNOCH

The Tunnel Tigers – the poet chief – Clan Atholl and the Highland Charge

Following the River Tummel west, I arrived at Loch Tummel. Situated at its western end is Queen's View, which offers one of the most scenic panoramas in Highland Scotland. Although many people believe the viewpoint is named after Queen Victoria who paid a visit on one of her many tours, it is also possible that the queen referred to is several centuries older – the 14th century to be precise. According to legend, Queen Isabella, the wife of Robert the Bruce, used this place to rest her weary old royal self while travelling through the Highlands.

The view is really spectacular – and certainly one worthy of royal appreciation – but it's not what Queen Victoria or Queen Isabella would have seen and I'm not talking about modern changes like forestry plantations, new houses and roads. There's been a more fundamental change than that. The landscape has been altered by the rising water levels caused the nearby Clunie Dam, which blocks the flow of water from Loch Tummel. It's part of an ambitious hydroelectric scheme that was developed in the 1950s to harness the power of water collected from a vast Highland catchment area. Seven enormous dams were built, and over 7,000 kilometres of tunnels were dug to carry the water to several power stations.

Working in appalling conditions deep underground, an army of men toiled day and night, drilling and blasting their way through solid rock to divert the flow of water into the scheme. On the opposite side of Loch Tummel is a memorial to the men who did the dangerous work. Called the Clunie Memorial Arch, this concrete structure has the same dimensions as the gigantic tunnel that was dug to bring water through the mountains. A bronze plaque inscribed with a list of names is a reminder of the human cost of the project. Those men – and the men who survived – are known as the 'Tunnel Tigers'. I met up with one of them a few years ago, while he was holidaying in the place where he had worked as a young man.

An Irish Gaelic speaker from Donegal, Gonna O'Donnell came to Scotland as a teenager, hoping to join a relative who was already working on the hydroelectric scheme. 'The first job you got was as a spanner man. That's the man who holds the spinning drill for the man drilling holes for explosive,' said Gonna. 'We had no gloves, no earmuffs. I was stone deaf in a week. Completely stone deaf! The men in the tunnels were mostly miners, some were plate layers looking after the railway lines. Then you had the powder monkeys looking after the explosives. Then you had the loco driver taking out the muck.'

'Was it dangerous work?' I asked.

'Everything is dangerous when you don't know. When I first went in, everyone was minding my back. When a new man came in, I minded his. We looked after each other and pointed out the dangers.'

Gonna lived on-site in a camp high on the mountainside, along with hundreds of other workers. Many like him had come from rural Ireland. Others were from Eastern Europe. They had

Gonna O'Donnell, right, one of the original 'Tunnel Tigers', with veteran engineer Brian Haslam.

escaped the Cold War to find work on the great hydro scheme.

'It's a funny thing,' said Gonna. 'I like to come back every other year or so to see what we built. Looking at it makes me feel 18 feet tall! And it makes me proud that I was a small part of it. It's our legacy, you could say. The legacy of the Tunnel Tigers.'

The land around Loch Tummel was once the centre of power for Clan Donnachaidh, later known as Clan Robertson. The most famous chief of the clan was Alexander Struan Robertson, the 13th chief, who was born in 1670. He became a legend in his own lifetime. An ardent supporter of the Stuart cause, Alexander was a writer of poetry, a misogynist, a celebrated drunk, and the

Opposite. The Clunie Memorial Arch, which commemorates the 'Tunnel Tigers' who worked on the massive hydroelectric scheme here in the 1950s.

Above. The eerie ruins of Dunalastair House on the banks of the River Tummell.

only clan chief to have fought in all the great Jacobite risings of the 17th and 18th centuries. He modelled himself on the great chiefs of old and was a self-styled keeper of the Jacobite flame, upholding ancient clan values and traditions, which were based on honour and ancestry.

Alexander lived in a remote setting close to the River Tummel, in a district with no roads, and isolated from the outside world. At a place known today as Dunalastair, close to the River Tummel, he designed and built himself a villa, which he called the Hermitage. It was destroyed after the 1745 Jacobite rebellion and later replaced by Dunalastair House – now an eerily spectacular ruin overlooking land flooded by Dunalastair reservoir.

A few years ago, I met up with a member of the clan, James Irvine Robertson, who has written about the 13th chief. 'Alexander loved it here. It was his spiritual home and it inspired him to verse,' said James. He recited:

Expand they gates thou blessed abode
They long neglected cells repair
Confess the bounteous care of God,
Our Strephon breathes his native air!

James went on to describe Alexander as a very convivial man. 'People travelled a long way to enjoy his drink and his company. But there was one pleasure they couldn't indulge – they couldn't enjoy the company of women at the Hermitage. There was a sign, written in verse at the gate, forbidding entry to members of the opposite sex. The Hermitage was a bachelor pad only, fuelled by brandy, conversation and humour.'

Curiously, perhaps, for a man of excess, Alexander had once been a student of divinity at the University of St Andrews. When King James II and VII was forced into French exile by his brother-in-law William of Orange, the young student Alexander turned his thoughts from heaven to war. Leading a force of clansmen to join 'Bonnie Dundee' (more on him later) at the Battle of Killiecrankie, Alexander was too late and missed the action. He then fled to France where he spent ten years in the court of the exiled Stuart king. Here he continued the good fight, using his pen to make verbal assaults on the new regime. Poetry was his weapon and imagination his ammunition. In a series of bawdy and sometimes obscene verse, he compared the effete new king William of Orange unfavourably with the virile but exiled James II:

The other un-performing prig
Could only with his page retire and frig.

The opportunity for Alexander to return to the battlefield came in 1715 with another Jacobite rising, which once again started in Scotland. This time Alexander wasn't late. He led his men onto the field at the Battle of Sheriffmuir, where he fought with distinction and honour. Although the Jacobite forces outnumbered the government troops two to one, they were unable to press home their advantage, and both armies retired claiming victory. Unfortunately, Alexander was captured during this inconclusive clash of arms and was imprisoned in Edinburgh Castle along with other Jacobite combatants. He was sprung from jail by his resourceful sister in an episode that reads more like farce than history. Disguised, and using a false name, she bribed her way into the castle prison and plied the guards with brandy, getting them so drunk that Alexander was able to make good his escape.

After another long French exile, Alexander returned for a third rebellion – this time to join Bonnie Prince Charlie in the rising of the '45. By now, Alexander was 75 years old, but age didn't prevent him from marching his clansmen to the Battle of Prestonpans, where the deadly and feared 'Highland Charge' overwhelmed and destroyed the government army. After this triumphant victory, Alexander seized the defeated commander Sir John Cope's carriage, claiming it as a trophy of war along with his gold chain and a wolf-fur cloak. On the way home to the Hermitage, the carriage wheel broke when it hit rough ground. Alexander ordered his men to carry the coach on their shoulders for the last few miles home, where he celebrated long and hard. But the sweet smell of success didn't last a year.

When the Jacobite dream of a Stuart restoration was destroyed at the Battle of Culloden, Alexander's estate was forfeited. His beloved Hermitage was torched by government troops, and he was forced into internal exile on his own land. In a house at Carie on the edge of the Black Wood of Rannoch, he eked out the rest of his life. When Alexander died in 1746, over 2,000 clansmen accompanied the poet chief's coffin some 15 miles to the kirkyard at Struan.

With fellow warriors of Clan Atholl.

In the hills of Clan Donnachaidh country I met up with a group of enthusiasts who wouldn't have looked out of place following the old Robertson chief Alexander on his Jacobite adventures, that is, if they'd lived in the 18th century and not the 21st. Calling themselves Clan Atholl, they take part in battle re-enactments and demonstrations of authentic Highland life. They have also appeared in several historical films and television shows, including some of my own, where the Highland Charge features as part of the action.

Alan Torrance is their leader. His red flowing locks and intimidatingly thick beard make him ideal for the part he has chosen to play in his double life as a Highland warrior. On that day, Alan wanted to initiate me into the 'clan'. But first I had to look the part. To do this, he asked me to drop my trousers and lie down. Alarmed at first, I was reassured when he only produced a six-yard length of tartan cloth.

'This will be your plaid,' he said.

Under the watchful gaze of the others, he instructed me in how to roll myself in the cloth, make pleats, then throw the remaining material over my shoulder, fastening it all together with my leather belt.

'This will keep you warm and dry – up to a point. And at night, you can use it like a sleeping bag.'

'Will it keep out the midges?' I asked.

'Nothing keeps out those wee bastards!' he replied.

Tartan leggings and a blue bonnet were added to the ensemble. Alan then handed me a dirk, a round leather shield called a targe, and a basket-hilted broadsword. Fully equipped, I was ready to practise the Highland Charge – that headlong, running assault that had such a devastating effect on government troops in Jacobite times.

'The idea was to use your speed and agility to shock the enemy. Surprise helped, but speed was essential. A government soldier could fire every 25 seconds. You had to get to the enemy line before they could reload. Sometimes, the clansmen would stay just out of range to provoke an early volley, then they'd run like hell, screaming their war cry, and get in about the enemy before they could fire again.' Alan sounded breathless. He was obviously enjoying this.

'But having run so far and so fast, wouldn't you already be exhausted before the bloody business of hand-to-hand fighting began?' I asked.

'No. Clansmen were fit. They had a hard physical life outside in the open air all their lives. If you were nae fit and strong, you'd no survive.'

The Atholl men were ready to charge now. About 20 of us lined up on the crest of a hill. We banged our targes rhythmically with the hilt of our broadswords. The beat was hypnotic. Then Alan gave the signal. Screaming the clan war cry 'Claymore!' we hurtled downhill where heathery tussocks hid dangerous holes to trap feet and topple the unwary. The man to my right fell, then another to my left went down. Still we charged on.

'Alan! 'I cried. 'Where's the enemy?'

'There isn't one. Just keep going and use your imagination!'

At the bottom of the hill we staggered to a stop. I glanced behind to see how many casualties we'd taken. Six men were pulling themselves upright having taken a tumble in the heather.

I'd been impressed by Alan's imaginative powers and his attention to authentic detail. But one thing bothered me. Not one of the clansmen was wearing period footwear. Some were wearing lightweight treadless shoes, which couldn't have helped. Perhaps that's why they'd slipped and fallen. I pointed this out.

'Aye well, I know,' Alan answered. 'The fact is, most clansmen would have been barefoot. And many of them would have thrown off their plaids and charged the enemy butt naked. But that's going a wee bit too far I think.'

It was a relief to discover that the pursuit of authenticity – even among battle re-enactors – does have its limits.

Loch Rannoch is a big loch, stretching east to west for almost 16 kilometres. On its southern shores, Rannoch Forest climbs the flanks of high hills towards distant summits. An area of this now commercial forest includes a remnant of the magically named Black Wood of Rannoch – one of the largest areas of ancient Caledonian pine forest left in the country. Here the Scots pine, *Pinus sylvestris*, is the dominant tree species.

Pinus sylvestris was recently voted Scotland's national tree. In the Black Wood of Rannoch are some ancient specimens. Some gnarled relics are thought to be up to 400 years old. It is amazing to think that they would have been vigorous youngsters when Alexander Struan Robertson was alive. Sadly, over the centuries the trees have suffered over-exploitation by human hands. A huge area of the original wood was felled and sold for timber by Robertson chiefs and later estate factors. In one part of the Black Wood I was shown traces of a canal, dug two centuries ago, to float logs for export, first into Loch Rannoch and then further downstream.

Kinloch Rannoch sits at the eastern end of the loch – at its foot, unusually, rather than at its head. Cycling through the village, it seemed a quiet, solid, respectable sort of place, but at one time, Kinloch Rannoch was the heart of a wild and rebellious community.

In 1746, after the Jacobite army of Bonnie Prince Charlie had been destroyed and dispersed at the Battle of Culloden, the fastness of Rannoch became a refuge for desperate men on the run. The British government, intent on retribution, pursued them, burned their homes and confiscated their land. This led to great poverty and hunger throughout the district. Because the people were starving, the returning Highland warriors resorted to theft to keep themselves and their families alive and Rannoch became a byword for cattle rustling and lawlessness. A captain in the army of occupation wrote: 'the people of this country are the greatest thieves in Scotland and were all in the late rebellion, except for a few. They have a great number of arms but they keep them concealed from us.'

Within a few years, peace and tranquillity were restored. The village of Kinloch Rannoch was established and schools and churches were built, all in the cause of civilising the wild Highland natives. From what I could see as I glided past on my Rudge Lever Tricycle, the pacification of the native seemed to have worked. I didn't see a rebellious Jacobite anywhere in the neat, orderly wee place.

Taking the southern road along the loch, I pedalled my way west towards the settlement of Bridge of Gaur, passing Dall House about halfway. For many years this was home to the fee-paying Rannoch School, which closed in 2002. The school seems to have produced alumni who were instilled with a healthy passion for the outdoors (I've met several in my time) – perhaps not surprising given its remote setting. At the Bridge of Gaur, where redcoat soldiers were formerly garrisoned during 'peacekeeping duties', I crossed the river and continued along its right bank to the end of the road at Rannoch.

To be honest, there's not much to see at Rannoch. Half a dozen houses and a hotel are scattered on peaty ground, facing Loch Laidon and the great solitude of Rannoch Moor which stretches for 15 kilometres towards the Black Mount and Glencoe. This is a haven for red deer, heather, bog cotton and wild flowers. It can also be a hell of oozing peat bogs, wind and rain, and, in the summer months, a purgatory of midges. The main feature of the village, if you can call Rannoch that, is the railway station, where an iron footbridge spans the line (incidentally, this originally came from Corrour, the next stop north). From Rannoch station it's possible to catch a train all the way to Euston in London. Standing on the platform listening to skylarks singing overhead, it was hard to imagine the contrast with the fumes and traffic of the metropolis. The two places hardly seemed to belong on the same planet, let alone in the same country.

With that thought, I stepped inside the station tearoom, which is run by an English couple who love their remote location. Their tearoom is a delightfully cosy place to shelter. Here I was able to gather both my resources and my strength before tackling the long return trip to Pitlochry.

Refreshments are offered at Rannoch, one of the most remote stations in the country.

SCHIEHALLION TO DALWHINNIE

Contours of a fairy mountain – the Battle of Killiecrankie – Cluny's Cage

Well fuelled with coffee and homebaking, I set off along the northern road around Loch Rannoch. The view was dominated by glimpses of Schiehallion's shapely peak, a mountain that I have climbed many times, and once quite painfully when I carried my four-year-old son Patrick on my shoulders for most of the way up and all the way down. I had a stiff neck for weeks afterwards.

Looking at Schiehallion from the lochside road, it seemed obvious from its aesthetic outline why it was considered to be a sacred mountain in ancient times – a magical place and the haunt of fairies. In the 18th century, such fey notions were put aside when science arrived and tamed Schiehallion with a series of measurements designed to determine the mass of the earth. But to do this, the men of science and mathematics first had to work out the mass of something smaller – like a mountain.

In 1775 the Astronomer Royal, Nevil Maskelyne and mathematician Charles Hutton chose Schiehallion because of its regular conical shape. If you look at the OS map of Schiehallion, you can clearly see how uniform it looks from the contour lines. Interestingly, contours, as a mapping technique, were actually invented by Charles Hutton to help him calculate the volume of the mountain; the first ever contour lines in the world

Schiehallion, the mountain that helped Victorian scientists calculate the mass of the earth.

were drawn for Schiehallion to make the wild mountain measurable. Contours have been used by nearly all map-makers everywhere ever since.

Once the volume of Schiehallion had been worked out, Maskelyne and Hutton were able to calculate what fraction of the earth's volume this represented. Then, using a pendulum, they established the pull of Schiehallion away from the earth. This enabled them to calculate the mass of Schiehallion and then by multiplying up by the ratio of mountain to the size of the earth they calculated the mass of the earth itself.

The experiment took 17 weeks to complete – partly because of the terrible weather that summer. But it was a brilliant success and got very close to the modern figure of 5.9 × ten to the power 24 kilograms. Unfortunately, it also proved to be a very costly experiment. It had taken so long, the expedition bankrupted the august body that had funded the research in the first place – the Royal Society. But this didn't stop the scientists celebrating their success. Maskelyn threw a party on the mountain for the locals who had helped him. It was quite a night by all accounts. The fiddler burnt his fiddle and then burnt down the bothy where they had all been staying. It's hard sometimes to be a rock and not to roll!

At Pitlochry, I swapped my vintage tricycle for a more modern contraption – a 1950s Humber bicycle complete with Sturmey-Archer gears, a dynamo light and a bell. With bicycle clips in place and doing their job, I set off north following the old road through the Pass of Killiecrankie.

The Pass of Killiecrankie, a name which comes from the Gaelic Coille Chneaghaidh, the 'wood of the shimmering Aspens', is a dramatic gorge filled by the roaring River Garry. *Black's* is its usual effusive self: 'Here and there the water runs at one time dark and silent and at another boiling and foaming. The mountainous bank rises like a wall from the dark chasm below, and to the very summit is covered with wood with trembling foliage.'

In 1689, Killiecrankie was the location for a bloody battle between the forces of the new king, William of Orange, and a combined force of Highlanders and Irishmen who supported the exiled Stuart king, James II and VII. Leading the Jacobites was James Graham of Claverhouse, the 1st Marquis of Dundee. Known as 'Bonnie Dundee', Graham was a brilliant leader but a ruthless commander, a fact that had earned him another sobriquet – 'Bloody Clavers'.

In July 1689, Dundee's army – outnumbered by two to one – faced a north-marching government force of over 5,000 infantry and cavalry. Dundee knew that his enemy would have to come through the Pass of Killiecrankie so he turned geography to his advantage. Occupying the high ground on the slopes of Creag Eallich, which stands above the House of Urrard, he formed his men up to be ready with their Highland Charge. As the red-coated government troops emerged from the Pass of Killiecrankie, their commander saw the Jacobite army on the hill above him. When the sun dipped below the hills, and was no longer shining in their faces, the Highlanders hurled themselves at the troops below. They cut their enemy to pieces. Surviving redcoats turned and ran in a chaotic rout. Highland triumph turned

quickly to tragedy – Dundee was hit by a bullet. According to legend, he bled to death, leaning against an ancient standing stone. Today this monolith is known as the Claverhouse Stone and can be seen from the road below the House of Urrard.

In the aftermath of battle, Bonnie Dundee's body was carried to the nearby church of St Bride, where he was buried. His untimely death quickly became the stuff of legend. One story suggests that Dundee had the protection of the Devil himself, and could never be killed by a lead bullet. So how had he died? What could kill one of Satan's chosen? Only precious silver had that sort of power. Perhaps the lead bullet had struck one of Dundee's buttons, which in turn had caused the fatal wound. This story has two propaganda advantages: it denigrates Dundee as a hellhound, while attributing his death to something intrinsically unheroic – a button.

Another story about the Battle of Killiecrankie tells how a government soldier escaped by leaping across the River Garry from a high rock. Known as Soldier's Leap, this 5.5-metre gap was crossed by the legendary soldier and adventurer Donald McBane, while he was being pursued by a mob of victorious Highland warriors. Donald survived his leap of faith and went on to become a prize fighter. Later in life, he wrote a manual of swordsmanship.

I remember being take to see the Soldier's Leap when I was a child. Looking at the enormous gap across the river, the distance to jump, the height of the rock, the trees and the steep ground all around, I wondered how it had been possible. Had Donald McBane's narrow escape been embellished to make it appear even more heroic? I suppose that's precisely how fact becomes myth, especially in the Highlands where reality shifts and changes with the retelling of events.

As I cycled towards Blair Atholl, and Blair Castle, I found myself following lines of cars through the village. The annual Highland Games had attracted both locals and tourists from far afield. The grounds of the castle were heaving as people thronged burger stalls, supped on stovies, gulped beer in beer tents, and generally milled around accompanied by an incessant medley of pipe tunes played by various 'lone pipers' dotted around the field of competition. As I settled down in the spring sunshine to watch, the Atholl Highlanders, some pulling a small cannon, marched into the area led by a pipe band. These men famously make up the only surviving private army permitted to exist in Europe. In 1839, the Duke of Atholl, George Murray, formed a regiment from his tenants to act as a personal bodyguard. When the young Queen Victoria came to stay with the duke at Blair Castle in 1842, the Atholl men guarded her day and night. Victoria was impressed. To reward them and to show her gratitude, she granted the Atholl Highlanders royal colours, thereby giving them an official status. Today, their function is purely ceremonial and recruitment is by invitation only.

After much marching, wheeling about and puffing at the chanter, the Atholl Highlanders fired their cannon. A muffled explosion and a puff of gunpowder smoke marked the start of the athletic competition. I went down to watch, and to chat to Bruce Robb who, amongst other things, has been tossing his caber for years.

'I've read that Highland Games are really an invention of the Victorian age,' I said, provokingly.

Soldier's Leap. Donald McBane leapt the 5.5-metre gap when fleeing the Battle of Killiekrankie in 1689.

Atholl Highlanders at Blair Castle.

'Before that, there were no Highland Games at all.'

'No, no. That's not the way of it at all,' said Bruce, who towered a good ten inches above me. 'It goes back thousands of years when clans competed with each other to see who was the strongest, the most athletic. It was a preparation for battle. The games were a proving ground for warriors.'

From his muscular physique, Bruce was clearly made of warrior material himself.

'Today, I'm doing the Scots Hammer, the Caber, Weight over the Bar, and the Shot-Put,' he said.

'Where does the caber tossing come from?' I asked.

'There's various myths about loggers working away in the forest. They used to throw whole trees into rivers to float them downstream. The sport comes from that, I think.'

Leaving Bruce to grapple with his caber – very successfully as it turned out – I made my way to the beer tent to sample the local ale and to talk to some thirsty pipers.

The striking white walls of Blair Castle can be seen for many miles around. This local landmark was originally built in the 13th century by the powerful Comyn family. It then changed hands over several generations, belonging first to the Campbells and then the Stewarts. In the 17th century it was granted by the crown to George Murray, who also acquired the title of Earl of Atholl.

When Sarah Murray came this way in 1796, she didn't have the opportunity to stay at Blair Castle, but she wrote admiringly of the duke's prowess as a deer hunter. 'The Duke is one of the best shots in Britain; but notwithstanding, his Grace is often obliged to be scrambling about the crags for eight or ten hours before he succeeds.'

Sarah dined on 'the venison of the wild deer' and found it to be delicious. As her man guided her carriage on the long road from Blair up Glen Tilt to Forest Lodge, Sarah passed great herds of these animals. Rocked from side to side on her upholstered seat, Sarah contented herself with the thought that a smooth new road 'would at some time or other' be built from Blair, through the glen, and down to Braemar on Deeside. Over two centuries later we are *still* waiting, although today the rough track that Sarah took is open to mountain bikes and walkers.

When Sarah reached Forest Lodge, which is still a hunting lodge on the Atholl estate, she was treated to the famous, health-giving Atholl Brose. 'Made of whisky, eggs and honey it is a delicious treat to a lover of whisky, and much prized by the people of Atholl.'

The recipe Sarah describes is an odd one. Oats are traditionally an important ingredient of Atholl Brose, along with whisky, honey and sometimes cream. Perhaps the whisky was so strong and the honey so sweet that Sarah didn't notice the oats. I bet she slept well that night.

As I left Blair and headed north-west, climbing towards the Drumochter Pass, I was glad to have swapped my Rudge Lever Tricycle for the sleek vintage Humber which was altogether kinder on the buttocks. The route I was following took the long-distance cycle path Route 7, which avoids the traffic on the A9, although the rumble of lorries and speeding cars occasionally drifted across the glen. At Calvine, I made a detour to Struan, which clan chief Alexander Robertson took as his middle name. Struan comes from the Gaelic for 'the meeting of two waters'. The old kirk at Struan occupies a peninsula of land bounded by Errochty Water where it joins the River Garry. This is where Alexander's body was carried by his faithful clansmen in 1746. Strangely, for a figure of such monumental significance in Highland history, Alexander's last resting place has been lost.

There's nothing to mark the grave of Alexander in Struan kirkyard, but here among the weathered headstones is an early medieval Christian inscribed stone. And inside the kirk, to protect it from the elements, is a stone that's probably much older. On a large, irregular block of slate is an elegant Pictish carving. Looking almost like a modern tattooist's handiwork, it consists of a double disc, circles within circles, and a 'Z' shape. Apparently, there was once another inscription beside it, but this has largely worn away.

The House of Bruar sits on the A9 and is a busy watering hole and stop-over location for drivers heading north and south. Perhaps because of its prices, it has been described as the 'Harrods of the North', and attracts tourists in droves into its

The Pictish carving in the old kirk at Struan.

merchandising halls and tearoom. Avoiding such temptations, I parked my bike at the nearby Clan Robertson Museum instead, where I met up with historian Ron Greer. I'd come to see the mysterious and beautiful *Clach na Bratach* – a crystal orb which, it is said, was found on the eve of battle by Clan Robertson's first great heroic chief, Duncan – or *Donnachaidh* as he was known in Gaelic. It was Duncan who gave his name to the original Clan Donnachaidh before they become known as the Robertsons.

Ron proudly showed off the ancient relic – a spherical rock crystal, about 3 centimetres in diameter.

'It looks just like a crystal ball, Ron,' I said.

'That's exactly what it is. It was found 700 years ago on the eve of one of the many battles between Clan Donnachaidh and their inveterate enemies Clan MacDougall. Legend has it that the night before the battle, Chief Duncan put the pole that held the clan's banner in the ground. In the morning when he pulled the banner out again, he found the *Clach na Bratach* in the hole left behind. Incidentally, *Clach na Bratach* in Gaelic means "the stone of the banner".'

'What an amazing find. And what a coincidence!' I said.

'That's why the clan thought there was something supernatural going on. Things like this couldn't just happen. It was meant to be found and was hailed as a great portent for victory.'

'And was it?' I asked.

'Indeed it was. For over 400 years the clan prospered with the stone in their possession. It was so powerful that the clan claimed it had helped defeat the English at Bannockburn when they carried it into battle for King Robert the Bruce. But it wasn't just for bringing good fortune in times of war. It also bestowed healing powers on the chief. If he placed it in water, the water would acquire potent healing properties.'

'What's the crack I see in the crystal?' I asked.

'Well, the stone was used to tell the future, just like a witch would use her crystal ball. When he was chief in 1715, Alexander Robertson consulted the stone to see if the Jacobite rebellion would be successful. The omens weren't good. That's when the crack appeared.'

'The rebellion was lost before it started, then,' I said.

'At least according to the *Clach na Bratach*.'

Musing on the shifting nature of past realities and the unreliability of history – especially in the Highlands, I continued on my way. The cycle path was much closer now to both the Inverness main-line railway and the A9 road, facts which made it difficult to appreciate the otherwise remote grandeur of my situation. To the south-west, the waters of Loch Garry sparkled in the afternoon sunshine under a lonely sky.

Rising ahead were two darkly prominent peaks known locally as the Sow of Atholl and the Boar of Badenoch, both guarding the Drumochter Pass. The pass is something of a bottleneck: here the main road, the railway, the cycle path, and General Wade's 18th-century military road are squeezed together beneath the heather-clad, scree-topped hills on either side. At the summit of the pass, which rises to 462 metres, I took a photograph of my Humber bicycle, and rested for a moment in the sunshine, remembering the trials of winter, and how I had often crept in my car over

My 1950s Humber bicycle, which was far more suitable for Highland terrain than the Rudge Lever Tricycle.

Drumochter on a dark night, following a red tail-light into swirling, drifting snow.

When Sarah Murray came this way it was summertime, but the desolation she encountered struck a chord in her soul. The solitary hotel at Dalwhinnie seemed lost in the vastness of the landscape: 'A person accustomed only to the scenes in the vicinity of London, or the greatest part of England, would be dismayed at the sight of this lonely habitation, the only one for miles around where not a tree or a shrub is to be seen; only desolate crags, and a boggy heath of great extent on every side. Dalwhinnie pleased me.'

The village of Dalwhinnie sits at the northern end of Loch Ericht, which fills a deep trough scoured out millennia ago by long-vanished glaciers. In the distant blue haze to the south-west, and holding onto its winter snows well into summer, the great bulk of Ben Alder dominates the view.

As you'd expect, Dalwhinnie has grown since Sarah Murray visited – though perhaps not by all that much – and her description of a 'lonely habitation' still holds true. This is still a desolate place. But seen from a distance, it's not the hotel that draws the eye but the tall white pagoda towers of the Dalwhinnie distillery.

I'm not sure if Sarah had a dram after she had settled into her room at the hotel, but she was ready to explore her new surroundings. 'Though the evening was chill, and a mist was coming on, I walked to the head of Loch Ericht, about three quarters of a mile across the boggy heath. The high bare crags swept precipitously to the loch's edge, with now and then, patches of wood creeping up their lofty sides.'

A couple of years ago I was lucky enough to take a 17-kilometre boat trip down Loch Ericht to Ben Alder Cottage, beneath the towering mass of Ben Alder. It was a long way – much further than I realised. The cottage is now run by the Mountain Bothy Association for the use of walkers, mountaineers and kayakers. In the past, it was home to a deer stalker and his family who were the only people living in this desolate area. When the family eventually left, the place fell into disrepair but it soon found a new role as a howf and drinking den used by navvies working on the Loch Ericht dam.

We were passing through very remote country. There are no public roads along either shore – there never have been – and history is silent on the subject of who might have occupied the lochsides in the distant past. Maps from the 17th century show no habitation at all. It seems Loch Ericht has been a wild and lonely place for a very long time.

The remoteness and inaccessibility of the area was used to great advantage by desperate men in the aftermath of the '45. Cluny Macpherson, a staunch Jacobite chief and the overlord of the lands around Loch Ericht, fought on the side of Bonnie Prince Charlie. After the Jacobite defeat at Culloden in April 1746, Macpherson and a band of faithful warriors concealed themselves for several years in various mountain hideouts. One of these was somewhere on the slopes of Ben Alder. Known as 'Cluny's Cage', it was supposed to have been constructed of branches and turf set around a natural chimney, which was formed by a giant boulder that had been split down the middle. It was to Cluny's Cage that Bonnie Prince Charlie came when he was on the run from government troops. The prince spent two weeks hiding with Macpherson on the slopes of Ben Alder before finally escaping to the west coast where a ship took him to France.

Cluny Macpherson continued to use his mountain hideout for a long time afterwards, but to this day no one is really sure where his cage was located. Robert Louis Stevenson wrote a fictional description of it in his novel *Kidnapped*. The action takes place some six years after Culloden, but Cluny Macpherson is still in hiding there: 'The trunks of several trees had been wattled across, the intervals strengthened with stakes, and the ground behind the barricade levelled up with earth to make the floor. A tree, which grew out from the hillside, was the living centre beam of the roof. The walls were of wattle and covered with moss. The whole house had something of an egg shape; and it half hung, half stood on that hillside thicket.'

The Cage is generally thought to have been somewhere close to the bothy of Ben Alder Cottage. Leaving the boat at Ben Alder Bay, I set off to try and find the site of Cluny's Cage for myself. From Stevenson's description, it was on a hillside covered with trees. But there were none that I could see today. Had Stevenson been using

The desolate country south of Dalwhinnie – lonely Loch Ericht and distant Ben Alder.

his literary imagination, or had the woodland been cleared by felling and overgrazing? On my OS maps there was a location marked with the name 'Prince Charlie's Cave'. This seemed a promising start. It lay a few metres north of the cottage and close to the burn that flows from the Bealach Breabag. I spent a frustrating hour or so scouring the hillside to no avail. And hadn't the prince stayed in a *cage* rather than a cave? Climbing higher up the steep flanks of Ben Alder, I came to a boulder-filled ledge several hundred metres above the loch with fantastic views of the country to the south. There were still no trees, but what a place for a lookout. What a place to hide! Perhaps Cluny had built his cage in a place like this. From here he would have felt like an eagle in his eyrie, able to see anyone approaching, be they a prince on the run or a party of pursuing redcoats.

PART FOUR

**FROM BREADALBANE, ACROSS RANNOCH MOOR TO
KINLOCHLEVEN, THE MAMORE FOREST AND ON TO CORROUR**

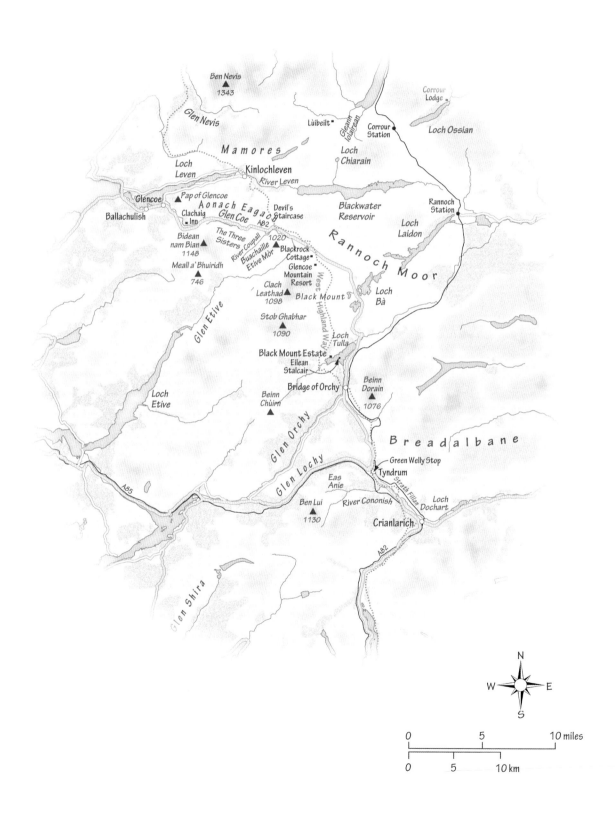

Ben Nevis
1343

Glen Nevis

Corrour
Lodge

Lùibeilt

Gleann Iolairean

Corrour
Station

Loch Ossian

Mamores

Loch
Chiarain

Loch
Leven

Kinlochleven

River Leven

Glencoe

Pap of Glencoe

Aonach Eagach

Devil's
Staircase

Blackwater
Reservoir

Rannoch
Station

Ballachulish

Clachaig
Inn

Glen Coe

A82

Loch
Laidon

Bidean
nam Bian
1148

The Three
Sisters

River Coupall

1020

Blackrock
Cottage

Rannoch Moor

Buachaille
Etive Mòr

Glencoe
Mountain
Resort

Meall a' Bhuiridh
746

Clach
Leathad
1098

Black Mount

Loch
Bà

Glen Etive

Stob Ghabhar
1090

West Highland Way

Loch
Tulla

Black Mount Estate

Eilean
Stalcair

Loch
Etive

Bridge of Orchy

Beinn
Dorain
1076

Beinn
Chùirn

Breadalbane

Glen Orchy

Green Welly Stop

Glen Lochy

Tyndrum

A85

Eas
Anie

Strath Fillan

Loch
Dochart

Ben Lui
1130

River Cononish

Crianlarich

A82

Glen Shira

N
W E
S

0   5   10 miles

0   5   10 km

CRIANLARICH TO TYNDRUM

The Gold Mountain – the Green Welly Stop – water cures and lofty verse

The A82 north of Crianlarich has been my gateway to adventure ever since I was a teenage hitch-hiker, heading towards the peaks of Glencoe, Lochaber and beyond. After passing beneath the old railway viaduct in the centre of Crianlarich village, the views quickly open up. The mountains seem higher and steeper and the views tantalise with glimpses of a wild, almost treeless landscape. There is excitement in the air.

Ben Lui, to my mind the most beautiful mountain in the southern Highlands, sits well back from the traffic on the A82 at the head of a long and lonely glen. The mountain's twin peaks soar above its great northern corrie making a fishtail summit that continually draws the eye and thoughts of ascent. But before a climber can reach the lower slopes, there's an 8-kilometre hike along a rough track beside the River Cononish, passing close to a fragment of Caledonian Forest whose gnarled pines recall more dangerous times when wolves hunted in packs and clan fought clan for supremacy. In such a landscape, it's hard to imagine that this glen was, and still is, a place of industry.

Beinn Chùirn, the hill on the northern banks of the Cononish, is home to Scotland's little known and only gold mine. In the 1980s a mining company drilled a thousand-metre-long tunnel into the flank of the ben in the hope of extracting gold. But precious metal prices fell, making further exploration uneconomic. The mine closed. It was later bought by another company with plans to

resurrect the mining operation and hopes to extract about 5,500 kilograms of gold and 673,000 ounces of silver. Conservationists opposed the mine, citing damage to both the scenic beauty and the tranquillity of the area, which is situated on the edge of Scotland's first National Park. But the counter-argument from the mining company, offering at least 25 jobs to the local community, won the day. It's always a difficult balancing act, weighing employment in a deeply rural area where there are few jobs outwith tourism against potential damage to the environment.

The Gold Mountain of Beinn Chùirn is also known for its lead mines. Now almost forgotten, they operated for nearly 200 years, from 1739 to 1923, at a place not far from the new gold mine. The workings can still be seen below the waterfalls of Eas Anie. During the 1745 Jacobite uprising, the lease was owned by an English Jacobite sympathiser. The Argyll militia, raised by the chief of Clan Campbell to oppose the Jacobite cause, feared that lead from Eas Anie would become lead bullets for the Jacobite army, then on the march through Scotland. In a pre-emptive strike, the Campbell militia sabotaged the mine workings and burned the miners' cottages to the ground.

Beyond the mines, the track comes to an abrupt end below the mighty north-east face of Ben Lui. From here, a faint footpath leads through the heather up increasingly steep ground towards the north-east ridge, where a sometimes airy scramble rises to the summit cairn at 1,127 metres. From this vantage point, the views well repay the effort of the long walk in. They are magnificent and all-encompassing.

Somewhere near the cairn is a set of car keys, lost by me on my first ascent of Ben Lui. It was a particularly cold January day when I left my mini-

Ben Lui, the most beautiful mountain in the southern Highlands.

van in a lay-by on the A82 to begin the long trudge up the glen towards Ben Lui. Walking with me were my pal Gus, and his then girlfriend Kirsty. When I complained of having a blister on my heel, Kirsty suggested a novel way of dealing with pain – that I should enjoy it. 'Pleasure and pain are just sensations, so really they amount to the same thing. Just try to fool yourself that the sensation in your foot is pleasure and you'll be fine.' I could tell by her smile that she wasn't kidding. A strange logic indeed, but perhaps one that proved useful when she became a nurse.

Because of the soft, deep snow on the track, it took much longer than anticipated to reach the base of the mountain. Using ice axes and crampons we made better progress up the steepening north-east ridge, but dusk was already gathering when we summited. After a quick sandwich, accompanied by a steaming mug of cocoa gulped in the icy air, we descended by torchlight. By the time we reached the minivan we were all exhausted,

and I was now limping because of my blister. So much for Kirsty's pleasure/pain principle, I grumbled as I rummaged for the car keys. Where were they? I turned out my pockets and rifled through my rucksack but failed to find them. Then the horrible realisation struck me. I must have dropped the keys when we'd stopped at the summit.

What to do? A return trip in darkness was out of the question. Phone somebody for help, Gus suggested. But how? This was before the era of mobile phones and there was no phone box for miles.

I noticed a point of light in the darkness indicating a house across a field. I followed its source to the door of a small croft. My knock was answered by a grey-haired and slightly suspicious Highland woman who let me use her phone; she refused to accept the 20p piece I proffered.

'Who is it you need to call?' she asked.

'The police', I replied.

'Has there been an accident?'

Glen Shira – part of the wilderness north of Tyndrum.

'No. I've lost my car keys and wondered if they might be able to help.'

'Och, I'm sure they will! The sergeant's always helping tourists.'

A brief call to the Crianlarich police station reassured me that all would be well. Thanking the woman for her kindness, I returned to the others.

Within minutes, a bemused police sergeant arrived in his patrol car as snow began to fall heavily. From his pocket he drew out a massive bundle of minivan keys. 'One of these will work for sure,' he said patiently trying them in turn.

And by a miracle, as my mother would say, the engine burst into life. We were saved!

As we slowly drove home through a blizzard, I kept on thinking about that damn key, lying in the snow somewhere up on the dark summit of Ben Lui. I've been back several times in summer, but haven't come across it yet. So if you are up there and happen to find an old minivan key, it's mine!

Tyndrum, from Tigh an Druim in Gaelic, meaning 'the house on the ridge', is an important Highland crossroads, where traffic heading north and south joins the road to Oban and the west coast. The village also boasts two railways stations on two separate lines: Tyndrum Upper on the West Highland Line to Fort William, and Tyndrum Lower on the Oban line.

The village grew during the great days of cattle droving, offering food, shelter and drink to thirsty drovers on their way to markets – or *trysts* as they were called – in the Lowlands. Back then the village would have been something akin to a Wild West frontier town. Today, a hint of this atmosphere survives and Tyndrum remains a busy place. Interspersed with a scattering of houses and B&Bs are hotels, eateries and a filling station.

Traffic on the A82 seems irresistibly drawn to the Green Welly Stop, a place well known to regular travellers and to long-distance bus passengers on routes to and from the far north and the

Hebrides. Tourists also pull over at the Green Welly to buy fuel and have a quick bite to eat. Coach parties browse the tourist souvenirs on offer, and bikers cluster around their machines outside. Here leather-clad men of a certain age talk torque and horsepower while chomping on sausage rolls and swilling mugs of tea.

Most visitors stopping for refreshment have little or no idea that Tyndrum once catered for an altogether different sort of traveller. Because of the clutter of signage and parked vehicles, it's hard to believe that people once came for reasons of health. For a thousand years, Christian pilgrims stopped on their way to take the waters of a nearby holy well. Tyndrum was a sort of Highland Lourdes, as Sarah Murray discovered when she spent a night at the village inn in 1796. She had come in search of the picturesque and the sublime, and was a little disappointed by what she found. She wrote: 'There is little to see or admire in Tyndrum: the landlord however wished me to see a holy well near Strath Fillan kirk, whose water, he told me, cured every disease but that of the purse.'

One of the many things I love about Sarah is her ability to poke fun at herself. During this exchange, she completely misunderstood the man's Highland accent, and thought that 'purse' must be a Gaelic word for some sort of disease. She asked what 'purse' meant in English?

'Money, madam,' he said. 'It will not cure the want of that.'

Indeed not!

Like Sarah, I was also keen to see the holy well. It's named after the local Celtic saint, St Fillan, and lies just down the road from Tyndrum in Strath Fillan, on a bend in the river of the same name. According to legend, Fillan came from Ireland as a missionary in the 7th century. His

evangelical powers were impressive, as was his ability to deal with wild and dangerous animals. He once hitched a marauding wolf to a plough to till the soil. On another occasion, he clubbed to death a wild boar that had been terrorising parishioners.

One day in springtime, I followed a couple of signposts along a muddy path and passed the ruins of St Fillan's Priory. Squelching my way further I arrived at St Fillan's holy pool, which turned out to be little more than a bend in the river. Hard to imagine that this unlikely spot had been a place of pilgrimage.

A stone dyke once divided the holy pool into male and female sections. Here devotees of St Fillan came to be dunked in the waters, which were reputed to have powerful healing properties. The water was especially beneficial to those suffering from a variety of mental health issues, but the cure must have been something of an ordeal. The afflicted were plunged into the icy water, then bound hand and foot and left overnight in the old priory, where St Fillan's ancient bell was placed upon their chest. If, by morning, their bonds had been loosened, it was interpreted as a sign from St Fillan that the patient had been cured. If not, they were thrown in the pool again. And so the process was repeated until a cure could be pronounced and another miracle proclaimed.

I think I'll let Sarah Murray have the last word on such 'miracles'. Back in 1776, she dryly observed that it was more likely, given the shock of repeated immersions in the icy river, that 'death, and no saint, in most instances, must break the cord of life, and thus release those unhappy sufferers'.

A couple of kilometres north of Tyndrum the A82 makes a big sweep as it climbs out of the village. At the apex of the curve, the road reveals

Beinn Dorain. The poet Iain Crichton Smith celebrated the mountain in verse.

the dramatic and elegant form of Beinn Dorain, a mountain whose steeply inclined grassy slopes rise to a rocky knoll on the summit.

The first time I saw Beinn Dorain, I was hugely impressed. I was on a hillwalking expedition with a group of school friends, led by our maths teacher – a sporting, outdoors type.

'What an amazing mountain,' I said, gazing up at Beinn Dorain. 'The slope is almost the perfect parabola.'

'And what's the definition of a parabola, young man?' asked the teacher.

I hesitated, not liking to be put on the spot. 'Er . . . y equals x squared?'

Typical of a maths teacher, I thought, to see everything, including the landscape, as a series of numbers. But ever since, an equation comes to mind whenever I see beautiful Beinn Dorain.

The Gaelic bard Duncan Ban MacIntyre was born in this area in 1724. Growing up in the shadow of Beinn Dorain, he sang the mountain's praises in verse. This is an extract from his celebrated poem 'Moladh Beinn Dóbhrain', translated by the poet Iain Crichton Smith:

Her gifts are so many,
her fruits are so bonny,
and rarer than any
her bushes and leafage

in flawless green raiment
as bright as the diamond
your blooms in agreement
like elegant music.

The buck small and nimble
quick on the green
neat as a thimble –
a clever machine!

When he's startled to motion
he's as swift as your vision
with speed and precision
he speeds through each forest
without seeming exertion
he's nearest, then furthest!

What is striking about the work of Duncan Ban MacIntyre is that all his poems, which were composed exclusively in Gaelic, were the product of an oral tradition. He was illiterate throughout his life and never wrote his compositions down. Instead, he committed them to memory. Only years later were they collected, recorded and eventually translated into English. 'Moladh Beinn Dóbhrain' is considered to be his finest composition and is a classic example of Gaelic praise poetry. In it, he eulogises the mountain and its wildlife. Unlike the southern poets and artists who came later, who saw the landscape through the filter of the picturesque, the sublime and the romantic, Duncan Ban MacIntyre looked at the world with eyes shaped by his native Gaelic tradition.

BRIDGE OF ORCHY TO THE KING'S HOUSE

Crannogs and cattle – Skyfall and a desolate moor – conquering the Buachaille

Hugging the bare flanks of Beinn Dorain is the railway track of the West Highland Line, which makes an extraordinary meandering loop to cross a viaduct over lonely Gleann Achadh-innis Chailein. From a carriage window, I have often watched walkers below on Scotland's most popular long-distance path – the West Highland Way – making their way from Milngavie outside Glasgow to journey's end at Fort William. The stretch of the path beneath Beinn Dorain follows the route of the old military road built by Major William Caulfield over two summers from 1751–52. The road was designed to allow the swift movement of troops from the south to a line of forts in the heart of the Highlands. After the Jacobite rebellion of 1745, the government wanted to ensure that further uprisings could be swiftly suppressed.

At Bridge of Orchy, where the wife of Duncan Ban MacIntyre was born, Caulfield's road crosses the River Orchy. As the sound of passing cars on the A82 faded into the distance, I tramped this section of the old route north, heading towards the quiet of Loch Tulla, and the ominous-sounding Black Mount.

Loch Tulla is familiar to anyone who has driven north from Glasgow on the A82 road to Fort William, or walked the West Highland Way. It is a beautiful stretch of surprisingly sheltered water, and acts as a great mirror to the moods of the ever-changing sky. Surrounding the loch are remnants of the great Caledonian Forest; tortured-looking pines stand like lone sentinels in a primeval landscape. Today the trees are a haven for wildlife. Although Loch Tulla has supported a human population for millennia, there's scant evidence of their presence. It often surprises me how little our ancestors left behind. Houses and whole communities have been absorbed into the landscape they emerged from and you need to look hard to see where people once lived.

One example is the tiny island lying in the

The remains of the crannog on Eilean Stalcair, Loch Tulla.

middle of Loch Tulla, called Eilean Stalcair, which once supported some of the first people to lead settled lives in this part of Scotland. I took a boat out to the island, and tied up to one of several large trees growing from a jumble of fist-sized stones littering the ground. These were evidence of the little island's origins. Eilean Stalcair is a crannog – an artificial island built of piled stones to keep the occupants safe from attack by wild animals or from human enemies raiding and plundering. During the Iron Age the crannog was home to an extended family living in a thatched timber house on wooden stilts above the water. It's amazing to think that people made their homes out here so long ago and in such a seemingly inhospitable place.

Crannogs were once very common. At least 600 have been identified by archaeologists in Scotland's lochs. The earliest belong to the Stone Age. Others were used successively for hundreds of years. The last were abandoned as recently as the 17th century, and it's known that Eilean Stalcair was used up until the 14th century by a branch of Clan MacGregor. When they lost their land to the Campbells, their bard wrote a lament that recalled happy days on 'Loch Tulla of the Sunny Slopes'.

The MacGregors were famous as cattle men – and notorious as cattle thieves – a reputation and

With Ali MacDonald, cattle farmer, Glen Shira.

tradition that is forever bound up with the history and mythology of the area. Near Victoria Bridge, at the western end of Loch Tulla, I met local farmer Ali MacDonald who runs cattle on the moor. The ruin of Achallader Castle sits on the land Ali manages. In 1602, the Campbell Earl of Breadalbane met several Jacobite chiefs here and attempted to persuade and bribe them to accept William of Orange as their new and rightful monarch. McIain, the chief of the Glencoe MacDonalds, wasn't persuaded by the earl's arguments. His opposition later became a thread in the web of tangled circumstance that culminated in the Massacre of Glencoe.

So perhaps ironically – or fittingly – it was a MacDonald who gave me a lift a short way up a Land Rover track to some rough pastureland above Glen Shira. Clambering out of his 4x4, Ali leaned on his shepherd's crook and gazed proudly at his herd of beef cattle, a mixture of Shorthorn and Luing. 'Aye, they're looking not too bad considering the winter we've had,' he said. 'But they are a hardy breed. They need to be. There's not much pasture for them out here.'

The elements are the great enemy. Winters can be arctic; even in the relative meteorological quiet of summer he has lost cows and calves in the bogs. 'It's impossible to free them unless you can get a tractor to pull them out,' he said.

Ali takes his cattle by truck to market in Stirling, but in the old days, before the coming of the internal combustion engine and the steam locomotive, cattle were driven to market on foot – a journey measured in weeks. Ali explained: 'Cattle droving was a tricky business. You didn't want to go too fast, otherwise the cattle would get too thin for market. But take too long, and you'd miss the best prices. To help them along and to preserve their feet, some beasts were shod with shoes – a bit like horseshoes.'

Ali went to the back of his 4x4 and filled a plastic bucket with pellets from a bag of cattle feed. He shook the bucket and called across the heather to his herd. The bull lifted his head and lumbered over. The rest of the cattle followed and we were quickly surrounded by a warm fug of beasts with slavering mouths and long probing tongues seeking a tasty morsel. Ali moved confidently among them. I could tell he loves his animals and the land he farms.

Before I returned to the West Highland Way, my curiosity was aroused by the low walls of a ruined house a short distance from where Ali had parked his 4x4. I wandered over to have a look and was surprised to discover that this unassuming heap of stones was in fact a literary location of national significance. According to a plaque on a stone inside, this was the birthplace of the bard Duncan Ban MacIntyre.

Back on the West Highland Way, the old military road gives way to an improved highway that was built in the early years of the 19th century by Thomas Telford. Having said that, the 'new road' is not much more than a dirt track and yet until the 1930s continued to serve as the main road to the west Highlands from the south. It follows a lower route than Caulfield's military road, winding towards the immense bleakness of Rannoch Moor.

Toiling uphill above the Forest Lodge and the sporting estate of Black Mount, I paused to take in the view. For several generations now, the Black Mount estate has been owned by the Fleming family, whose most famous member was Ian Fleming, the creator of 007, James Bond. The main

estate house occupies a commanding position overlooking Loch Tulla, which gleamed in the late afternoon sunshine. It seemed an inspirational setting for Skyfall, the fictional Highland home of James Bond.

Cresting the ridge above Loch Tulla walkers get their first view of the Black Mount – Am Monadh Dubh. This huge area of treeless, lochan-studded bog is ringed by a range of impressive mountains including Stob Ghabhar, Clach Leathad and Meall a' Bhuiridh. Together they form an impenetrable wall at the western extremity of Rannoch Moor – one of the wildest places in Britain.

In 1796, Sarah Murray came this way with her maid and her manservant. Bumping along in a horse-drawn chaise they negotiated the Black Mount, heading towards the lonely hostelry of King's House. Peering out at the wild moorland, Sarah found it almost too much for her romantic sensibilities to bear. 'Stretching to the east and Rannoch is nothing but a dreary black boggy moor, the loose soil of which is quite black, broken by pools and small lakes and very thinly covered, where the water does not remain, with the coarsest brown heath, rushes and bogs.'

This epic landscape covers an area of 132 square kilometres and was once described by the early traveller and geologist William McCullough as 'an inconceivable solitude; a dreary, joyless land of bogs; a land of darkness and desolation'.

For centuries, there were no roads across this wilderness. Only sinuous paths threaded through the heather and oozing ground – ancient rights of way used by cattle drovers, occasional peddlers and other itinerants. But the moor wasn't entirely without a human population. On its fringes lived the 'broken men' of outlawed Clan Gregor – the

Rannoch Moor and the Black Mount. The moor was described by William McCullough as 'an inconceivable solitude'.

'children of the mist' along with other fugitives from justice or poverty. It was from this band of desperadoes that the soldiers building Caulfield's military road armed themselves for protection, keeping a primed musket at the ready while they dug their way across the moor, an activity that would have unearthed large quantities of bog pine.

Protruding like bleached bones from the black peat are ancient tree roots. They are mostly of Scots pine, which grew on the moor thousands of years ago. Just after the last ice age, the climate in Scotland was warmer and drier than at present, creating conditions that encouraged the spread of forest cover. Then the climate changed. It got wetter and cooler, promoting the growth of moss, which developed into layers of peat, which even-

tually suffocated the forests but preserved the remains of trees. This is why so many tree roots can be seen on an otherwise treeless moor.

The dried wood from these ancient pines was considered a valuable resource in the past. Broken into splinters, the prehistoric sap inside burns brightly, a source of light to spin wool by on a dark winter's night. Not that most people had any choice in the manner of illumination – candles were beyond the means of most local folk at the time.

About 10 kilometres or so out from Victoria Bridge, I spotted a monument on a knoll near the road. It's to the memory of Peter Fleming of Flemings bank. Peter was the elder brother of Ian Fleming of 007 fame. During his lifetime Peter was the

Blackrock Cottage, owned by the Ladies Scottish Climbing Club.

more famous of the two, being a successful author before Ian had put pen to paper. Peter was primarily known for his travel writing, but one of his novels *The Sixth Column: A Singular Tale of Our Times* is an early spy thriller. It has been regarded by some critics as a precursor to his younger brother's first Bond story, *Casino Royale*. Later, Ian acknowledged the influence of his brother and admitted that the name Miss Moneypenny in the Bond stories was suggested by Peter.

Peter Fleming was typical of his class: Eton, Oxford, the Grenadier Guards. After the Second World War he retired on a private income and indulged his passion for hunting, shooting and fishing. He loved being on the family's Black Mount estate, and it was on the spot marked by

the monument that he dropped dead of a heart attack while stalking deer. Apparently, the friends who were with him that day decided the manner of his death was just as Peter would have wanted it – so they left him where he'd fallen and continued shooting. Why spoil a terrific day's sport?

After another couple of kilometres, the old Telford road joins a single-track public road leading from the A82 to the Glencoe Mountain Resort; set back from the junction is Blackrock Cottage, probably one of the most photographed locations in the UK. The cottage is one of several premises owned and run by the Ladies Scottish Climbing Club and occupies a superb setting, with the mighty bulk of Buachaille Etive Mòr towering impressively behind.

Glencoe Mountain Resort continues to defy expectations by staying open for snow sports in an ever-changing and unreliable climate. This is no Val d'Isère, so don't expect immaculate pistes. This is Scotland and it is a little rough around the edges, with steep, rugged, often ungroomed runs and a good deal of ice. But without doubt, the Glencoe Mountain Resort is my favourite of all the five Scottish ski resorts. This is partly because of its setting and partly because I learned to ski there (it's true what they say: learn to ski in Scotland and you can ski anywhere). To take the chairlift and the series of ski tows up to the top of Meall a' Bhuiridh is an adventure in its own right, with a superb 360-degree vista of trackless Rannoch Moor and the surrounding snow-covered mountains.

Passing below Meall a' Bhuiridh 200 years ago, Sarah Murray wasn't interested in snow. She was looking forward to a well-deserved rest. She had spent the best part of her day bumping along the old military road towards the King's House. Exhausted and jolted by her journey, she was desperate to stop. Only a couple more miles, she thought, gazing with incredulity at the approaching scene. 'The inn at King's House as I approached it looked like a dot in the midst of a barren wilderness; surrounded by the most craggy, bare, stupendous mountains that the mind can form an idea of.

Sarah was somewhat disappointed by the accommodation she found at the King's House, an establishment that was more accustomed to catering for cattle drovers than ladies from Kensington. To Sarah's eyes, the inn was a dirty hovel full of rowdy, drunken Highlanders who made her stay there a misery. But despite her discomfort, she was still overawed by the scenery: 'There is a crag to the west of the Inn of a stupendous height, in some degree conical, of grey rock over rock, which as the sun shone upon it, assumed a most beautiful tint, contrasted with the dark russet of everything beneath it.'

This 'crag' was Buachaille Etive Mòr, the 'great herdsman of Etive' – my first and favourite 'true mountain' where I tested my nerve as a 14-year-old.

It was early December. I was a member of a school climbing party organised by my English teacher, known teasingly as 'Ned' because he shared the same surname as the notorious Australian outlaw Ned Kelly. We left the minibus parked in a lay-by and marched over the moor towards the towering rocks of the Buachaille. If ever a mountain has frowned down on you, this is the one, I said to myself.

The Buachaille grew more intimidating the closer we drew to the base of its great cliffs. It looked like a vast pile of ancient, mouldering masonry: a huge ruin, riven with deep, snow-filled gullies, plunging to obscurity between soaring ridges and buttresses. Vertical rock walls – hundreds of feet high – disappeared into gloomy clouds from which flakes of snow were beginning to fall.

We stopped for a breather beneath the Water Slab – a massive ramp of wet stone – where a waterfall dropped 30 feet over an overhang. It was a cheerless place, made even gloomier by a small cairn and a plaque commemorating the death of a young climber who had been killed in a fall a couple of years earlier.

We roped up just above the Water Slab, Ned leading, a lad in second year following him, and I played tail-end Charlie. Our route up Curved Ridge took us into the heart of the mountain. It

Buachaille Etive Mor, the first mountain I ever climbed.

was a spectacular situation. On the eastern horizon a pyramid-shaped mountain drew my eye.

'That's Schiehallion – the fairy mountain of the ancient Caledonians,' Ned explained, following my gaze as I clambered onto a narrow ledge beside him.

At the top of Curved Ridge, the rocks disappeared beneath a snowfield. The way ahead presented an intimidating spectacle – a narrow snow-filled gully, which tapered and steepened until it ended in a gap between a huge tower of rock and the summit cliffs.

It was getting dark; snow continued to fall from a leaden sky.

'We can't hang about here long,' Ned said. 'Let's go.'

We moved together, trying to kick steps in the iron-hard snow. My boots made little impression so I edged my way up, putting my weight on my ice axe for balance and support. I felt frightened. I knew if I – or any one of us – slipped, we'd all be pulled off. I pictured us sliding uncontrollably over the snow, and then hurtling down the cliffs.

I was breathless with fear by the time I reached Ned. He was perched on a narrow ledge of snow in the gap between Crowberry Tower and the summit. It was a very exposed position. Behind him, the deep slit of Crowberry Gully plunged a thousand feet into darkness. The only way was up.

Ned left me, climbing out of sight around the rocks above. I shivered as a sudden gust of wind blew a flurry of snowflakes through the gap where I crouched in a state of fear and nervous excitement. This was a truly amazing place to be: dark, forbidding and deathly dangerous. I felt utterly alone.

The rope moved in my gloved hand. Ned was climbing again. He was moving quickly and I had to feed the rope out faster and faster to keep up with his ascent.

A few moments later I heard Ned's voice, small and faint in the deepening twilight: 'Climb when you're ready!'

I felt the rope pull reassuringly tight around my waist. 'Climbing!' I called back to him.

Secure on the rope, I climbed towards the summit. I was triumphant. I had conquered the Buachaille – and my own fear.

Walking off the mountain by headtorch we followed a decent path back to the minibus. Before we began the long drive home, we stopped at the King's House for a spot of refreshment – a beer for Ned and cola for the boys. The tiny climbers' bar was a heaving mass of raucous mountaineers, crowding around the open fire, propping up the bar and knocking back pints. Glowing with success, I looked at the faded framed photographs hanging on the walls. These were of past mountaineering exploits. There were signed portraits of climbing greats and dramatic shots of their achievements: Dougal Haston on The Bull Roarer; W. H. Murray crossing a Himalayan glacier. These were images that inspired me with thoughts of greater conquest.

After my ascent of the Buachaille, W. H. Murray became a hero to me. His book, *Mountaineering in Scotland*, written in unbelievably harsh circumstances when he was a prisoner of war in Germany during the Second World War, became my bible

and inspiration. Between its covers, Murray gave a beautifully written account of climbing adventures in the 1930s, interspersed with philosophical musings on the nature of the sport and the poetry of the natural environment.

Sadly, the old King's House has gone, and along with it the climbers' bar and its happy memories. It was demolished in 2017 and completely rebuilt, with the exception of the entrance, which retains part of the original 18th-century building. A tragedy surely. The old King's House had a unique character and played an important role in Scottish mountaineering history. The atmosphere of the place had literally soaked into the fabric of the building. It might have needed refurbishment, certainly, but demolition? That seems a step too far.

GLENCOE TO BALLACHULISH

The Glencoe Mafia – massacre – a wooden goddess

Buachaille Etive Mòr marks the entrance to Glencoe, where so much of Scottish mountaineering can trace its origins. Beside the River Coupall, which sweeps around the base of the Great Herdsman, is an undistinguished-looking bothy made of railway sleepers and scrap wood, and covered in black roofing felt and tar. This is the Jacksonville bothy – a famous place in the annals of Scottish mountaineering, and one which has a place in my own personal mythology.

According to legend, the Jacksonville bothy was built by members of the notorious Creag Dhu Club, men who had grown up in the poverty and unemployment of Glasgow during the Great Depression of the 1930s. In the mountains of the north they found respite from the monotony of their urban lives, forming friendships while exploring new climbing routes that tested their nerve, fitness and ability. After the working week, members of the Creag Dhu – aka the Glencoe Mafia – hitch-hiked to Glencoe and based themselves at Jacksonville. A column of smoke rising from the chimney was a sign that the bothy was occupied. But the Creag Dhu Club had a fearsome reputation. It was an 'invitation-only' organisation. Membership depended on fitting in and demonstrating fearlessness on the mountain. All others were excluded.

As a teenager, I lived in mortal fear of the Creag Dhu Club. I was told that anyone using their bothy without permission would be torn limb from limb. Which is why, when in the area, I always camped. But one October night, I arrived long after dark with my pal Gus. We were exhausted, and the weather was foul. A gale was driving horizontal rain across Rannoch Moor and funnelling it down the glen. In a moment of recklessness, we decided to risk the wrath of the Creag Dhu Club and seek the sanctuary of Jacksonville instead of trying to pitch our tiny tent.

Tripping over clumps of heather in the darkness, we nervously approached the bothy and crept up to the windows. There seemed to be no light inside. Was it empty, or had the occupants already gone to sleep? Gus carefully put his head torch to the window. The narrow beam of light illuminated the interior. The wooden sleeping platforms were unoccupied.

We pushed open the heavy door and entered the musty atmosphere inside. We daren't light a candle or use our torches in case we betrayed our presence: a club member might this very minute be making his way through the darkness towards us. Such imaginings grew more vivid as we tried

– and failed – to get some sleep, convinced that the Glencoe Mafia were about to burst in on us at any moment.

When Sarah Murray left the King's House in the summer of 1796, her sights were set beyond the Buachaille to the dark entrance to Glencoe, which even then was a byword for infamy. Because her own horses were tired, she took alternative transport: resourceful as ever, she hitched a lift with a local man in his peat cart. In this undignified conveyance, she made her way through the wild and romantic glen. 'I determined on an 18 mile's drive in a peat cart across which was fastened a board by way of a seat. As soon as I had taken my short meal and secured my pig hole to sleep in [she really didn't think much of the King's House!], I mounted my cart. And away we went.'

She must have been quite a sight. But Sarah cared little for appearances or other social conventions of the age. She was on a mission to explore Glencoe, and she was transfixed by the scale of the glen: 'Huge towers upon towers of rock, forming a multitude of stages to the greatest height, and all in a drizzling state; which in some degree looked like thousands of icicles dropping from innumerable points of rock upon every stage . . . The whole mass, to an eye below, appears an immense and inaccessible ruin of the finest architecture, mouldering, defaced, and become uneven by the vast lapse of time . . .'

Sarah Murray's dramatic prose was the product of an eye tutored by Romanticism. Glencoe epitomised the sublime – the very purpose of her Highland adventure, and its reward. Her reaction is also common enough today. Two hundred years later, traffic through the glen slows down not because the driving gets any harder, but simply because drivers and passengers can't resist admir-

Glencoe – looking up to Stob Coire nam Beith, where I climbed a route called The Sphinx.

ing the fantastic mountain landscape. Visitors and tourists crane their heads and gaze with awe no matter how many times they might have made the journey before. Quite simply, Glencoe is a place of superlatives and still turns heads, whether you are in a peat cart or behind the wheel of a modern SUV.

For me, to descend through the glen is to pass through a landscape coloured by memory. To the north lie the massive ramparts of the implacable Aonach Eagach ridge, with memories of dizzying rock towers and improbable pinnacles. To the south are the Three Sisters that hide the great corries of Glencoe: the Lost Valley where the MacDonald clan once hid stolen cattle, Corrie nan Lochan where I kicked steps up snow-filled gullies as a kid, and Corrie nam Beitheach where I was hauled up a rock climb called The Sphinx. But this is to look upon the mountains purely for their climbing potential. Most modern visitors see the peaks as a landscape phenomenon and reach for their cameras. And ever since Sarah Murray bumped and rattled her way through the glen, writers and artists have been inspired by the scenery. Landscape artists like Horatio McCulloch came with sketchbook and paints. The images that he and others produced became iconic, encapsulating the magical essence of the Highlands for a Victorian audience. Art has helped to make Glencoe a 'must-see' destination on a tourist's itinerary for 200 years.

Scenery apart, there is another allure to Glencoe, one that Sarah Murray was keen to experience for herself: 'the scene of the cruel massacre in King William's time'.

At the bottom of the glen and facing Bidean nam Bian, the highest mountain in Argyll, is the Clachaig Inn. For many years the inn was owned by members of the MacDonald family, who put up a sign on the bar door: 'No Campbells'. The reason for this antipathy dates back to a bloody incident, which took place in 1692. In popular mythology, it's known as the Massacre of Glencoe when the Campbells slaughtered the MacDonalds. But as with most things in history, it is more complicated than that.

After the Catholic King James II and VII was forced into exile in 1688, William of Orange and his wife Mary, the sister of James, became joint Protestant monarchs of the United Kingdom. But amongst Highland clans there remained considerable support for the exiled Stuart king, who launched an invasion of Ireland in 1689 in an attempt to regain his throne. After James was defeated, King William offered the Jacobite clans an amnesty on condition they signed an oath of allegiance. In case they failed to comply, letters of 'fire and sword' were drawn up authorising death and destruction to recalcitrant Stuart sympathisers. By an extraordinary series of mishaps and bad luck, MacDonald of Glencoe was late in signing the oath. He was then grievously misrepresented as a thief and a rebel by the Campbell Earl of Breadalbane, and singled out for punishment.

Orders were dispatched, which included the ominous sentence: 'If McKean of Glencoe (the clan chief) and that tribe can be well separated from the rest, it will be a proper vindication of the publick justice to extirpate that sept of thieves.'

It turns out that the MacDonalds of Glencoe were less ardent Jacobites than they were enthusiastic cattle thieves, which is why they had incurred the wrath of the Campbell Earl of Breadalbane, whose beasts they had frequently lifted and taken to Glencoe. It's clear that the Campbell earl had a prior grudge against the MacDonalds – one which had little to do with politics. Motives became confused when the earl was asked to dispatch 70 men from the Campbell-controlled Argyll regiment to execute the orders of the government. For nearly a fortnight, the soldiers, most of whom were not from Clan Campbell, were billeted with the people of Glencoe. By all accounts they got on well together, socialising and playing cards with their hosts. Then, on 12 February 1692, their commander captain Robert Campbell of Glenlyon received his final orders: 'To fall upon the Rebells, the MacDonalds of Glenco, and put all to the sword under seventy.'

At five o'clock, on the morning of 13 February 1692, the butchery began. At least 38 members of the clan – men, women and children – were brutally murdered. Those who weren't slain on the spot escaped in a blizzard. Without shelter, many died in the snow.

From Glencoe, the A82 runs to Ballachulish on the shores of Loch Leven, a village once dismissed by *Black's Guide* as: 'a dirty and unpicturesque little place, chiefly inhabited by the workers of the neighbouring slate-quarries'.

The slate quarries closed decades ago. In their heyday, they produced over 20 million roofing

slates a year and employed a workforce of over 300 men in a very dangerous industry. *Black's* disparaging remarks about the now-flooded quarries are quite telling. Heaven forbid that tourists might come away with the wrong impression of the Highlands. There can be no place for dirt, poverty and industry in *Black's Picturesque* view of 'Caledonia, stern and wild'.

A few hundred metres from the shore at Ballachulish and its slate quarries is a group of small islands and skerries. One of them, Eilean Munde, is an ancient and sacred burial ground for several clans: the MacDonalds of Glencoe, the nearby Stewarts of Ballachulish, and the Camerons of Callart. The island was used for generations, until it became too full of the dead. Their headstones still cluster around a ruined medieval chapel dedicated to the Celtic saint St Munde. Close by is Eilean a' Chòmraidh commonly known as the 'Isle of Discussion'. For hundreds of years, disputes among local MacDonalds were settled there. The feuding parties were told by their chief to remain on the island until an agreement had been reached, a process apparently aided by a supply of whisky and cheese. When a resolution to their differences was found, the clan members rowed up the loch to Eilean na Bainne ('the Isle of Covenant'), where agreements were drawn up and sealed.

At South Ballachulish, a bridge carries the A82 across the narrow kyle to North Ballachulish. Before the bridge was built in 1975, a ferry shuttled across with cars and foot passengers, but the volume of vehicles created queues of traffic, especially in the tourist-busy summer months. As a child, I remember a lone piper who entertained

A replica of the mysterious Ballachulish Goddess, which dates back to the Iron Age.

On the Pap of Glencoe.

people while they waited for the ferry.

In 1880, not far from where the bridge spans the kyle, a labourer was digging in a peat bog overlooking Loch Leven when he made a remarkable discovery. Lying face down in the black earth was the carved figure of a woman. A photograph taken shortly afterwards revealed a five-foot totemic representation of the female form. Unfortunately, the wood wasn't properly conserved at the time and rapidly deteriorated. Known today as the Ballachulish Goddess, the wooden figure has become something of a mystery. The original, which has been carbon-dated to the Iron Age over 2,600 years ago, is on display at the National Museum of Scotland.

FROM THE PAP OF GLENCOE TO CORROUR LODGE

The Electric Village – the last great monument to the navvy – from bothy to lodge

Retracing my steps towards the village of Glencoe, I followed a path towards the shapely summit of the Pap of Glencoe. Sitting in the sun on the lower slopes were two elderly gentlemen. One looked familiar for some reason. He said 'hello' as I passed but it was only after I'd walked further that I realised he was Hamish MacInnes, the famous 'fox of Glencoe', mountaineer and climbing legend whose exploits I'd followed in various books and journals since I was a teenager. Thrilled to be walking in the footsteps of the great man, I slogged up the steep path with renewed vigour, scrambling over the rock-strewn upper mountain to the summit of the Pap where I looked down vertiginous scree slopes to Loch Leven – a narrow fjord-like arm of the sea, which forces its way into the mountainous country of the Mamore Forest.

At the head of the loch, nestling below the high summits is the village of Kinlochleven. Today, Kinlochleven is perhaps best known as an outdoor pursuits base where a whole range of activities is on offer. There's a rock and ice climbing arena, 150 kilometres of downhill bike trails, and some glorious mountains to lure summit-lovers and Munro-ists ever higher. But just over a century ago, there was nothing much here apart from a couple of shooting estates on either side of the River Leven.

All that changed with the coming of electricity and the development of a huge factory complex. In the first decade of the 20th century, this part of the Highlands was valued more for its industrial potential than its romantic scenery. In 1907 a state-of-the-art aluminium smelter opened using hydro-electricity from a dam built on the moorland high above.

Pipes from the distant dam can still be seen on the hillside, carrying water to a hydro power station where 20 Swiss-made turbines once generated electricity for the smelter. Today, modern turbines continue to produce power from the plant, feeding it to the Lochaber smelter and into the National Electricity Grid. When the smelter was operational, raw materials were shipped in from overseas. An entire new town was built to house more than 500 workers and their families. Kinlochleven was born, becoming known as the 'Electric Village' – the first village in the world to be connected to a mains electricity supply.

It's clear to see that Kinlochleven was once a company town. Architecturally, most of the houses are from the same mould and built to the same company design. But there's little left of the giant smelter, which was once the focus of the whole community. Before the First World War, it produced over a third of the world's aluminium. Sadly the plant couldn't maintain its supreme position in the smelting world. By the 1970s, it was too small and too inefficient to compete with modern overseas super-smelters. It finally closed in 2000. The smelter site is now empty and only a few brick buildings remain.

Avril Watt, a local woman in her early eighties, is fiercely proud of Kinlochleven and its industrial history. I met her in the library of the new education campus. She told me that Kinlochleven was a great place to grow up when it was owned by the British Aluminium Company, which, by her account, was a benevolent if somewhat paternalistic organisation.

'The company kept the welfare of its workers and the whole village high on their agenda,' Avril told me. 'They organised dances and ceilidhs in the village hall. There was a football club, and there was an annual Highland Games to which Olympic athletes were invited to compete, making us feel at the centre of the world. And for the long dark nights before we had the television, there was a cinema. It attracted people from the entire district to come to Kinlochleven for an evening at the Electric Village.'

The loss of the smelter left a huge hole in both the social and the built fabric of the village, forcing Kinlochleven to reinvent itself as an outdoor adventure capital. In 2003, a new venture began when the Ice Factor opened in an old carbon factory silo building. Advertised as the world's largest ice-climbing facility, thousands of visitors come every year to its artificial ice walls and rock-climbing pitches.

Taking a path out of the village, I set off to explore the surrounding countryside. The mountains that ring Kinlochleven are a mecca for outdoor enthusiasts, from climbers and walkers, to downhill bikers, and those who trudge the West Highland Way. But few who follow the tracks and trails behind the village know about the existence of a German prisoner of war camp that dates from the First World War.

Avril Watt had already told me a little of its history and where to find it, although she'd warned me that there was not much to see and that the site is fast becoming lost to encroaching birch and alder.

After walking for about 2 kilometres I came to a level area of ground on the north bank of the River Leven. A couple of metal piers lay in the water, all that's left of a railway bridge that ran to the camp. Exploring among the young birches I came across some crumbling brickwork and the concrete bases of prison huts.

Avril had told me that most of the prisoners were Bavarians captured after the Battle of the Somme in 1916. According to Avril, one eyewitness account describes the German POWs creating quite a stir when they first disembarked at the steamer pier: 'We were children at the time. I remember seeing them as they marched towards us with heads held high. In the silence we watched them march past, some of them doubtless thinking of their own children, looked at us sadly.'

The German POWs had no idea where they had been sent to, but seem to have had a relatively comfortable time during their internment. They were put to work building a new hydro pipeline for the expansion of aluminium production at the smelter. For their labour they were paid '1d per hour; 1.5d for good work; 2d for good work of a skilled type'. In their spare time, some prisoners carved wooden toys for local children. For the most part, the Bavarians were well liked and trusted by the locals and were even billeted with villagers when the camp flooded. Because of their good behaviour, they needed few guards. On one occasion, a pair of locksmiths escaped to Glencoe where a farmer found them sleeping in his byre. He said he wouldn't turn them in. Instead, he asked them to consider the difficulties of getting back to Germany and what would happen if they managed to return home, where they'd most likely be sent back to the front line. Might not the option of being a POW be the better one? Taking the farmer's advice, the two fugitives gave themselves up to the police.

After the armistice of 1918, and the Spanish Flu epidemic (which took the lives of 26 prisoners) the Bavarians left Kinlochleven. They were laden with gifts from villagers. One mother baked a huge farewell clootie dumpling, which was presented to the former captives as they boarded a ship that took them home.

Leaving the site of the old prison camp I continued along the course of the River Leven, climbing high above the village. The German POWs were not the first soldiers to labour and battle against the elements in these hills. The track I was following was a former military road. It was constructed over two centuries ago and formed part of the same road built by Major Caulfield's soldiers across Rannoch Moor, over the hairpins of the Devil's Staircase, and on to Fort William and beyond. Even today, the road is an impressive feat of engineering. Hugging the steep hillside above the river, it reaches a height of over 550 metres. Although no longer of strategic value, Caulfield's road is still a still a busy route, forming part of the West Highland Way.

The old road seemed to get steeper with every step as I plodded laboriously towards the great concrete dam that holds back the 13-kilometre-long Blackwater Reservoir. When it was finished, the 1-kilometre concrete barrier was the biggest of its kind in Europe.

Over the course of five years, from 1904 to 1909, over 3,000 men laboured day and night in appalling conditions to build the dam and the pipeline carrying water to the turbines at Kinlochleven. It has been said that the dam is the last great monument to the navvy – the itinerant labourers – mostly Scots and Irish, who moved from one construction site to another. Their experience is brilliantly told by Patrick McGill in the autobiographical novel *Children of the Dead End*. He arrived in Scotland from Ireland aged 12. After a variety of labouring and agricultural jobs, he eventually made his way across Rannoch Moor to the 'waterworks' as the construction site was known. He describes his first view of his future home and place of work as 'a muddle of shacks huddled together in bewildering confusion. These were surrounded by puddles, heaps of disused wood, tins, bottles and all manner of discarded rubbish. It looked as if the buildings had fallen out of the sky by accident and were just allowed to remain where they had fallen.'

In the shadow of the dam, enclosed by a wooden palisade fence, is a burial ground where neat rows of concrete headstones mark the graves of those who lost their lives to accident, disease or to the freezing weather. Surprisingly, among them is the name of a woman, Mrs Reilly, one of several women who also lived and worked on the site. Most were wives or camp followers. To make a little extra, they washed clothes and cooked meals. There was even a school where they taught the labourers' children. Other headstones in the cemetery have no name at all – just the word 'Unknown'. Such was the nature of the largely anonymous workforce that it was possible for a man to work and lose his life without anyone in authority knowing his identity.

Leaving the forlorn burial ground, I crossed over the great dam of the Blackwater and headed towards Gleann Ioliareann – 'the glen of the eagles'. I was now walking through some truly remote country where there's so much space it makes you feel almost agoraphobic: tiny and insignificant in the empty vastness. After tramping across a sodden peat bog for half an hour, I followed a faint track through the heather. My map told me there was a bothy somewhere ahead at Loch Chiarain.

The bothy at Loch Chiarain was originally built as a shepherd's cottage about a century ago and replaced one that was lost to the rising waters of the Blackwater Reservoir. Today it is run and maintained by the Mountain Bothy Association. The MBA is supported entirely by membership subscriptions and donations, and exists to maintain remote bothies for public use. I've used them on several occasions. They are as basic as you can get. And that is their charm. The Loch Chiarain bothy is quite spacious, and boasts two big rooms downstairs with an open fire, and two rooms in the upper storey. Unfortunately, there was no fuel when I arrived tired and footsore. This was a bit awkward because there was not a stick to burn outside for miles. But such inconveniences don't

The Blackwater Dam, built between 1904 and 1909. Working conditions for the 3,000 men were appalling.

The last resting place of many who lost their lives building the dam.

The bothy at Loch Chiarain.

seem to deter visitors. The guestbook was full of entries from around the world.

Having slept like a baby, I rose early next morning. I crossed the burn by some slippery stepping stones and reached the opposite bank from where I toiled up a trackless hillside for 400 metres until I reached the crest of a ridge.

From the giant cairn on the summit of Leum Uilleam – just 5 metres short of Munro status – I could see Loch Ossian and in the foreground the station of Corrour on the West Highland Line. Apart from that, there was a whole lot of Nothing.

Coming off the hill, I followed a path beside the single-track railway line that links Glasgow and Fort William. As I walked beside it, I remembered the weekend when my mate Gus and I hiked across Rannoch Moor to Glen Nevis – including a painful, hobbling trek along this same stretch of track.

I'd recently celebrated my 17th birthday. We'd crossed the moor from the King's House to Rannoch station and were now walking on the railway line. It was a ghastly experience. The sleepers were wrongly spaced for the human stride. Every third step our boots hit the ballast between sleepers: step, step and crunch, a tedious and exhausting rhythm which went on for mile after mile – all seven of them. There was little to relieve the monotony except playing a game: who could spot the oldest date stamped on the steel plates holding the rails? There was one from 1939, another from 1920. Gus found the oldest. It dated from 1912.

As we walked, we anxiously listened out for approaching trains, especially when we entered the snow tunnel. This is a deep cutting, roofed with corrugated iron to prevent snow drifts forming and blocking the line. Emerging safely on the other side (incidentally, we didn't see a single train throughout the duration of the walk), we left the line at Corrour station and followed a path through the boggy wastes to the head of Glen Nevis, where we spent the night at a ruined shooting lodge called Luibeilt and which, I have to say, was a lot more rudimentary than the Loch Chiarain bothy. In total that day, we walked over 30 miles. We were exhausted. We lit a fire in the grate and bandaged our bleeding feet.

Luibeilt is now a complete ruin. Back then it was still watertight and made an excellent refuge. A couple of years after our first visit, we returned with some friends to celebrate New Year, walking in from Corrour station with supplies which included a small bag of coal. On Hogmanay, a blizzard roared around the ruined house, blowing in stray snowflakes as we huddled by the fire, sipping beer and trying our best to feel festive.

The storm exhausted itself overnight. In the morning we emerged into the brilliance of a winter wonderland. Wading through snow drifts we scaled a nearby summit, from where we surveyed the arctic scene. I was captivated by the sight of a large herd of red deer. Their antlers were covered in snow, and they chased their shadows as the sun set behind them. It was a powerful and exhilarating spectacle.

When we left Luibeilt the sky was grimly overcast. Blinding squalls of snow obscured the path back to Corrour station where we had to wait for about three hours for our return train. It was dark when it arrived and it was equipped with an

enormous snowplough up front. The engine and its carriages were wreathed in clouds of hissing steam, which leaked from old heating pipes. The sight was like a scene from the film *Dr Zhivago*. The stationmaster, who lived at Corrour with her family, had changed specially to meet the train. Wearing her full British Rail uniform, she stood on the dark platform in the falling snow, backlit by the headlight of the approaching locomotive. With theatrical deliberation, she raised her left arm. In her hand she held the passkey for the next section of single track. The locomotive slowly drew alongside her. The driver leaned out of the cab and took the key, unlocking us from this frozen but romantic wilderness.

Things at Corrour have changed a lot since then. The old waiting room and ticket office have gone. There is no longer a stationmaster and the signal box is an expensive holiday let. But Corrour is perhaps better know today than it once was, having been a location in the cult film *Trainspotting*.

Corrour is just about as remote as you can get in Scotland by using public transport. The nearest road is the B848, which is ten miles away by hill track. Other than that, you have to take the train. Passengers on the West Highland Line to Fort William may well ask what a station is doing out on this desolate moor over 400 metres above sea level. The answer goes back to the golden age of sporting estates, eye-watering wealth, and a time when the super-rich of the Victorian era came out to play – with guns.

In the 1890s, the owner of the nearby Corrour estate persuaded the directors of the West Highland Line, which was being laid across the moor, to build the station. This would enable his friends to step off the London train and join him hunting,

Corrour Lodge, reflected in water.

shooting and fishing. Having disembarked, the guests were conveyed by pony and trap to the shores of lovely Loch Ossian, from where they took a private steamer to their host's splendid shooting lodge. Close to the steamer pier, a wooden waiting room was erected for the convenience of guests. Today, this wooden building is a youth hostel. I have spent many a comfortable night there listening to stags roaring in the gloaming as I drifted off to sleep.

It's many years since the steamer ran the length of Loch Ossian. To reach Corrour Lodge, I followed a Land Rover track for 6 kilometres to the eastern end of the loch. The lodge is now in its third incar-

nation. The original was on the moor. It fell into ruin. The second, built by Sir John Stirling Maxwell (a founder member of the National Trust for Scotland and an early, influential figure in the Forestry Commission) burnt to the ground in the 1940s. The present building, which some have likened to a Bond villain's lair, has a strangely futuristic appearance. It dates from the 1990s and was built with imported Portuguese granite, steel and glass at a cost of over £20 million. Its owners are the fabulously wealthy Swedish Rausing family who are the heirs to the Tetra Pak empire.

Passing the unexpected sight of an Antony Gormley statue gazing across Loch Ossian, I was met by David Taylor, who runs the lodge with his wife. 'There is a permanent staff of nine at Corrour – more in the summer,' David explained. 'That's when we get busy.'

David is an excellent chef who learned his craft in Italy. He has worked at top-class restaurants and hotels around the world, and once cooked for wealthy passengers on the Royal Scot tourist train. Now he provides for the Rausing family and their guests.

'How often do the Rausings come and stay to enjoy all this?' I asked as he ladled homemade Cullen skink into my bowl.

'They simply love the place and come whenever they can. Summer usually – about three weeks every year – and then they have the whole, wild estate to themselves.'

When the family are not in residence, Corrour can be rented by discerning folks with money. It makes an ideal hidey-hole; celebrities like Bono and Gwyneth Paltrow have enjoyed David's cooking while admiring the views through the lodge's massive windows.

'Those sort of people don't come by train. They fly in,' said David. 'Having said that, one New York hedge fund manager did hire the entire Jacobite steam train when he came with friends to celebrate his 30th birthday.'

When David's wife gave me a guided tour of the luxurious splendours on offers, I couldn't help myself asking how much it might cost to rent for a week. It would be ideal for one of my own large family's get-togethers.

'Well,' she said, 'depending on the time of year, you wouldn't get much change out of £35,000.'

Sadly, that was a bit out of my price range.

The statue by Antony Gormley which looks out over Loch Ossian.

PART FIVE

**FROM FORT WILLIAM TO NEWTONMORE, IN SEARCH OF THE
CENTRE OF SCOTLAND VIA SPEAN BRIDGE AND LOCH LAGGAN**

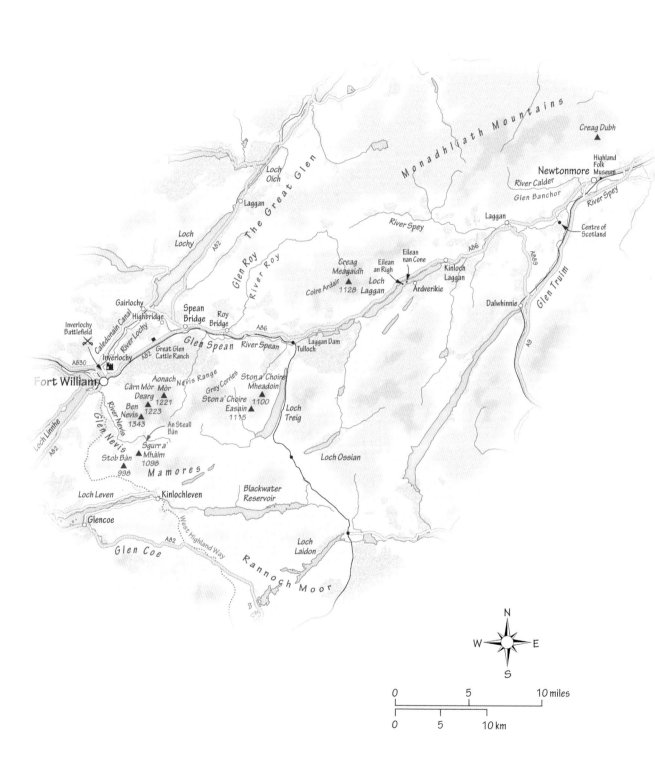

Creag Dubh ▲

Monadhliath Mountains

Loch Oich

The Great Glen

Newtonmore

Highland
Folk
Museum

River Calder

Glen Banchor

River Spey

Laggan

Laggan

River Spey

Centre of
Scotland

River Roy

River Spey

Glen Truim

Loch
Lochy

Glen Roy

A82

Creag
Meagaidh

Eilean
an Righ

Eilean
nan Cone

Kinloch
Laggan

A86

Coire Ardair

1128

Loch
Laggan

Ardverikie

Dalwhinnie

A889

A9

Gairlochy

Highbridge

Spean
Bridge

Roy
Bridge

Caledonian Canal

Inverlochy
Battlefield

River Lochy

A82

Glen Spean

River Spean

A86

Laggan Dam

Tulloch

A830

Inverlochy

Great Glen
Cattle Ranch

Fort William

Càrn Mòr
Dearg

Aonach
Mòr

Nevis Range

Grey Corries

Ston a' Choire
Mheadoin

River Nevis

1221

Ston a' Choire
Easain

1100

Ben
Nevis

1223

1115

Loch
Treig

1343

An Steall
Bàn

Glen Nevis

Sgurr a'
Mhàim

Loch
Ossian

Loch Linnhe

Stob Bàn

1098

A82

998

Mamores

Loch Leven

Kinlochleven

Blackwater
Reservoir

Glencoe

West Highland Way

Loch
Laidon

Glen Coe

A82

Rannoch Moor

N
W   E
S

0   5   10 miles

0   5   10 km

The Strange Plate – Neptune's Staircase – the road of death

Fort William lies within striking distance of some of the finest mountain scenery in the Highlands, including, of course, Ben Nevis, the highest summit in the whole of Great Britain. 'The Fort' – as it's known locally – is the capital of the west Highlands, and is a surprisingly lively place with a cultural heart that boasts an excellent bookshop, a new cinema and arts centre, and an array of interesting shops and places to eat. Anyone in the Highlands heading north or south, east or west, will eventually pass through the town, mingling with tourists, climbers and walkers in the pedestrianised Main Street which also marks the end of the West Highland Way. In Fort William today, there is no obvious physical evidence of the town's military origins, but the Gaelic-language road signs are a clue. For some distance, they have been pointing the way to An Gearasdan, which in English means 'the garrison'.

The Inverlochy Garrison, as it was originally known, was established in the 17th century by the army of Oliver Cromwell. Its purpose was to supress the local clans – especially Clan Cameron, led at the time by the indefatigable Sir Ewen Cameron, 'the Ulysses of the Highlands'. This old warrior was involved in conflict and rebellion all his long life (he lived to be 90). At the Battle of Inverlochy he infamously bit out the throat of an enemy soldier who'd wrestled him to the ground. Sir Ewen later fought at Killiecrankie and sent his men to support the Stuart cause at the Battle of Sheriffmuir.

Previous spread. Ben Nevis

In the 1690s the Inverlochy Garrison was rebuilt, strengthened and renamed Fort William in honour of the new king, the Protestant William of Orange. The town that grew up in its shadow was called Maryburgh in honour of William's wife, Queen Mary.

I was surprised to discover that parts of the old fort still exist. I'm not alone. Thousands of people drive past it every day without ever realising the fact. The inconspicuous ruins lie beside the main road skirting the shore, hemmed in by a retail park and a roundabout. It was here early one spring when I met up with local historian Chris Robinson. As is often the case in Fort William, a blustery wind was driving rain showers off the loch. At first glance, there wasn't much to see.

'We've tried to make more of a feature of the place,' said Chris shrinking into his coat as a blast of rain hit him in the face. 'We've put out flower planters, a couple of benches and an information board.'

Chris led me around the site, which occupies a once strategic position where the River Nevis enters Loch Linnhe. 'There were over a thousand men stationed here in the 18th century. They were essentially an alien presence in an otherwise traditional, Gaelic-speaking Highland society. It was a colonial venture to pacify the natives.'

'And did they succeed?'

'Ultimately, yes they did. One of the most notorious acts of "pacification" came soon after the fort was completed. From here, troops were marched to Glencoe to sort out the troublesome MacDonalds. It's an episode everyone remembers today as the Massacre of Glencoe.'

By now, Chris had led me down to a shingle bank above the tideline. Viewed from this angle, it was much easier to visualise the fort as it once was. The stone walls of the old gun bastions were quite obvious, and there was an arched postern gate leading down to the lochside. 'The fort was eventually turned into housing and would have survived for longer had it not been for the railway company. They demolished most of it in the late 19th century and pushed the railway line right through the middle, which accounts for the fact there's not a lot left to see.'

Chris led me from the windswept fort to the comfort of the cosy museum in the centre of town. On the way we passed a rather pleasing sculpture of a man driving a Model T Ford.

'That was commissioned to commemorate the occasion, in 1911, when a young Edinburgh man, Henry Alexander, drove a Model T Ford up the mountain and back again,' said Chris.

'Why did he do that?' I asked.

'Apparently it was for a bet, but it was probably more of a publicity stunt to promote his dad's garage business. Anyway, it took several days to get the car up to the summit of the Ben – nearly 4,500 feet. Alexander was then filmed by the press making his descent in the car. It was quite an achievement and hundreds of people turned out to applaud when he returned to Fort William. After that, he drove home to Edinburgh. Not a bad day out!'

Stepping inside the West Highland Museum, it was a relief to be out of the rain. Chris enthused as he led me through the Jacobite collection, reminding me that to be a supporter of the Stuart cause in the 18th century was a dangerous, treasonable business. To communicate with those of a like mind, a coded language of symbols and artefacts was developed. Among the many objects of sedition on display were snuff boxes with hidden images of Bonnie Prince Charlie which could be discreetly shown when required. There was also a Jacobite 'fan' to signal a lady's political sympathies and a portrait of the prince himself whose image magically appears when a glass column is placed on a coloured mat. But the exhibit that piqued my interest most was the 'Strange Plate'.

'This obviously has nothing to do with crockery,' said Chris. 'It's an engraving plate created by a man from Orkney called Strange.' When the Jacobite campaign faltered in 1746, Bonnie Prince Charlie went broke. In order to pay his men and keep them fighting, he decided to issue his own Jacobite banknotes. Strange was commissioned to produce a printing plate; by the time it was ready to print the banknotes, the Jacobites had already lost the Battle of Culloden.

'If you printed one of those notes now, how much do you think it would be worth?' I asked.

'Well, in 1928, the museum had a limited print run made to raise funds. One was recently sold for nearly £900. So I think the notes are keeping up with inflation at least!' said Chris.

A couple of kilometres north of the centre of Fort William, the famous Road to the Isles heads west, crossing first the River Lochy, and then the Caledonian Canal. From the bridge there's a dramatic view of Neptune's Staircase – a series of eight canal locks which lift vessels to a height of nearly 22 metres. Boats entering the 'staircase' can sail along a 60-mile canal system that connects Fort William to Inverness. The route provides a shortcut between the east and west coasts, avoiding the difficult and dangerous passage around the north of Scotland.

The Caledonian Canal was designed by the civil engineering genius Thomas Telford. Construction began in 1803; it was part of a government-led infrastructure scheme which

The eight locks of Neptune's Staircase, on the Caledonian Canal.

aimed to provide work for local people following the Highland Clearances. At least that was the hope. Unfortunately, it failed on several counts. The canal took 17 years to build – far longer than expected. By the time it was finished, steam engines had revolutionised shipping, and bigger ocean-going vessels were unable to use the canal. And meanwhile, thousands of Highlanders had emigrated after suffering eviction and injustice at the hands of oppressive landlords.

Despite these setbacks, the canal received the royal stamp of approval when it was graced by the young Queen Victoria. Again, things didn't go quite as planned. When the royal yacht passed through Neptune's Staircase, the queen's patience was tried by the length of time it took – six hours – to complete the passage through all eight locks. As time dragged by, the queen was heard to remark, perhaps not for the first time, 'We are not amused.'

Ironically, the canal is busier now than it was in the past, but most of the vessels are for leisure rather than commerce. Tourism has led to a boom in yachts, pleasure boats and day-trippers heading to destinations up and down the Great Glen. The last time I took a stroll along the canal, I saw only one commercial vessel – a solitary fishing boat called the *Crystal Stream*, registered at Port Seton on the Firth of Forth. As the water level rose between two lock gates, the skipper told me about the terrible winter he'd had trying for prawns on the west coast. They had given up but a pal had called him to say that prawns had been found in the Moray Firth. 'That's where we're heading now,' he said. 'To try our luck!'

On the outskirts of Fort William, to the west

Inverlochy Castle, built by John Comyn, Lord of Badenoch.

of the distillery and the aluminium works, is Inverlochy Castle, a rare 13th-century survivor from the reign of King Alexander III. It was built by John Comyn, the powerful Lord of Badenoch, whose family became deadly rivals of Robert the Bruce in the race for the Scottish crown. It was said that to hold Inverlochy was to control a huge swathe of the north-west Highlands. The castle has been a roofless ruin for centuries, and little altered since it was built beside the River Lochy.

The most significant military engagement at Inverlochy took place during the Wars of the Three Kingdoms. In February 1645 a Royalist army under the flamboyant Duke of Montrose utterly crushed the army of 'God and Covenant' led by Archibald Campbell, the 1st Marquis of Argyll. The marquis was still reeling from an attack on his castle at Inveraray. The assault had been led by a blood-thirsty and ruthless warrior called Alasdair Mac Colla – a MacDonald from the Hebridean island of Coll. Mac Colla had lands and interests in Ulster. When war erupted between the monarch Charles I and the forces of parliament in England and the Covenanters in Scotland, Mac Colla sided with the Royalists. Landing from Ireland with 300 men, he burned and butchered his way through the west Highlands, taking every opportunity to wreak havoc on his enemies, especially Clan Campbell. When Mac Colla sacked Inveraray, the marquis was forced to flee his burning castle in a rowing boat.

Bent on revenge for this humiliation, the marquis regrouped and assembled his forces at Inverlochy. Meanwhile, Mac Colla and his warrior band of MacDonalds joined Montrose and the Royalist army in Scotland. What happened next was one of the most decisive military encounters in the entire civil war in Scotland. In a brilliant move, Montrose and Mac Colla surprised the Covenanting army of Clan Campbell just outside the old castle at Inverlochy.

A few years ago, I met up with military historian John MacFarlane – an ex-soldier and a Gaelic speaker – to explore the field of battle. Together we climbed a hill facing the lower slopes of Ben Nevis. The castle stood to our left. Behind us a steep escarpment fell away to some railway sidings where a steam engine was getting ready to pull the *Jacobite Express*.

'The Marquis of Argyll had no idea that his forces were about to be attacked by the whole Royalist army,' said John. 'They only realised when they heard the first trumpets blow and saw the Royalist banners being unfurled in the dawn light. The Royalists attacked immediately. In the onslaught, both flanks of the Covenanting army collapsed, leaving the centre exposed on the escarpment. But as the Royalists charged, there was nowhere to retreat to because of the steep ground behind them.' John gestured to the land now occupied by the railway sidings. As if on cue, the steam engine below blew its whistle. The forlorn sound reverberated against the walls of old Inverlochy.

'What happened next?' I asked.

'A rout took place. That's what happened. More than half the army of "God and Covenant" were killed – almost 1,500 men – mostly Campbells. It was carnage. The officer class of Clan Campbell were decimated.'

Archibald Campbell, the Marquis of Argyll, watched the destruction of his clansmen from a war galley moored in Loch Linnhe. The army that he'd assembled for 'God and Covenant' had been cut to pieces, and as the scale of the defeat became apparent, he slipped his moorings and sailed away. The men he deserted were left to a terrible fate. Alasdair Mac Colla gave them no quarter: 'The Royalist army lost just 20 men with about 200 wounded,' said John 'Relatively unscathed, they continued on their bloody rampage, pursuing and cutting down those who fled.'

Survivors from the Campbell army were channelled along a route that now forms part of the West Highland Way. But in February 1645, it was a road of death. The wounded and the weak from the defeated army were quickly overtaken and put to the sword by Mac Colla's bloodthirsty men. As the bodies mounted up, the MacDonalds wearied of their butchery and eventually stopped the hunt. Today, few visitors to Inverlochy have any idea of the horror and the bloodshed that took place.

GLEN NEVIS TO LUIBEILT

Pan bread and a toy tent – Gardyloo Gully – Luibeilt and pants on fire

The West Highland Way tracks the western side of Glen Nevis, which is overshadowed by the slopes of Ben Nevis to the east. To the south, the Mamores rise like a threatening geological tidal wave. About 3 kilometres from Fort William and sitting on the left bank of the River Nevis is the Glen Nevis Youth Hostel – a place frequented for generations by walkers hoping to scale the UK's highest mountain.

Although I've rested my weary bones there myself, my pal Gus and I were too poor as teenagers to afford the luxury of a shared dormitory when we made our first ascent of 'the Ben'. Instead, we pitched our tent in the campsite opposite, having hitched a lift from Glencoe in a Mother's Pride bakery van delivering pan bread to Highland shops. As we dropped from the cab, the driver tossed a loaf in our direction. 'That's for yer tea boys!' he said. 'You'll need to build up your strength if you want to climb the Ben.'

We walked to the campsite and wrestled with what I can only describe as a miserable excuse for a tent. Gus's much-vaunted expedition tent was basically a toy. He'd got it by saving up coupons cut from the back of a Weetabix packet. It certainly didn't look robust or well suited to Caledonian meteorological conditions.

Of course, it was freezing cold that night – made worse by the lack of a groundsheet – and we hardly slept at all. At dawn, we gave up the battle for repose and packed the tent away. We were now both starving. I chewed on the heel of the Mother's Pride loaf while Gus looked disconsolately at the campsite shop which, according to the sign, was not going to open for another three hours. Hunger seemed a poor way to start our climb. Then I noticed a recent delivery of milk. Pint cartons were sitting very temptingly in a red plastic crate by the door. Somewhat guiltily, we helped ourselves, promising to pay on our return.

Gus, wrapped in his duffel coat, led the way forward. I followed in my anorak and wellies. Although it was June, the weather felt more like winter. After a couple of hours slogging up the tedious path, the view disappeared completely when we climbed into cloud. Occasional snowflakes blew past in the grey light. Ahead I could make out dark shapes. These resolved themselves into tall cairns, which I hoped were marking the route. At this height the path was buried under old snow, but the silent presence of the cairns showed the way. Eventually, the ground levelled

out. We'd reached the plateau.

Snow was falling more heavily now. 'We need to be careful not to walk off the cliffs in this cloud,' Gus shouted into the rising wind. 'There are huge drops – 1,500-foot – somewhere in front of us.'

Moving forward cautiously – and almost blindly – we saw something looming out of the mirk. It was the summit cairn, topped off with a trig point. We had made it. We had conquered the Ben.

Since that first ascent, I've got to know Ben Nevis in many of its different moods: mist-shrouded and wet, when you have to work hard to convince yourself that climbing is a joy; in summer, in shorts, hopping along the Càrn Mòr Dearg arête; in winter, front-pointing up a gully; in spring, feeling the welcome warmth of the sun while squinting into the reflected glare of a melting snow pack. These are all memorable moments. But the mountain isn't one to show off its charms easily. Ben Nevis is a secretive place and saves the best to last, rewarding those who put in the effort to get acquainted.

The last time I ventured onto the Ben I took the climbers' path into the corrie below the great north face. Ahead of me was the world-class climber Dave MacLeod. We were being filmed making an ascent of Gardyloo Gully, a snow and ice route which cuts up left between Tower Ridge and Observatory Ridge.

The Ben was looking fierce that morning and I was reminded that 'Ben Nevis' is Gaelic for 'evil mountain'. Reading *Black's Guide* before setting out hadn't made me feel any better: 'A strange scene of desolation presents itself. A terrific precipice on the north-eastern side makes a sheer descent from the snow-capped summit of not less than 1500 ft.'

We were moving up the path at something

approaching jogging speed. I was already struggling to keep up. As I wheezed along behind him, Dave spoke effortlessly about the history of Scottish mountaineering. He explained how Ben Nevis had been enormously important to the development of the Scottish sport. 'The great cliffs of the Ben are as close as we can get to the big rock faces in Switzerland and the Alps, and in winter they can be hugely challenging. It might be a small mountain in terms of height, but a winter climb on the Ben is a serious undertaking and ranks with the best of the Alps for technical difficulty.'

It was a relief to eventually stop for a breather beside a small building known as the CIC Memorial Hut. It sits beneath the enormous cliffs of Càrn Mòr Dearg and was built in memory of a young climber, Charles Inglis Clark, who was killed in action during the First World War. Dave said that the CIC hut is the only real example we have in the UK of an Alpine hut – probably because Ben Nevis is the only UK mountain big enough to need a place where a mountaineer can get a head start, to be on the mountain early in the day in order to complete the big routes before nightfall.

Long before the real mountaineers arrived on the Ben, tourists were making the long slog up to the summit – just as Gus and I had done years ago – walking a route that completely bypasses the spectacular cliffs. Those who were keen to avoid perspiration altogether could hire a pony and a guide for the return trip. The tourist route proved so popular that a small hotel was built at the summit, offering rudimentary accommodation to weary walkers, who could also purchase souvenirs and even send a postcard.

The route that Dave and I were going to climb

Dave MacLeod at the start of Gardyloo Gully, Ben Nevis.

– Gardyloo Gully – owes its name to the occupants of both the hotel and the weather observatory who for many years had used the gully as a waste disposal chute. 'We've pulled out all kinds of rubbish from there in summer. It's like an archaeological dig,' said Dave as we headed up a slope of ever-steepening snow.

Sadly for Scottish national pride, English climbers made the first winter ascents of the Ben's great cliffs. In April 1897, three Englishmen climbed Gardyloo Gully for the first time, while another first ascent was made of Tower Gully, witnessed by mountaineer John Begg: 'Up this with ropes and ice axes came three members of the English Alpine Club. It certainly seemed a rash and foolhardy experiment, but their coolness and courage were rewarded after six hours of hard work by their reaching the summit in safety.'

Dave and I had gained a good deal of height by now, but I was beginning to feel slightly nervous. The sheer scale of the towering cliffs was very intimidating. I'd experienced a similar feeling once before when I'd climbed the gully as a teenager, practising my snow and ice techniques before leaving for the Swiss Alps. Back then, fear gripped me when two jet fighters flew at low level through the corrie. They were actually below me as they screamed past. For a terrifying moment, I mistook the roar of jet engines for the sound of an avalanche.

The crux pitch of Gardyloo Gully is sometimes a steep wall of snow and ice. At other times, it can be a curious ice tunnel, which forms a couple of hundred feet below the summit. When Dave and I got to it, we discovered an almost chimney-like feature of polished ice rising vertically between projecting rocks on either side. Wriggling up this unusual feature was a weird experience. To be confined in a tube of ice with no view and knowing I was almost 1,500 feet up on Britain's highest mountain was surreal.

As I emerged from the frigid confinement of the ice tunnel, I was caught in a torrent of powder snow. It completely blinded me. I was swallowing snow and gulping for air as I struggled to the safety of Dave's belay position. When I reached him, he quickly clipped me in before I peeled off from exhaustion.

After the final pitch, with no great cornice to negotiate, we reached the summit snow field where the ruins of the old observatory were plainly visible. Of the hotel, there was nothing to be seen at all. Shame – I could have done with a pint.

From the youth hostel in Glen Nevis, the single-track road heads south-east for about 4 kilometres before it crosses the River Nevis and then makes a dog-leg east. Here the glen narrows between the heights of Ben Nevis and the highest mountain in the western Mamores, Sgurr a' Mhàim, which is connected to its neighbour by the delightfully airy and exposed Devil's Ridge.

From the car park at the road end, a path winds through beautiful deciduous woods above the cascading River Nevis. The path emerges beside river flats in an almost Alpine setting, where the focal point is the spectacular waterfall of An Steall Bàn ('the white spout'), which drops over a 120-metre cliff, creating a dazzling white fan of water as it falls. I've camped at Steall on several occasions while tackling the wonderful high ridges of the Mamores, whose summits have evocative but hard-to-pronounce names: An Gearanach ('the complainer'), Na Gruagaichean ('the maidens') and An Garbhanach ('the rough ridge') to name just three of the ten Munros in the range.

It was on one the Mamore peaks, Stob Bàn,

The old observatory, Ben Nevis.

whose white quartz-covered summit is often mistaken for snow, that I once had an eerie and mysterious encounter. It was a cold day in early May, with squally snow showers blowing in from the north. I had spent the morning with a friend, Andy, traversing the ridge from Mullach nan Coirean. We were now in thick mist negotiating a switchback of tops. In the muffled silence, we heard a distant sound – a rhythmic, percussive clattering. We stopped to listen. The noise grew louder and seemingly closer. Then a figure emerged through the fog – an old woman with snow-white hair and equipment that seemed to match her age. Dangling from an antique rucksack was a metal canteen and a tin mug. Every time she took a step forward, they banged together: clang, clunk, clink, clang. When she saw us, she stopped. The noise stopped too.

'Are you lost?' she asked in a thin voice.

'No,' I said. 'We're heading for Stob Bàn.'

'I'm looking for a place to camp – to bivvy,' she said. 'But it's not easy in this mist.'

'Have you been camping up here for long?' I asked.

'Oh yes indeed. For a very long time.'

She then turned and disappeared into the swirling mist again, the sound of her clattering canteen getting fainter with every passing moment.

Andy and I looked at each other.

'She must be at least 80 years old,' said Andy. 'But did you see the speed she was travelling at? I'm not sure I could keep up with her!'

There was definitely something 'different' about that woman. She seemed out of place – and out of time – almost as if she didn't belong to our world. Then again, in the Highlands, reality is often not quite what it seems.

The boggy path from the Steall heads east over rough terrain, following the course of the River Nevis to its source in an area of desolate country between the Mamores and a range of high mountains called the Grey Corries. From here, it's just a couple of kilometres to the now ruined shooting lodge of Luibeilt.

Today Luibeilt is a roofless ruin, but long before it was vandalised by careless hikers who broke up its timbers and floorboards for firewood, Luibeilt was a desirable destination where I've stayed on

The waterfall of An Steall Ban, which drops over a 120-metre cliff.

a number of occasions. On one memorable night, my pal Gus and I arrived having walked from Rannoch. We were on a cross-country trek to Spean Bridge in the company of two young French women, Veronique and Marianne. Gus had met them at a teacher-training college a couple of weeks earlier. They were just the sort of mademoiselles every young male learner of the French language dreams about.

The weather had been appalling – wind and rain had swept the moor – and we were soaked through. After lighting a fire, we hung our wet clothes as close to the flames as we dared. Later in the evening, having shared a bottle of wine, I became aware of a burning smell. I saw Gus poke a stick into the fire and retrieved my britches. They were now ablaze. Mockingly, he held them aloft, almost as if in triumph. The flames had burned a hole through the seat of my pants. I howled with dismay as Gus, Veronique and Marianne giggled at my predicament. I still haven't entirely forgiven Gus for this outrage.

THE AONACHS TO THE EASAINS

Cattle ranching – the Parallel Roads – blizzards and Lemsip

The A82 road north from Fort William passes the Nevis Range ski centre, where a gondola takes snow sports enthusiasts in search of excitement on a mountain known as Aonach Mòr. When the weather's right, the sky bright and the snow white, much fun is to be had slipping and sliding on its groomed pistes. I have spent many happy days skiing with friends and family on Aonach Mòr, where the mountain environment offers superb views of Ben Nevis and the surrounding peaks. But this being Scotland, the weather is fickle, and 'blue bird' days can be a rare event, especially since global warming has reduced the chances of a good,

cold winter with a decent covering of snow.

Less of a hostage to climate change is the sport of mountain biking. In summer, the Nevis Range gondola switches to carrying bikes and their riders to the top of the UK's longest downhill bike track. Since 2002, the UCI Fort William World Cup has been held there, attracting riders and spectators from around the world.

The A82 from the Nevis Range closely follows the route taken by General Wade's 18th-century military road, which linked Fort William to other military bases in the Great Glen. In 1796, Sarah Murray came this way. Stopping in her chaise for refreshment, she bought a cup of milk from women who were herding cattle: 'The country is very thinly inhabited; and notwithstanding its non-productive appearance. I never drunk finer

Skiing Nevis range. Lifts and tows provide access to backcountry skiing on Aonach Mòr.

milk than I did there, from cows I found milking on the road's side; and what was still more extraordinary, though I gave but a trifle more than the value of what was drunk, the honest creatures thought it too much, although they seemed the poorest of the poor in Scotland.'

Cattle were traditionally a measure of wealth in the Highlands. For centuries clans had fought and raided each other for them. Today, the humble Heilan' coo plays a less important role in the local economy. But in the 1940s and 1950s, an ambitious attempt was made to ranch cattle in the Highlands.

Travellers following the A82 north from Fort William may notice a couple of curious structures, which appear to be out of time and out of place. They look as if they might have been left over from a Western film set – two black-and-white buildings, standing a couple of miles apart, each with a courtyard and a wide main gateway with the words Great Glen Cattle Ranch emblazoned on their whitewashed walls. I first saw them when I was a child driving with my father from Fort William to Inverness.

The Great Glen Cattle Ranch was the brainchild of an energetic and flamboyant man called Joe Hobbs. Originally from Hampshire, Joe emigrated at the age of nine with his family to Canada, where they settled on a prairie farm. During the First World War, Joe visited Scotland for the first time with the Royal Navy Air Service. When he returned to Canada, he became a whisky salesman. During the years of Prohibition he made a fortune smuggling whisky into the USA. He became so wealthy he was able to buy several distilleries in Scotland.

Joe came to Fort William because of the town's whisky distillery. He liked the country so much that he decided to stay and in 1945 bought a large

swathe of land between Fort William and Spean Bridge. But instead of retiring to enjoy his wealth, he embarked on a new enterprise. To the bemusement of his neighbours and others in agriculture, he set up his Great Glen Cattle Ranch. Over the next decade, he broke in the land – just as his family had done in Canada – digging ditches, draining bogs, liming the soil, erecting fences and seeding grass. Eventually, he began producing high-quality beef in great quantity, rounding up his herds of hill-grazed cattle on horseback. After five years, he made a good return on his investment. But Joe's vision was even greater. He wanted to develop Fort William as a deepwater transatlantic port. He planned pulp and paper mills and an improved rail infrastructure to open up the area to tourism. Joe Hobbs died in 1963 aged 72. He had been ahead of his time for most of his life, but his great vision for the Highlands never really materialised. Today, the two cattle shelters alongside the A82 are a reminder of his bold, ambitious plans.

When Sarah Murray entered the Great Glen, she was following the military road and heading for the High Bridge, which spanned the River Spean. Built by General Wade's men, the High Bridge was an impressive sight. Unfortunately, Sarah was prevented from sketching the 'stupendous' scene because dark clouds threatened rain, but she was sufficiently impressed to create a word picture for her readers: 'As I stood upon the ground higher than the bridge, it appeared to be a region of the utmost wildness; bare craggy mountains, one above another, on every side, and a dreary rough moor before me. The river Spean, which, as if glad of its escape through the arches of the bridge, was dashing with rapid bounds from one bed of rock to another; eager to finish the remainder of its tortured passage to the foot of Loch Lochy, deep below.'

At the High Bridge, Sarah once again found aspects of the romantic and the sublime. Sadly today the object of her artistic gaze isn't in great shape. All the arches have collapsed and only the stone uprights remain. In some ways, this makes the old bridge an even finer candidate for Sarah's admiration. I wonder if her response would have changed had she known of its significance to Jacobite history. It was at Highbridge that the first shots of the '45 were fired by a small party of clansmen who took on the British army and won.

Paul MacDonald was using a metal detector when I met him at Highbridge. He was scouring the site for evidence of the battle, which took place on 16 August 1745. Taking a break, Paul described what he knew about the clash. 'To be honest, it was more of a skirmish than a battle,' he said. 'Just after the raising of the Jacobite standard at Glenfinnan, which marked the start of the campaign, the British army sent two companies of soldiers down the military road from Fort Augustus, just north of here, to Fort William. They were ambushed here by 11 MacDonalds and their piper.'

Paul told me that the MacDonalds tricked the soldiers into believing they were a much larger force. They did this by running about, shouting, hiding among the trees and spreading out their plaids. They were so successful that the commander of the soldiers sent two men forward to negotiate with the 'superior' Jacobite force. These men were immediately captured by the rebel clansmen. Still fearing they were outnumbered, the government soldiers retreated over the bridge, but were fired on by the Jacobites. One of the musket balls wounded the officer leading the troops. Although the soldiers returned fire, they were captured, to

The earliest shots of the Jacobite Rising of 1745 were fired at Highbridge.

a man – all 80 of them – defeated by just 12 MacDonalds. In triumph, with their piper leading the way, the MacDonalds marched their prisoners to the main Jacobite army. The wounded officer's horse was presented to Bonnie Prince Charlie, and became his mount for the early part of the campaign.

Close to Highbridge is the village of Spean Bridge, which lies at a crossroads. Traffic crossing Telford's bridge over the River Spean (built in 1819) can either turn left towards Inverness, or take a right onto the A86 towards Newtonmore. Just outside the village on the A82 to Inverness is the famous and much-photographed memorial to the commando forces. These elite soldiers trained for battle in the hills and glens of the surrounding area during the Second World War.

A few kilometres east of Spean Bridge is the village of Roy Bridge, which sits at the entrance to Glen Roy. This glen would be unremarkable

The Parallel Roads at Glen Roy, thought to have been the work of giants but which were actually caused by the changing water levels of a glacial lake.

except for a geological mystery that puzzled some of the greatest intellects of the past – including the formidable Charles Darwin. The feature that Darwin and others travelled to the area to see is known as the Parallel Roads of Glen Roy. Seen from a distance, the Parallel Roads look like just that: bold lines, one above the other, following the contours of the hillside as if bulldozed into shape by a rogue plant operator.

Early inhabitants mythologised these curious landscape features as the work of giants or even the mighty Fingal himself. When Charles Darwin and the geologist Charles Lyell visited in 1838, they decided that the Parallel Roads were evidence of rising and falling sea levels. They were getting close to the truth in suggesting ancient shorelines, but it took the work of Swiss geologist Louis Agas-

siz to solve the mystery. In the late 19th century he demonstrated that glaciation had had a profound effect on the landscape. According to this account, the gigantic ice sheet that covered most of Scotland 17,000 years ago had blocked the entrance to Glen Roy. When temperatures rose, glacial meltwater had been trapped in Glen Roy by a dam of ice. As the rate of melting increased or declined, the water level of the icebound lake rose or fell, leaving the scars of three separate shorelines on the hillside. Eventually the glacial ice dam had burst and the ice lake drained with sudden, catastrophic force. Today only the Parallel Roads remain – evidence on the hillside of Scotland's very own glacial lake.

Further up Glen Spean, and graced by its own mainline railway station, is the tiny hamlet of

Tulloch. If you have the inclination – and money – you can catch a train from here straight to London Euston. Tulloch station also boats an independent hostel – a bunkhouse for walkers and climbers and other wanderers of Lochaber. The first time I availed myself of its facilities was in January 2001, just before the foot-and-mouth epidemic shut down much of the Highlands. Four of us, my pal Gus, my neighbour Andy, and a student of environmental science called Gavin, met at Tulloch station where we'd booked a night's accommodation. We'd planned to climb two Munros – Stob a' Choire Mheadhoin and Stob Coire Easain – known collectively as the Easains, whose snow-covered peaks are bold landmarks in the country to the west of Loch Treig.

As we drained the last drops of alcohol from our carry-out, a freight train rumbled past the station. 'I hope there won't be many more like that to wake us,' I said, climbing into my bunk and switching off the light.

Next morning was bright and cold. The low sun cast long shadows across the snow-covered world, where every frost crystal became a prism, scattering the light into miniature spectrums every time I moved my head. After breakfast, we packed our gear for a long day on the hill. Our plan was to stay overnight in a bothy below Stob Bàn in the Grey Corries. Consequently, our rucksacks bulged with provisions and camping equipment. Before we left, the hostel owner came to collect payment. He was obviously very proud of his neat little establishment. It turned out he was a railway enthusiast, trainspotter, and something of an expert of the history of the West Highland Line.

'Did you know that the civil engineer Sir Robert McAlpine almost lost his life surveying the line?' said our host. 'He and a party of fellow engineers

set out from here in January 1889 to walk to Corrour up on Rannoch Moor – a distance of about 28 miles. But it was further than they thought and very tough-going across trackless country. Then the snow came down and they were caught in a blizzard. Fortunately, they were found – completely lost and half frozen – by a search party led by a local shepherd.' Our host paused as if for dramatic effect. 'They were completely unprepared and wearing city clothes. They were lucky – very lucky – to have survived.'

It was an interesting story, but I wondered why he was telling us. Was it a thinly veiled warning not to underestimate the weather in Lochaber?

Pondering this thought, we set off and gained height rapidly. We soon reached the steep slopes of Meall Cian Dearg, where we experienced a number of unexpected technical challenges that forced us to 'tool up' earlier than expected. Kicking crampons into snow and ice we made good progress towards the summit of Stob a' Choire Mheadhoin. The weather was still beautiful, but a subtle change was taking place in the upper atmosphere. Fingers of cloud began to drift in from the north-west, slowly filling in the blue sky above us. About an hour later, the first snowflakes blew past. Another hour and we were in the teeth of a full-scale blizzard and navigating by compass. This is a laborious process where one in the party walks on a bearing, counting his steps as he goes, until he almost disappears into the mist. His companions then walk up to him – and then, following the same bearing – continue until they too just about disappear. Despite religiously counting every step over the ground and sticking to our bearing the best we could in the howling wind, we failed completely to find the summit cairn of Stob a' Choire Mheadhoin.

The summit of Stob a' Choire Mheadhoin.

Dropping out of the cloud in a rapid descent to the saddle between the two Munros, we debated whether we should turn back or press on. Since we were about halfway to the bothy we decided to plough on.

As luck would have it, the cloud lifted before we reached the summit cairn of Stob Coire Easain. In the late afternoon sun, we watched as pink-tinged clouds and trailing vapours parted like a curtain on a scene of arctic wonder. Somewhere in the world of white below us was our bothy.

We didn't have much time to appreciate the view. It would soon be dark and we had a long way to go to reach shelter. We descended as fast as we dared. Nearing the bottom of a steep snow field, Andy decided to speed things up by sliding down the mountain on his rear end. As he shot off, he lost control. He tried to break his fall with the pick of his ice axe, but his crampons caught in the snow and flipped him into the air. With amazement, we watched as Andy performed a surprisingly acrobatic somersault before crashing to an abrupt halt. We hurried to his rescue. He seemed okay, except for a badly twisted ankle. Even with our help, he could only move at a snail's pace. By the time we reached the bothy, it was dark and snow had started to fall again.

Inside was very primitive – nothing more than four stone walls and a roof. The only fuel on offer was three lumps of coal – medium-sized – lying

The Loch Laggan dam, built in 1934 to power the aluminium smelter at Fort William.

in the grate. We managed to light them with some old candle stumps and bits of cardboard, but our blaze only gave the illusion of heat. Altogether, it was a pretty miserable experience, even after cooking a rudimentary meal on our camping stove. With nothing much to do, we went to bed on a platform under the roof timbers. Sleep was a long time coming. The rising wind blew snowflakes through gaps in the slates, which settled in the folds of our sleeping bags. I was just beginning to nod off when Andy started complaining about the pain in his ankle. Eventually, I was forced into action. Putting on my boots I went outside into the night, and stumbled through the blizzard to a burn where I broke the ice and filled a pan. Back

inside the bothy, I boiled the water, dissolved three Lemsips into a mug and handed it to Andy. 'Drink your medicine,' I said angrily. 'And go to sleep!' He slept like a baby after that. But in the morning, he needed help to walk, and used the bothy broom like Long John Silver's crutch to escape the mountain.

Back on the A86 and heading east for a couple of kilometres, the road comes to the impressive Laggan Dam. Built in 1934, it blocks the River Spean at the western end of Loch Laggan and creates a reservoir of energy for the aluminium smelter at Fort William. It is an impressive sight, especially when the river is in spate. Excess water is released through pipes in the centre of the dam wall,

Creag Meagaidh National Nature Reserve is home to many species, including the mountain hare.

creating gigantic and mesmerising plumes of water. Tunnels connect Laggan to Loch Treig 5 kilometres away. From there, another tunnel system carries the water for 24 kilometres through the mountains to the slopes of Ben Nevis, where it drops down the mountainside in five steel pipes to the powerhouse beside the aluminium smelter.

LOCH LAGGAN TO NEWTONMORE

Ancient kings – Creag Dubh and Cluny Macpherson – poverty and porridge

Much of Creag Meagaidh is a National Nature Reserve with a range of habitats that extend from the shores of Loch Laggan to the vast summit plateau – the haunt of mountain hare and ptarmigan. It's a wonderful wildlife haven. Rory Richardson, who works as the reserve manager, wanted to give me a tour of the land that he clearly

loves. As we walked along the path to the woods of Coille a' Choire, Rory told me that his route into conservation and environmentalism had been something of a long and winding road. Raised locally, he became a soldier in the guards before returning home to work as a stalker on one of the estates.

'My priorities were completely different then. I was actually against conservationists. I thought they were meddlers from outside who didn't understand the community, our way of life, or the environment they were so keen to protect,' Rory said. 'But after I took a short-term contract with the National Nature Reserve, I was won over. I've been working for the "old enemy" for 22 years now.'

Today, Rory looks after 4,000 hectares of wild land that is being restored to the way it was several hundred years ago.

'Back then there was an abundance of wildlife.

And people. They lived closer to nature. It's amazing to think that there were animals alive then that are now extinct. There were wild boar, wolves, beaver and maybe even lynx.'

'Did they not go extinct for a reason?' I asked. 'People and wolves don't go well together.'

'I'm not saying bring back wolves to Creag Meagaidh,' said Rory. 'But Scotland is big enough for some selective and cautious species reintroduction. It would be nice to know that somewhere in the country a wolf is watching from the heights.'

From the edge of the wood, we admired the view of Coire Ardair – the 'corrie of the high water' – before returning to the shores of Loch Laggan. In the middle of the loch are two small islands, Eilean an Righ and Eilean nan Cone. Rory explained that according to the old stories, they were used by the ancient kings of Dunkeld when they came to Loch Lagganside.

Boarding a boat, we headed out to the first of the islands – Eilean an Righ – the 'isle of the king'. As we drew closer, Rory warmed to a royal theme. A thousand years or more ago, the kings of Dunkeld were the first to call themselves kings of Scots when the ancient Gaelic kingdoms of Dalriada and the Picts were united. 'The kings came to Loch Laggan and the area round about for sport – for hunting and feasting.'

Rory pointed to a fairy-tale baronial mansion on the opposite shore.

'That's where they filmed the television series *Monarch of the Glen*. It's called Ardverikie House. The name Ardverikie translates from Gaelic as the "promontory of Fergus". The Fergus in question was probably King Fergus of Dunkeld. Legend claims he's buried somewhere close to where the big house now stands.'

Reaching the tiny island, we clambered ashore.

Rory showed me the remains of some very ancient walls. Some archaeologists believe they are among the oldest medieval walls still standing in Scotland. They belonged to a castle that was used by the king and his retinue when they came to Loch Laggan. A couple of hundred metres to the west is Eilean nan Cone, the 'isle of the dogs', and is where the hounds were kept when the king came a-hunting.

A thought occurred to me. 'What did the king and his men hunt for?'

'Anything and everything, I suppose. Deer, wild boar, bear perhaps. And lynx too.'

'So the kings of old would have done their bit to eliminate the animals you want to bring back?'

'You're right. But they didn't know any better. Environmentalism wasn't exactly a big thing in the 9th century.'

Rory produced a picnic. Together we sat down in the ruins of the castle's great hall, each chewing on a cheese sandwich. It was odd to think that a millennium and more ago, kings and huntsmen of old had feasted here and drunk themselves silly, while wolves called from the shore.

Heading north-east from Loch Laggan, the A86 winds through the flat lands beside the meandering River Spey. About 4 kilometres west of Newtonmore is a prominent crag, which rises above fields and birch woods. This is Creag Dubh – the 'black crag'. Today, it's the haunt of rock climbers but it was once a hideout for the outlawed Highland chief Cluny Macpherson.

After the failed Jacobite rebellion of 1745, Cluny Macpherson was a man on the run with a price on his head. To evade capture, he used several hideouts (one on Ben Alder was known as 'Cluny's Cage'), including a cave high on the rock face of Creag Dubh. I've tried on several occasions to find

The view from Creag Dubh, a favourite destination for rock climbers. Cluny Macpherson hid in a cave on the lower cliffs.

it, but have never succeeded, beaten back by steep ground, a sea of bracken, and the fact that the cave is very well hidden.

While Cluny Macpherson was hiding, he probably reflected on the life he'd been forced to flee. Not far from his refuge on Creag Dubh is the ancestral seat of Macpherson chiefs. The original Cluny Castle was destroyed by government troops in 1746 while Cluny himself was on the run. A new Cluny Castle, built in 1805, now stands in its place.

The Macpherson name comes from the Gaelic meaning 'son of the parson', not because they were necessarily related to any parsons, but because an early ancestor had once had the collection of parsonage tithes in the parish of Laggan. Clan Macpherson is part of a larger confederation of Highland clans known as Clan Chattan, which was embroiled in a feud with neighbouring Clan Cameron – a bloody contest that lasted for 350

years. In 1396, a gladiatorial contest was held in a field called the North Inch at Perth to settle the differences between them. A fight to the death took place in the presence of King Robert III and his court. According to the story, Clan Chattan knocked lumps out of their rivals, quite literally. They killed all but one of the Camerons, with the loss of 19 of their own party of 30 clansmen.

The village of Newtonmore, with its own railway station, lies just north of the A9. Newtonmore is an attractive village. About halfway along the main street is an independent hostel offering cheap accommodation to walkers and climbers. I've only used its facilities in the depths of winter when it's very quiet, except for one occasion when several rooms were occupied by a Georgian chanting choir and their hosts from the Findhorn community. The owner of the hostel kindly invited me to a private choir recital in his home. I was

spellbound by the extraordinarily beautiful music which radiated an ancient, earthy energy.

The history of Newtonmore isn't a long one. Before the early 19th century it didn't exist at all. Most people in the immediate area lived in townships in Glen Banchor to the west – an area I know well because it gives access to the peaks and high plateau of the Monadhliath Mountains. Tramping hill paths on the north bank of the River Calder, I've often come across the ruins of these townships, and tried to imagine what life would have been like for the folk who lived there, before the village of Newtonmore was built, with its neat rows of solidly built, slate-roofed houses.

Sarah Murray described similar Highland townships or clachans in 1796.

Through the vast moor, there was nothing but the road to be seen, except a few scat-tered huts; some of them in such bogs, that it seemed impossible for any thing human to exist in such places. The huts are very small and low and consist of four stakes of birch, forked at the top, driven into the ground; on these they lay four other birch poles, and then form a gavel at each end by putting up more birch sticks, and crossing them sufficiently to support the clods with which they plaster this skeleton of a hut all over, except a small hole in the side for a window, a small door to creep in and out, and a hole in the roof, as they call a chimney. The covering of these huts is turf. I hardly saw any difference between the huts and the moor; for what heath there was on either, was equally in bloom. In these huts they make a fire upon the ground, and the smoke issues in columns at every hole;

The Highland Folk Museum shows the kind of houses that Sarah Murray saw on her journey to the Highlands in the 1790s.

notwithstanding which, the cursches (caps of Highland women) were as white as snow, and the faces of the children mostly fair and blooming. At night they rake out the fire, and put their beds of heath and blankets on the ground, where the fire had been, and thus keep themselves warm during the night. The chief of their furniture is an iron pot, a few bowls, and spoons of wood, and pails to put their milk in.

A person accustomed to the comforts and luxuries of life, cannot conceive how it is possible for human beings to exist, in a state so near that of the brute creation.

It's still possible today to get a glimpse into the domestic world that Sarah Murray so vividly described. Just outside Newtonmore is the Highland Folk Museum – a 'living' museum that provides a home to a number of traditional build-

ings that have been rescued and relocated. The centre of the collection is taken up with a recreated Highland township called Baile Gean built to look as it would have done in 1700. The timber-framed buildings are pretty much like the ones seen by Sarah. A peat fire smoulders on the ground in most of them, with an iron pot hanging above it. When I visited, the scene was brought to life with the help of re-enactors dressed in period costume. I sat down beside one of them in front of the peat fire. It was hard to see her properly through the smoke-filled, gloomy room.

'Was it always this dark?' I asked.

'It would have been pretty dark all year round. Most of them couldn't afford oil lamps or candles. Their only light came from the fire, or from bits of ancient bog pine or dried heather which they could ignite for a few seconds of illumination,' replied the museum attendant.

'And they would have kept their animals – their

livestock – in the house with them?' I asked.

'That's right. Animals were kept at one end of the house, separated by a wicker hurdle of woven willow. Haymaking as a way of providing animal feed hadn't been invented at that time, so grazing animals kept over winter were horribly thin when they were released in the spring. They'd have been kept alive on a diet of gorse and broom. There are accounts of cows being so weak they had to be carried outside. Life was pretty harsh for both animals and people.'

I thought about Sarah Murray's verdict on Highland life for the poor. It was indeed impossible to conceive how human beings could exist in such circumstances. But exist they did.

Hanging over the fire in front of us was an iron pot with something bubbling inside. It looked like porridge. This, I thought, must be the authentic 18th century, fully organic wonder food that had kept Highlanders alive. Almost without thinking, I lifted the wooden spoon to my lips and tasted the oats that had sustained the Highland population for generations. It was disgusting.

The museum attendant looked at me incredulously. 'You never just ate that, did you?'

'I had a wee taste. But I'm not impressed.' I felt I'd transgressed badly.

'It's not for human consumption. It's for show. It has been gently warming – along with a lot of suspect bacteria – for months!'

I suddenly felt rather unwell.

Before I left Newtonmore, I wanted to find a place that is unique in Scotland – the geographical centre of the country, as defined by the furthest point from the North Sea and the Atlantic Ocean. I'd been told that it was marked by a cross carved into in a stone in a drystone dyke. It was on the north side of the road down Glen Truim near a

At the centre of Scotland.

farm called the Mains of Glentruim. After spending a couple of hours walking up and down that section of the road, which incidentally was built by General Wade in the 18th century, I eventually found it. To be honest, after all my efforts it was a bit of an anticlimax – an inconspicuous monument to such a geographically significant location. The incised cross was barely visible through the lichen and moss. That was some years ago. Since my 'discovery' a much more substantial stone has been placed on the roadside opposite. It's more of a boulder, really, and is adorned with a commemorative plaque making the claim to be 'the centre of Scotland'. But how can this be true when there now appears to be two centres, one on either side of the road? Alternative centres of Scotland are, of course, available, including Aberfeldy, Pitlochry, and the Ordnance Survey's current favourite – a location close to the A9 at Dalnaspidal. Take your pick!

PART SIX

**FROM ACHNACARRY TO CULLODEN VIA INVERGARRY,
FORT AUGUSTUS, LOCH NESS AND THE GREAT GLEN**

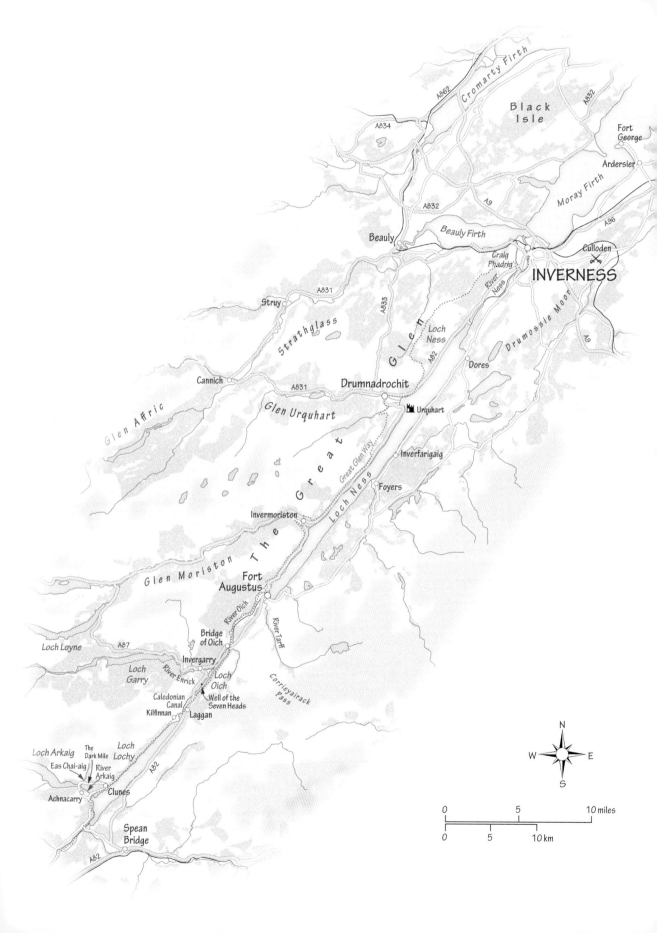

ACHNACARRY TO THE CORRIEYAIRACK PASS

The Dark Mile – Jacobite gold – Fort Augustus and the prince's double

Not far from the southern end of Loch Lochy, and close to the River Arkaig which flows through ancient woods bordering a narrow road known as 'the Dark Mile', lies Achnacarry House, where the oil cartel OPEC was founded over dinner in the 1920s. More famously, Achnacarry is also the ancestral home of the chiefs of Clan Cameron and a place that I've visited on a couple of occasions: once when Achnacarry was undergoing extensive restoration to save it from the ravages of dry rot, and later when I came to speak to the present clan chief, Donald Cameron of Lochiel. It was a cold, wet and blustery day in early June when we met.

'Welcome to Achnacarry – and to the glories of a Highland summer!' he said cheerily as we wandered beneath a canopy of dripping beech trees. These were partly the reason for my visit.

'You'll notice,' said Donald, 'that the trees are planted somewhat haphazardly.'

They were indeed. The mature beeches crowded together in separate clumps on either side of the grass avenue.

'There's an old family story to explain it,' continued Donald. 'In 1745, when my ancestor Ewen Cameron, known as the "Gentle Lochiel", was planting out the trees to make an avenue, he received the astonishing news that Bonnie Prince Charlie had landed on the west coast of Scotland. Appealing to the traditional loyalty of the clans, the prince asked them to join him in an uprising against the government in order to restore the

Previous spread. Urquhart Castle and Loch Ness.

Stuart dynasty to the British throne. In his haste to meet the prince, Lochiel temporarily heeled the beech saplings into the ground, intending, of course, to plant them out properly on his return. But he never came back. The Jacobite rebellion happened instead and he was swept away by the tide of history. In his absence, the trees rooted and grew.'

Seeking shelter from rain and the first of the season's midges, Donald led me inside the newly restored Achnacarry House. On a wooden chest in the hallway I spotted two antique pistols and a basket-hilted broadsword laid out on a piece of tartan cloth.

'We are just doing an inventory of all the weapons we have,' said Donald. 'The sword belonged to Lochiel and he carried it at the Battle of Culloden when his ankles were shattered by cannon fire. Miraculously, he survived and even-tually fled to France with Bonnie Prince Charlie.'

I had an irresistible urge to handle this relic of Jacobite history. Donald read my mind.

'Go ahead. It's very well balanced.'

A sensation like electricity flowed through me as my hand made contact with the sword. To be in touch with history and the Gentle Lochiel, in such a direct and tactile way, was amazing. The sword in my hand felt just as it must have done to Lochiel when he charged towards the lines of redcoats at Culloden. I felt connected to that fateful moment. And privileged beyond words.

'Lochiel was a key figure in the uprising,' said Donald. 'He was the man responsible for capturing Edinburgh for the prince, and when the Jacobite army was later forced to retreat, he also saved Glas-gow from being burnt to the ground (Glaswegians hadn't been great supporters of the Jacobite cause). The grateful people rang the bells in the Tolbooth

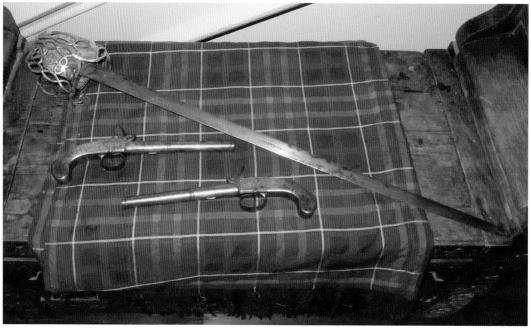

Historic weapons at Achnacarry House. The sword was used at Culloden by Ewen Cameron of Lochiel.

in Lochiel's honour. Two hundred years later they rang the same bells for me when I was a guest of the Lord Provost.'

'I can see you are proud of your ancestor,' I remarked.

'Well, wouldn't you be? But it can sometimes be a bit awkward. My wife's ancestor was also at Culloden, but on the other side. He was cleaved in two by a Cameron. We remind her of that from time to time – with a gesture.'

To demonstrate, Donald brought an imaginary sword down on my head.

During the Second World War, Achnacarry was at the centre of a different kind of military enterprise. The ancestral home of Clan Cameron chiefs was requisitioned and served as a major commando training ground. From 1942 to 1945, 25,000 men endured five weeks of the toughest

training on earth to prepare them to fight Hitler's armies. At Achnacarry, they learned to kill; they took part in simulated amphibious landings with the added excitement of live rounds and grenades being fired at them. It was a dangerous education in the art of war and several men lost their lives preparing for the real thing. Donald told me that when one soldier landed on the beaches of occupied France, he was heard to say, 'This is nearly as bad as Achnacarry!'

When I first visited Achnacarry, the place had been a building site. Scaffolding sprouted from the ground to roof level, and workmen were busy in every corner rescuing the old house from death by dry rot. In one of the rooms was a mural that had recently been uncovered behind a stud wall. It dated from the time when Achnacarry was being used by the commando forces and depicted a scene

Achnacarry House. The estate was a commando training ground during the Second World War.

of mayhem. War planes flew overhead dropping bombs; troops scrambled from a landing craft; battleships fired on the coast. These bloody illustrations of war seemed an odd choice of decoration for men about to face the real thing. It turned out that the artist was one of the men training the commandos. His name was Lance Corporal Brian Mullen, and he'd spent his free time replicating in paint the amphibious assaults he'd practised with his men during the day. Tragically, Brian was killed in a scene very like the ones he'd painted on the walls of Achnacarry. On D-Day – 6 June 1944 – he died on a Normandy beach while attacking German positions.

Leaving Achnacarry, I walked along the single-track road that bears the mysterious name of the 'Dark Mile' or Mìle Dorcha in Gaelic. Twisted trees shut out the light. Here moss and lichen cover everything in a dense green carpet that softens all contours and deadens all sound. I walked over a picturesque bridge of the sort admired by Sarah Murray, where the Eas Chia-aig waterfall tumbles delightfully down a cliff before flowing into the River Arkaig. A few kilometres further along the road, I met up with a group of metal detectorists at the ancient burial ground of Murlaggan. They were hunting for Jacobite gold – part of a treasure trove that was buried in 1746 when two French ships landed gold coins to fund the Jacobite rebellion. In today's money, the treasure trove would be worth more than £10 million. The money never reached its destination. When Bonnie Prince Charlie fled, he ordered the gold to be buried. Initially, it was hidden somewhere near Loch Arkaig and its location only divulged to the Jacobite Ewen Macpherson of Cluny. But could Cluny be trusted?

Margaret and Tony Sargent. Margaret tried to photograph Lizzie, the monster said to live in the depths of Loch Lochy.

In France, Bonnie Prince Charlie later heard that Cluny Macpherson was spending the hidden booty. Outraged, the prince sent his loyal supporter Dr Archibald Cameron – the brother of the Gentle Lochiel – to recover the treasure. But Dr Cameron was captured and executed for his part in the rising. According to records in the Clan Cameron archives, the doctor managed to hide the prince's gold at the Callich Burn before he was captured.

The metal detectorists were now searching the rough ground close to the burn. Robert Cairns of the Lochaber Archaeological Society seemed to have found something. He began carefully probing the earth. Disappointingly, his find turned out to be a rusty old spade.

'It's the hobby of the eternal optimist,' said Robert. 'But the treasure is out there somewhere. I'm certain of that. It's just a matter of time and someone will find it. Hopefully, me!'

Returning to the Mìle Dorcha, I joined the Great Glen Way long-distance path at a place called Clunes and continued north-east along the banks of Loch Lochy. As a name for a loch, Loch Lochy seems about as original as calling a boat Boaty Macboatface. Having said that, the name is apparently a corruption of the Gaelic for the 'loch of the dark goddess', which sounds suitably mysterious. Interestingly, the 'dark goddess' of Loch Lochy might turn out to be an early reference to 'Lizzie' – the monster who is said to live in its deep waters.

Like the world-famous Nessie in Loch Ness, the much less famous Lizzie is also an elusive and mysterious creature. Over the last century there have been only nine recorded sightings, and one photograph.

In 1975, Margaret Sargent had a close encounter with Lizzie. She, her husband and their four-year-old son were driving along the lochside when they saw a great disturbance on the water. A large aquatic animal with three humps was moving at great speed across the loch. Margaret jumped out of the car and ran to take a photo. Just as she raised the camera, the 'monster' disappeared beneath the surface. Her photograph failed to capture an image of the beast, but did capture the wake left behind – a line of mysterious waves in the loch. It seems that Lizzie didn't relish publicity and had taken the hump, quite literally, leaving the Sargent family with no real proof to back up their monstrous tale.

For almost the entire length of Loch Lochy, the Great Glen Way passes through dense plantations of spruce, which mostly obscure the view of the high peaks to the north that rise above it. A few years ago, I joined a party of friends who were staying with a young teacher based at Clunes. Together we enjoyed a fabulous winter's day

Invergarry Station, built to serve a line intended to connect Fort William with Inverness.

climbing Meall na Teanga and Sron a' Choire Ghairbh. Meall na Teanga means the 'hill of the tongue', a name that may have subconsciously inspired us to conversation, which I remember was extremely wide-ranging, taking in subjects as diverse and abstruse as the origins of the Jacobite uprisings, James Clerk Maxwell's Field Theory, Chomsky's linguistics, and why Scotland had lost again at rugby. Looking at the steepness of the upper slopes of Meall na Teanga from below, I wondered how we'd had the breath for such inflated talk. I do remember we were all pretty worn out when our teacher friend picked us up

in the dark at Kilfinnan, close to the Laggan Locks on the Caledonian Canal, which leads to Loch Oich, the next loch in the chain that fills the Great Glen.

Not far north from Laggan, where the A82 road crosses the canal by means of a swing bridge, is the old Invergarry station. It once served passengers of the branch line that ran from Fort William to Fort Augustus until it was closed in 1947. The station is the only one to survive and today is home to a group of enthusiasts dedicated to preserving the memory of the old railway line. One of the volunteers, Chris Ellis, told me how the restoration

project began in 2012 to preserve the old platform and create a museum to the age of steam.

The station opened for the first time in 1903. It was built to serve a railway that had been planned to continue through the Great Glen, connecting the Highland capitals of Fort William and Inverness. Unfortunately, the line never got any further than Fort Augustus, where passengers travelling further north were transferred to a steamer on Loch Ness. Because the line was a 'dead end' it was little used and failed financially. When it closed, the rails were lifted, but now they are being gradually replaced. I was impressed to see the throbbing, reeking hulk of a 1947 diesel shunter waiting at the platform. It was bought on an impulse by railway enthusiast Mark Bowman, who invited me to ride on the footplate. Pulling the chord that sounded the horn, we were off to a rattling start. It proved to be an exciting ride for about 400 metres until we ran out of track. Mark and Chris both hope to raise enough money to eventually extend the line further.

Loch Oich marks the highest elevation of the Caledonian Canal. It's a thin ribbon of freshwater and looks more like a broad, flooded river than a loch. For most of its length the shores are thickly wooded and only glimpses of its shimmering surface can be seen by traffic on the A82. About a kilometre north of the Laggan swing bridge is a monument at Tobar nan Ceann, the 'well of the seven heads'. Often missed by motorists grinding along the main road, it commemorates a grizzly event that took place when this Highland district was no stranger to bloodshed and murder.

In 1663 the 13th chief of the Keppoch Macdonalds

Tobar nan Ceann, the 'well of the seven heads', commemorates a grisly story of revenge.

and his brother Ranald held a feast to celebrate their return from France. Tempers flared, however, and the men were slain in a drunken brawl with their cousins. The killers were well known: Alexander Macdonald and his six sons from Inverlair, near Roy Bridge. But there seemed no one to bring them to justice. In those days, the rule of law had no writ in the Highlands. Bloody vengeance and retribution often took its place.

Pursuing his own form of rough justice for the victims, Iain Lom, known as the Keppoch Bard, petitioned several Macdonald chiefs for their support in bringing the murderers to book. He was refused help until he travelled to Skye where Sir James Macdonald of Sleat was swayed by the Keppoch Bard's oratory and desire to avenge his kinsmen. On their behalf, Sir James wrote to the privy council in Edinburgh and secured letters of fire and sword against the killers. Iain Lom then guided 50 men to Roy Bridge, where Alexander Macdonald and his six sons were killed and decapitated. Iain Lom carried the heads away, dangling on willow rods, to Invergarry, where he presented them to the clan chief Lord MacDonnell. Before he reached his destination, he washed his gory trophies in the waters of a well beside Loch Oich.

Invergarry Castle stands guard where the River Garry enters Loch Oich. The castle is now a ruined shell, but it once played a significant part in both the history of the MacDonnell family and the Jacobites. In the 16th century, MacDonnell lands were often raided by their neighbours, Clan Mackenzie. To defend themselves, the MacDonnells built a castle in 1602 on the Rock of the Raven – Creag an Fhithich. The name became the clan war cry. In 1654, Cromwell's troops burned the castle to the ground. It was then repaired in time for the first Jacobite rising, when the castle was occupied by the supporters of James II and VII. They were eventually forced to surrender to the new king, William of Orange, in 1692. In 1715, Jacobites again held the castle on the Rock of the Raven. The Bonnie Prince himself was twice a guest during the rising of 1745 and after his defeat at Culloden, Invergarry Castle was blown to pieces by government troops under the Duke of Cumberland.

At the northern end of Loch Oich, the Great Glen Way crosses the River Oich by means of a wonderfully elegant suspension bridge. The 46-metre bridge was erected in 1854 after flood waters destroyed the old stone bridge that had formerly carried the road. The new Oich Bridge was designed by the engineer James Dredge and was used by all traffic travelling on the main route between Fort William and Inverness until the 1930s. It then fell into disrepair; Historic Scotland restored it in the 1990s. Since then, it has served as a crossing for walkers.

The route north along the Great Glen Way follows the canal and the river all the way to Fort Augustus, where six lock gates carry canal traffic down to Loch Ness. The village was originally named after the Celtic saint St Cummein who built a church here. A settlement developed around this little religious centre and was known as Cille Chumein. The present name derives from the fort that was established after the Jacobite rising of 1715. It stood on a promontory between the River Oich and the River Tarff, where both flow into Loch Ness. The fort was named after Prince Augustus, the youngest son of King George II. In 1746, after Culloden, Augustus, then the Duke of Cumberland, went on to 'pacify' the rebellious Highlands with a series of punitive measures that left thousands dead – actions that earned him the sobriquet 'Butcher Cumberland' (of whom, more later).

When Sarah Murray arrived in town half a century later, she was not impressed. 'Fort Augustus is in a state of great neglect, and appears to be going very fast to decay. There were only a few old invalids in it when I was there: and the sight of these old firelocks, on the parade, rehearsing their exercises before the Governor's house in a morning, was quite a burlesque scene of soldiering. The creeping sentinels hailed us with "who goes there?" I was admitted over the thundering drawbridge, and through the dark gateway, to the parade ground and the Governor's door who received me with every mark of kindness and hospitality.'

Today, I'm happy to say that Fort Augustus, the village, is a busy and rather pretty place, having refocused itself on the canal and its system of locks; of the fort, which was demolished in the 1860s, only a fragment is left to be seen and you have to know where to look to recognise it at all.

The site that the fort stood on is now occupied by an imposing and sprawling building, which for over a century was a Benedictine abbey and boarding school. The Victorian edifice was designed by Peter Paul Pugin, whose brother Augustus Pugin had co-created the Palace of Westminster. Peter Paul Pugin didn't completely erase all traces of the original Fort Augustus. Incorporated in the walls of the Victorian abbey is part of the old fort – one of the four, angled bastions which would have been defended by six-pounder guns. It's amazing to think that the surviving bastion witnessed a siege by Jacobite clans in 1746. They blew up the gunpowder store and forced the garrison of 300 men to surrender.

My old *Black's Picturesque Guide to Scotland* claims that the fort held 'a host of Highland lairds' after the Jacobite defeat at Culloden. *Black's* goes

on to say that 'here also the bleeding head of Robert Mackenzie was brought and delivered to the Duke of Cumberland'.

Roderick Mackenzie was a zealous Jacobite from Edinburgh who'd joined the Bonnie Prince's army at the earliest opportunity. He was well liked by the prince. It was also noted that there was a close similarity between the two men. When the prince was on the run with a bounty of £30,000 on his head and hiding in a cave in Glen Moriston, Roderick Mackenzie acted as a lookalike decoy. Playing prince's double, he led a platoon of pursuing government troops away from their quarry, giving the prince time to escape. Mackenzie was eventually cornered in Glen Moriston. He refused to surrender and bravely drew his sword to fight to the death. But he was hit by a volley of fire from the soldiers. It's said that his dying words were, 'You have murdered your prince!'

As evidence of the kill, the soldiers cut off Mackenzie's head and presented it to the Duke of Cumberland, who then took it to London as 'proof' that his mission to track down the prince had been accomplished. By the time he arrived for the formal identification, the head had decayed beyond all recognition. Shortly afterwards, new reports from the Highlands suggested that Bonnie Prince Charlie was still alive and on the run. But Mackenzie hadn't died in vain. His actions as a royal decoy had enabled the prince to escape.

The strategic importance of Fort Augustus lay in its position at a crossroads where major Highland routes converge. In addition to the Caledonian Canal, which runs through the village, the old military road built by General Wade's soldiers leads south to Fort William. The military road to the north shadows the eastern shore of Loch Ness to Inverness. Both of these single-track roads

The former Benedictine abbey at Fort Augustus.

continue to be in use today. But another section of Wade's road, which leaves Fort Augustus from the south-east, has not been used by public vehicles since the 1830s. This is the Corrieyairack Pass, a 45-kilometre, high-level route that once connected the fort at Fort Augustus to the Dunkeld to Inverness military road.

For centuries, the Corrieyairack Pass had been used by travellers in the Highlands, including drovers herding cattle to southern markets, but in 1731 work began to create a properly engineered road. This would allow soldiers to move swiftly through the Highlands to suppress lawlessness and insurrection whenever and wherever they occurred.

It was an ambitious scheme. The Corrieyairack

Pass climbs to 770 metres above sea level. Work started in April 1731 and was completed by October the same year – an impressive rate of progress over trackless moor. The cost to the Exchequer was reported to be the princely sum of £3,281 4s 9d. A bargain, I'd have thought. Ironically, when the road was finished it was first used by Bonnie Prince Charlie and his Jacobite army on the march south to Edinburgh at the start of the '45.

In 1796, Sarah Murray followed in the footsteps of the Bonnie Prince. Braving the elements, she took her horse-drawn chaise over the pass. She'd spent the previous day sheltering from a storm that had swept the Highlands with wind and torrential rain. At the inn where she had sought refuge, she talked to a young man who had crossed

the pass on horseback during the height of the bad weather. He strongly advised Sarah against attempting the pass, and said it would be impossible in a carriage.

The following day, the indefatigable and ever-resourceful Sarah Murray got her man to hitch two plough horses to help her pull the carriage up the pass. To relieve their burden, and to suffer less from the continuous jolting of her carriage, Sarah walked for most of the way until close to the summit cairn. 'Having arrived at the top, I got out of the chaise, that I might be a judge of the climate there. It was certainly cold enough for my great coat; but I became neither torpid nor frozen. I began to examine the surprising scene all around me. I had been before on many high mountains, whence I had seen lakes, plains, and far distant objects; but the view from Corryarraick is totally different. No lakes, no glens, no plains; all is a boundless space of a rough ocean of mountains; whose tops seem to wave, one beyond the other, to the distant sea in the west; and on every other side, as far as the eye can reach. The whole scene was cold and dismal;—it was uncommon;—it was astonishing, but not at all terrific. My mind was raised to a state of awe and seriousness, that led to the great Creator of all; and I almost forgot I belonged to this world.'

The Corrieyairack Pass proved to be an impractical route. It was closed for most of the winter due to the depth of lying snow. Because of the number of travellers who perished from cold and fatigue, or who got lost in blizzards, a safer alternative had to be found. In 1830 a new road opened between Laggan and Spean Bridge. It avoided most

Opposite. The road that snakes through the Corrieyairack Pass was built by General Wade over six months in 1771.

of the problems of the higher pass. Corrieyairack then reverted to a drove road before eventually falling into disuse. In recent years, it has found a new lease of life as a route for intrepid mountain bikers and walkers, although the sense of wilderness experienced by Sarah Murray has been marred somewhat by a line of huge electricity pylons that follow its course almost the entire way from Fort Augustus.

FORT AUGUSTUS TO DORES

The Loch Ness Monster – The Crusader – Urquhart Castle

The views of Loch Ness from Fort Augustus stretch north-east for more than 36 kilometres. Loch Ness is the biggest Scottish loch by volume and is said to hold more fresh water than all the lakes and reservoirs in the whole of England and Wales. It is also tremendously deep, reaching 230 metres, giving it the status of Scotland's second deepest loch after Loch Morar. It's perhaps not surprising that these cold, dark depths hold many mysteries – the most famous, of course, being the Loch Ness Monster. Loch Ness draws thousands of visitors every year, all hoping to catch a glimpse of the primordial and preternatural beast.

Curiously, my *Black's Guide* makes no mention of the world's most celebrated aquatic enigma. Neither does Sarah Murray, who is usually the first to describe sublime encounters, especially those involving water. In fact, none of the early travel writers discuss Nessie at all. So where do the stories come from? I joined Nessie researcher Adrian Shine in a small boat on the loch.

Adrian, who could pass for Gandalf with his white flowing beard, has studied Nessie since the

Loch Ness, the biggest volume of fresh water in Britain, seen from Fort Augustus.

1970s. In the bright sunlight of a summer morning, we gazed over the glistening waters of the loch. 'Until the 1930s there was no Nessie as we understand it,' said Adrian, 'although there had been a long tradition of a big fish in the loch. At one time, this was thought to be part of the water horse "kelpie" tradition of Highland folklore.'

Adrian told me the first mention of a creature that could be the ancestor of the modern Nessie appeared in a book written by the Celtic monk Adomnan who recorded the life of St Columba. Adomnan described how Columba, who was on a mission to convert King Brude of the Picts to Christianity, encountered 'the beast' in the River Ness. When Columba and his companions arrived,

a funeral was taking place on the opposite bank of a man who'd been killed by a strange water beast. When one of Columba's companions swam across the river to fetch a boat for the rest of the party, the beast rose out of the water and attacked him. According to the legend, Columba made the sign of the cross over the monster and commanded it to depart, which, very sensibly, it did.

'Apart from this one story, which goes back over 1,400 years or so, there is no mention of beasts or monsters, at least none were reported by visitors to the area,' Adrian continued. 'Perhaps such superstitions were suppressed and deemed uncouth. They were not the sort of thing that was considered palatable for early tourists guided by principles of the picturesque. Primitive beliefs showed Highlanders in a bad light.'

Then, out of the blue, in 1933 the hotel manager at Drumnadrochit, Mrs Mackay, claimed to have seen 'the beast' after a local historian had written an article about the kelpie tradition.

'I met Mrs MacKay many years ago,' Adrian explained. 'She told me that she'd been driving back from Inverness with her husband when she saw something in the loch and shouted, "Stop! The beast!" The fact that she used the words "the beast" demonstrates that she must already have been aware of a tradition of some sort of creature in the loch.'

Adrian described what happened when the press got hold of the story. Despite Mrs MacKay trying to prevent news of her sighting from spreading, a series of 'silly season' articles appeared and the modern myth of Nessie was born – along with fake photographs.

Such determined fabrication and myth-making reminded me of an incident in our own family. In the 1950s my wife's great uncle was involved in an attempt to hoodwink the public with an account of a Nessie sighting. He and his son were paid by a London film crew to be interviewed on camera about their encounter with the monster during a fishing trip to the shores of Loch Ness. It was fantasy, of course, entirely made up, but Great Uncle Luke gained a fee and an all-expenses-paid trip to the Highlands for his contribution.

After the press hype and obvious hoaxes came a more serious approach to the subject of Nessie. In the 1960s, a radical time when old orthodoxies were challenged, people began to think there could be truth in local traditions like Nessie. A period of serious scientific research then began, and Adrian Shine was part of this.

'My problem is that I have had thousands of reported sightings from members of the public, over the course of several decades,' said Adrian. 'These are ordinary people, trustworthy people, sober people! They all insist that they have seen a creature – or creatures – in the loch but science has never found them.'

After 40 years of scientific study, Adrian has concluded there is no monster. 'People "see things" and want to attribute them as proof that Nessie exists. It's all wishful thinking – a desire to believe that there is a place in the modern world for "the wild things". Loch Ness is a lost world, in the same way that Jules Verne's great cavern at the centre of the earth was a lost world. And the idea of such a thing as Nessie can still be living with us – something so mysterious, so elusive and potentially so terrible – appeals to something deep in human nature.'

Despite all that, the Nessie tradition has its own momentum. People come in their droves, if not to catch a glimpse of the monster, then to catch a mindset that makes monsters possible. And the value of Nessie to the local economy can't be underestimated. It's worth tens of millions of pounds annually.

In Victorian times, tourists taking steamer trips on Loch Ness were not Nessie hunters. They came for a different sort of monster altogether – the monster-sized Falls of Foyers, sometimes known as the 'The Falls of Smoke' from the misty vapour produced by the cataract, which free-fall 60 metres or so into a deep linn at the bottom of a dark gorge, hemmed in by gigantic perpendicular rocks. Robert Burns visited in 1787 during one of his Highland tours and was moved to verse. Written with a pencil while standing by the falls, he composed:

The Falls of Foyers were celebrated in verse by Robert Burns when he visited in 1787.

Among the heathy hills and ragged woods
The roaring Fyers pours his mossy floods;
Till full he dashes on the rocky mounds,
Where, thro' a shapeless breach, his stream
    resounds.
As high in air the bursting torrents flow,
As deep recoiling surges foam below,
Prone down the rock the whitening sheet
   descends,
And viewless Echo's ear, astonished, rends.
Dim-seen through rising mists, and
   ceaseless show'rs,

The hoary cavern, wide sounding low'rs:
Still thro' the gap the struggling river toils,
And still, below, the horrid cauldron boils.

Perhaps not one of his more accomplished poems, it was nevertheless quoted by my *Black's Guide*, to encourage tourists to visit the 'the roaring Foyers'.

I don't know if Sarah Murray had read Burns before her visit, but she was similarly inspired by the noise and sublime chaos of the spectacle. On a day of heavy rain, she left her chaise and descended the slippery and dangerous banks of the falls with 'a very clever intelligent Highland-man' acting as her guide. After a lot of effort, she managed to get to a place where she had the best possible view – a projecting rock high above the gorge. By now she was covered in mud and wet through, but in a state of high excitement: 'I was in ecstasy with all around me; but to get to this station was a bold adventure for a man (or a woman). The noise was beyond belief. The spray deprived me of sight and breath; and every now and then, by gulping and shutting my eyes for relief I was by intervals enabled to look and breathe: to admire, and I might say, almost adore.'

Sarah was obviously very pleased with her plucky self for getting so close to the monster waterfall. Climbing back up the dangerous ground she had earlier descended, she met a party of 'four males not very active in body, who came tumbling and slipping down the banks, with fright and dismay, that made me smile. When they saw me they stared, as much as to say how come you there!'

When she finally and breathlessly reached the shelter of her chaise, Sarah pulled down the window blinds, stripped off her wet clothes and changed, while her man Allan discreetly held the horses.

When I visited the Falls of Foyers for myself, I was a little disappointed. I'd been to many places visited by Sarah Murray and had come to trust her descriptions. She might use rather excitable language, but generally her word pictures are more accurate than some of the Victorian landscape prints reproduced in *Black's Picturesque Guide to Scotland*. There was something not quite right about her account on this occasion. Her description is just a bit over the top – even for her. It turns out there is a good reason for this. In 1895, brilliant Victorian engineers decided to exploit the power

of the water that Sarah had found so thrilling. They built a hydroelectric scheme for an aluminium factory on the shores of Loch Ness. To turn the turbines of the factory, the Falls of Foyers were robbed of their water – and also of their power to thrill sensitive souls like Sarah Murray.

On the north side of Loch Ness, the Great Glen Way continues towards Inverness along forestry tracks above the busy A82. At Invermoriston the A887 road to Lochalsh and Skye passes through Glen Moriston. In 1746 Bonnie Prince Charlie hid somewhere in the glen after his defeat at Culloden. This is also where his 'double' Roderick Mackenzie gave his life while acting as a decoy. Mackenzie's headless corpse was buried close to where he fell. His grave is marked today by a cairn and a simple cross bearing the inscription: 'At this spot in 1746 died Roderick Mackenzie, an officer in the army of Prince Charles, of the same size and similar appearance to his Royal Prince. When surrounded and overpowered by the troops of the Duke of Cumberland, gallantly died in attempting to save his fugitive leader from further pursuit.'

Just a couple of kilometres south of Urquhart Castle is a stone cairn commemorating the tragic story of John Cobb, who attempted to set the world water speed record on 29 September 1952.

Cobb, who was known as the 'Gentle Giant' because of his height, was a fur trader from Surrey. His wealth allowed him to indulge his passion for speed and fast cars. By the time he arrived on the shores of Loch Ness he had already broken the land speed record three times. A rival had recently set a new record for a power boat. Cobb rose to the challenge hoping to regain the title of the world's fastest man on water.

Cobb spent £15,000 designing and building a

jet-propelled boat called *The Crusader*, which he brought to Loch Ness. The distance of a mile was measured from Urquhart Castle to a spot in the loch in line with the present memorial cairn. On the first run, Cobb was clocked at 206.89 mph, and became the first man in the world to exceed 200 mph on water. On the second attempt, tragedy struck when *The Crusader* hit the wake of another boat, causing Cobb to lose control. *The Crusader* nosedived and suddenly broke apart, throwing Cobb from the cockpit. He was killed instantly. The whole ghastly incident was filmed and watched by crowds on the shore.

Cobb hadn't been in the area for long but the Gentle Giant's brief presence had made a big impression on local people, who got together to raise funds for the memorial cairn. The inscription on the plaque reads:

John Cobb
having travelled at
206 miles per hour
in an attempt to gain the
World's Water
Speed Record
lost his life
in this bay
Sept 29th 1952
This memorial is erected as a tribute
to the memory of a gallant gentleman
by the people of Glen Urquhart

Urquhart Castle, one of the most photographed ruins in Scotland, sits on a rocky promontory jutting into Loch Ness. For centuries, it commanded a strategic position in the Great Glen, and throughout much of its long history was a royal stronghold. Archaeologists have speculated that the site was occupied during the Dark Ages by Pictish kings. In his *Life of St Columba*, Adomnan says the saint stopped off at Urquhart and converted the Pictish chieftain and his family to Christianity.

Despite the new religion, it seems that Christ's message of peace wasn't fully adopted and embraced in the Highlands. Urquhart Castle was the focus for violence and bloodshed for centuries. During the Wars of Independence, it was held by Edward I – the 'Hammer of the Scots' – and his English forces. Later it was taken by Robert the Bruce, becoming a royal castle, and held by a number of constables on behalf of the king. With the rise of influence of the powerful MacDonald Lords of the Isles who ruled the west coast and the Hebrides, Urquhart Castle came under attack again. In 1395, it fell to the MacDonalds, who held it for 15 years. Possession passed back and forth for 200 years, until King James III gave the castle to the Earl of Huntly, who in turn passed it on to Clan Grant. Over four decades, the castle was lost and won in the struggles between Clan Grant and Clan Donald, until the power of the Lords of the Isles waned. During the first Jacobite uprising of 1689, Clan Grant sided with William of Orange and held out in Castle Urquhart against a force of Jacobites. When the occupying Grants left, they blew up the castle to make it strategically worthless. The castle has been a spectacular ruin ever since. *Black's Guide* helpfully observes, 'The antiquary will notice an unusual arrangement in the windows for pouring molten lead on the heads of assailants.' Painful but effective.

Just around the corner from Urquhart Castle is the little village of Drumnadrochit, a name which comes from the Gaelic meaning 'the ridge of the bridge'. The bridge in question spans the

Steve Feltham has been seeking the Loch Ness Monster since 1991.

River Enrick and is the reason the village developed. Today, Drumnadrochit is something of a tourist trap, dominated by the Loch Ness Centre and Exhibition, which is largely devoted to all things Nessie. The village also commands the entrance to Glen Urquhart and a route to magnificent Glen Affric. When Sarah Murray visited, she seems to have been in something of a rush because she has little to say about its environs. However, she does report: 'I have been told that the inhabitants of Glen Urquhart are so wedded to it, that no one native has quitted it, nor one foreigner taken up an abode therein for ninety years.'

At the northern end of Loch Ness is a village called Dores. The view from the bay is to die for – it stretches the entire length of the loch to distant Fort Augustus.

Dores is now home to a man who has spent three decades on the lochside looking for Nessie. Steve Feltham gave up his job in England, sold his house and converted an old library van into his mobile home. In 1991, Steve arrived on the banks of the loch with a mission to discover the Loch Ness Monster. Shortly afterwards, he aroused the interest of the BBC who made a documentary about his endeavours called *Desperately Seeking Nessie*. After a brief moment of fame, Steve began making Nessie figurines out of modelling clay and selling them to passing tourists to raise funds. At the turn of the millennium his van failed its MOT. Since then, his mobile home has been a stationary one, based in the car park of the Dores Inn, where he continues to scan the loch for Nessie and to sell his figurines.

Steve said, 'People ask me if I've ever seen the monster in all the years I've been looking at the loch. I have to tell them that I haven't. I've seen lots of other things, though, including strange ripples on the water. In the absence of the monster, my life is very full. I get lots of visitors – even film crews – who all want to ask me about Nessie. It's understandable I suppose – but I do get frustrated. The important thing in life is, if you have a dream – no matter how hairbrained others might think it – then it's worth trying to make it come true.'

INVERNESS TO CULLODEN

King Brude at Craig Phadrig – Fort George – Culloden Moor

Inverness has a population of approximately 47,000 souls, and is by far the biggest town in the Highlands. As the capital of the region, it has boasted city status since the millennium and continues to be a focal point of economic and population growth. The origins of today's city go back to the Dark Ages when an important centre was established by the Picts on the western side of the River Ness. On a now wooded hill called Craig Phadrig, Pictish kings built a citadel. Archaeologists have since identified the remains of a large vitrified fort. According to tradition, Craig Phadrig is where King Brude and St Columba met, when the latter was on a mission to convert the Picts of the north to Christianity. King Brude was apparently unwilling to entertain the holy men from Iona and closed the gates of the citadel against them. But Columba is said to have invoked the power of Heaven, forcing the gates to open. Suitably impressed by this miraculous display, Brude and the Picts quickly converted to the new religion. All that remains of the fort in the 21st century are grass-covered mounds and ramparts enclosing a flat area at the top of the hill. A path leads to the summit, making a pleasant 2-kilometre walk with views of the Beauly Firth.

The imposing edifice of Inverness Castle, situated on a hill overlooking the River Ness, may look medieval on first inspection, but was in fact built in the 1830s to accommodate court rooms, a county hall and a jail. These buildings occupy the site of several much older castles, going back to the 11th century and possibly earlier. According to legend, one of these belonged to Macbeth. When he was overthrown, King Malcolm Canmore built a new castle. It was used for centuries, being modified and adapted by successive occupiers, including Oliver Cromwell who built a fortified citadel to consolidate his power in the north of Scotland. After the Jacobite rebellion of 1715, the citadel became a government fort. This was the original Fort George. It was blown up by the Jacobites shortly before their crushing defeat at Culloden in 1746.

When Sarah Murray rumbled into town in her chaise, she liked what she saw: 'I was very pleased with the appearance of Inverness, and

The present Inverness Castle, built in the 1830s, stands on the site of several older castles.

found it a neat town, charmingly situated. There was not a trace of the ancient castle; some person lately removed the small remains of its ruins to build offices, or some such for his own convenience . . . !'

Nevertheless, Sarah was impressed by the people of Inverness, their manners, and especially their accent. 'There is a decency in the appearance, manners and deportment of the people of Inverness, and the accent of their language is so soft, it charms the ear, being very pure English, accompanied with a sort of foreign tone, which is very pleasing; in short, it is like broken English, proceeding from the soft voice of a beautiful female foreigner, taught English purely and grammatically.'

I was a student when I visited Inverness for the first time, travelling in the company of two American chums. We had decided to skive off from our respective classes at the University of Aberdeen and were embarking on a tour of the Hebrides. We'd borrowed three barely serviceable bicycles from some friends and had arrived in town too late to find accommodation. I had a tent with me but reasoned that it was impractical to camp in the city centre. It goes without saying that hotels were beyond the slender means of a student budget. So what to do?

As we were debating this amongst ourselves, a strange figure dressed in a patched overcoat sidled over. His hair was long and grey and a thick beard sprouted from his face. We stopped talking and stared at him as if he were a ghost. He looked like a 'gentleman of the road' from a bygone age.

He introduced himself: 'I'm Cat Weasel. I couldn't help overhearing – if it's accommodation you're after, I can help you boys!'

Cat Weasel didn't quite fit Sarah Murray's description of a native of the city. He smiled, his eyes sparkling in his dirty face. I threw my friends a sceptical look, but they were more trusting.

'You know somewhere we could stay?' Dave was hopeful.

'I do,' said Cat Weasel. 'Just follow me!'

He hurried on ahead, while we pushed our bikes in his wake. I was wondering what dreadful dosshouse he might be leading us to when he stopped at the entrance to a multi-storey car park. He opened the door to a stairwell. We followed him inside, where a pungent aroma of urine hung in the air.

'This is where I often doss,' said Cat Weasel,

indicating a corner where a sheet of cardboard was propped up against the wall. 'That's what I use as a mattress.'

'Thanks,' I said, beginning my retreat. 'It's . . .'

Gordon interrupted. 'Seems kinda pokey in here. Maybe we'll check out an upper level. See if it's more spacious.'

And so I spent my first ever night in Inverness, sleeping on the second floor of a multi-storey car park, while Cat Weasel watched over us, gently humming to himself with knees pulled up, sitting on his cardboard mattress.

About 18 kilometres east of Inverness, not far from the city airport, is the peninsula of Ardersier, which juts into the Cromarty Firth at its narrowest point. At the seaward tip of the peninsula is Fort George, a magnificent relic from the 18th century and probably the biggest fortification of its kind in the UK to have survived almost intact into the present. It was built in the immediate aftermath of the Jacobite rebellion of 1745 to provide a final solution to the problem of the Highlands. It was hoped that its formidable fortifications, combined with the permanent presence of 2,000 troops, would pacify the rebellious Highlanders for good.

Work began in 1748. It took 1,000 soldiers 15 years to complete the complex of buildings within its hugely thick walls. Shortly after the first troops arrived in this part of 'North Britain', Fort George became obsolete. The threat of the Stuart kings in exile had finally disappeared and the project to create a united kingdom was now fully underway.

Remarkably, after well over two and a half centuries, Fort George is still an active army base.

Opposite. Fort George was built after the Jacobite defeat in 1745 and manned by 2,000 troops.

It has changed very little in that time and provides a fascinating day out for anyone interested in the military history of the Highlands.

Sarah Murray stayed at Fort George as a guest of the commander in 1796 – just a decade after the fort had become operational. The display of military might startled the good lady from Kensington: 'The entrance to Fort George struck me with awe; for as the carriage drove to the outer gate, "stop!" was the word, with fierce sentinels on every side crying, "Who goes there?" Thump, thump, thump went the horses' feet over the drawbridge, sounding like thunder. When I was fairly in the fort, they closed the huge gates, grinding on their hinges, leaving me in the midst of red coats, cannon, muskets and bayonets. I felt a little unusual on the occasion, something like being shut up in a prison, whence I may never escape.'

To the south-west of Fort George, and about 7 kilometres east of Inverness, the ground rises in folds towards the distant Cairngorms. Traffic on the A9 crests one of these folds – a long ridge between the Moray Firth and the green trough of Strathnairn. This is Drumossie Moor, the 'stinking hog's back', and at its centre, Culloden Moor. Because of the blood that was shed on its sour, sodden ground in 1746, Culloden has become the most emotive place in Scotland.

To mark the 250th anniversary of the Battle of Culloden, I was privileged to work with the celebrated historian and writer John Prebble on a BBC film about the Jacobite rebellion of 1745, which ended with the 'last battle' to take place on British soil. John was a wonderful wordsmith and evocative writer and we met several times at his London home to work on the script. His interpretation of Highland history had already had a strong influence on my own understanding. He told me how

he'd been inspired to write his now legendary and influential book *Culloden* after a visit to the battlefield in the 1960s. He'd wanted to tell the story from the point of view of the ordinary combatant – whether redcoat or Highland warrior – to produce a vivid and authentic account of the battle and the events that led up to it. His version of Culloden was informed by his own experience of war. John had fought his way across Europe with the Royal Artillery in 1945 and knew conflict and death first-hand.

John brought these insights into the writing of our script *Rebellion*, which I'll quote from to give a flavour of John Prebble's view of the Highlands:

Two hundred and fifty years ago, the Scottish Highlands were ravaged in the bloody aftermath of a conflict that threatened England and the constitution of the United Kingdom. Thousands of men left their homes and their families all over Scotland to join this rebellion. But what were they fighting for? Principles or a prince? Their clan chief or their country?

In 1745, Charles Edward Stuart, who is known to history as Bonnie Prince Charlie, arrived in Scotland with no money, no army and few weapons. But his ambition was great – to reclaim the thrones of the United Kingdom for the royal Stuart dynasty – exiled on Continental Europe for two generations. Defying all the odds, the charismatic prince gathered a Highland army, and moved south, winning battles and taking Edinburgh. In his boldest move, he led his forces into England, causing the government in Westminster to panic. But at Derby, just two days' march from London, the prince was persuaded by his generals to retreat. His campaign hadn't recruited enough English Jacobites to boost the cause, he was told. Furthermore, his generals erroneously believed that a large government army was marching towards them. The prince was urged to retire across the border. But in his heart, he knew that there could be no 'fortress Scotland'.

The Jacobites retreated and spent the early winter of 1746 in the lowlands. Despite their tactical victory at the battle of Falkirk in January, the prince was losing men – many were drifting away from his ranks as winter began to bite.

The prince came to Culloden House in the third week of February, having entered Inverness some days before. His army was sadly worn and reduced by the long march from the lowlands. Of the five thousand men he had taken to Derby, many were away home to their glens. Others were sick or exhausted. The Highlanders had crossed the mountains dragging carts of supplies through deep snow drifts, fierce snow storms freezing the breath in their throats.

The Hanoverian government army under the Duke of Cumberland had followed the Jacobites northward throughout the winter, never fully engaging – always threatening. In the second week of April, the red-coated army was now camped outside the town of Nairn, fifteen miles east of Drumossie. It was well equipped and harshly disciplined and a large part of it was composed of veterans of the European war. Ten thousand men

now moved eastwards towards Culloden, among them, four Scots regiments, spoiling for a fight.

At breakfast time on the 16th of April, over a thousand Jacobites were still asleep in the grounds of Culloden House below the moor. They were exhausted after a bungled attempt to surprise Cumberland's camp during the night. Some were bitter, some confused, others were angry. They were also hungry.

A cruel north-east wind was blowing as Cumberland's men advanced. Watching from across the sodden moor, four thousand Jacobites stood shivering in their plaids against the wind. In the next 40 minutes the lives of every one of them would be touched and changed forever.

At 12.30 p.m. the battle began. First, a cannonade from the Jacobites, answered immediately by the rolling thunder of the Royal Artillery, cutting swathes in the Jacobite lines. Provoked beyond endurance by artillery fire the clans at last surged forward against cannon and musketry, falling first on the left flank of the British. They broke the redcoat line, but it was then closed against them and the tartan tide fell back in a stumbling run. In the forty minutes that had passed since the first gun fired, upwards of fifteen hundred Highlanders – almost half the Jacobite Army – lay dead and dying on the field, the victims of the prince's ambition, and the overwhelming superiority of the government's military machine.

As the cries of the wounded filled the air, now clearing with the smoke of battle, the redcoat lines moved forward to take possession of the Jacobites' ground. What happened next secured Cumberland's reputation as a vicious and ruthless military commander. The wounded and the dying were systematically shot, clubbed or bayonetted where they lay. A group of wounded men found sheltering in a barn were burnt alive. Cumberland's dragoons galloped after the fleeing Jacobites, running them down on the Inverness road like vermin. Cumberland's men gave no quarter and assumed that anyone in Highland dress was a rebel. Like latter-day horsemen of the apocalypse, the dragoons killed all they met, including women and children, in an orgy of blood and vengeance.

Cumberland justified himself in proud letters to London: 'All the good we have done is a little blood-letting. If we had destroyed every one of them, such is the very nature of the soil here that rebellion would sprout out again, if a new system of government is not found in this country. I thank God that I was an instrument in this affair. I really believe that a month or six weeks will enable me to do all the things that would be necessary.'

Influential men in England, still alarmed by the early success of the rebellion, urged Cumberland on to do his punitive duty. The cultivated wit Lord Chesterfield declaimed, 'Starve Scotland! Put a price on the heads of all their chiefs, and let the Duke put all to the fire and sword.'

Cumberland and the government were intent on a final solution to the Highland problem. Their approach verged on genocide and ethnic cleansing. Their policy of savage and indiscriminate attacks on Highland areas terrorised the people and destroyed their food supplies. Those who had survived Culloden now faced starvation as the whole of the north suffered at the hands of a vengeful government.

With all Scotland under military occupation, Cumberland returned to London in mid July 1746 to a riotous welcome. Thanksgiving services were held in St Paul's Cathedral, and a choral work written by Handel, 'See the Conquering Hero Comes!' But in the Highlands, 'Butcher Cumberland' was a figure of hate.

Opprobrium spread. One hundred and fifty years after Culloden, the prime minister, Lord Rosebery, summed up the conduct of Cumberland like this: 'No blacker, bloodier page will be found in the history of any country than that which records the atrocities against a brave but vanquished enemy perpetrated at the command and under the eyes of a British monarch's son.'

Today, the battlefield remains a highly atmospheric and emotionally charged place. On the bleak moor, where flags mark the dispositions of the opposing forces, are several headstones. These were erected in 1881 by Duncan Forbes of Culloden to mark the mass graves where the dead are buried: Clan Mackintosh, Clan Stewart of Appin, Clan Cameron. A stone above another mass grave reads: Clans MacGillivray, MacLean, MacLachlan, Atholl Highlanders. Another two undressed headstones bear the simple message, Mixed Clans.

Culloden battlefield is owned and run by the National Trust for Scotland. The modern visitor centre and museum includes a 360-degree battle immersion theatre, which is designed to put the visitor at the heart of the action. But for me, the

A poignant reminder of the slaughter that took place at Culloden in 1746.

most moving and emotional experience is to wander over the ground where the Stuart cause was so brutally crushed. It's said that Bonnie Prince Charlie was shocked and in tears when he was led from the field on horseback.

The last time I visited it was the anniversary of the battle. A group of Highland re-enactors, dressed in tartan and holding aloft a Jacobite flag, processed slowly towards the giant memorial cairn. At their head, and negotiating a bumpy path in his electric wheelchair, was Donald Cameron of Lochiel whose ancestor, the Gentle Lochiel, had supported his prince to the end. There was a short service. Heads were bowed in solemn reflection. A wreath was laid, and some posies of heather placed on the headstones. The effect was very poignant.

PART SEVEN

**FROM KINGUSSIE TO AVIEMORE AND THE CAIRNGORMS, ON TO GRANTOWN-ON-SPEY
AND OVER THE LECHT TO COCK BRIDGE AND CORGARFF CASTLE**

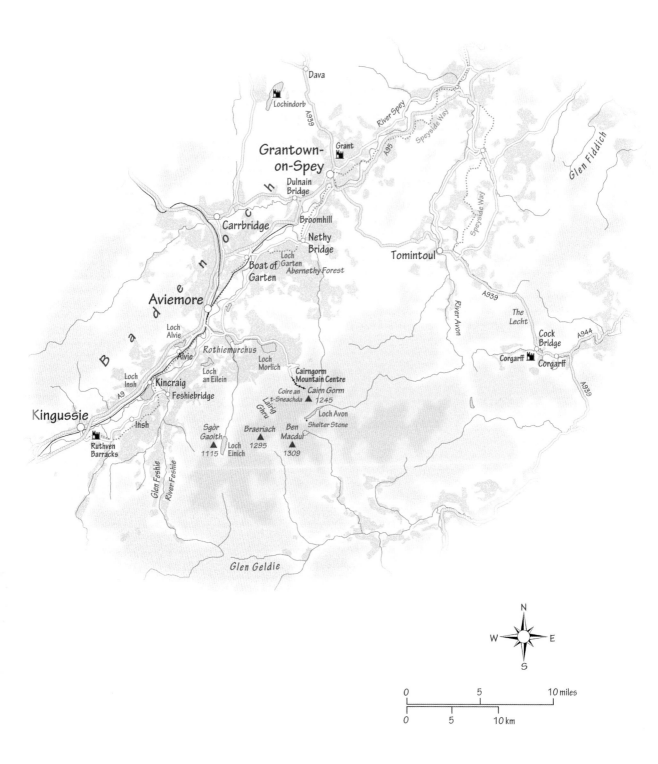

KINGUSSIE TO GLEN FESHIE

The Wolf and the Bishop – 'wild, wicked heiland men' – the peak of the wind

Kingussie is an attractive village lying on the northern edge of the River Spey flood plain. When I was a youngster, I often wondered who King Gussie was and imagined that his court must have been in the ruins of the nearby Ruthven Barracks. But of course, history has no King Gussie of Badenoch. The name Kingussie comes from the Gaelic Cean a' Ghiuthsaich, which apparently means 'the head of the pine wood'. The original settlement would have been a traditional Highland township consisting of turf-built, thatched houses surrounded by an extensive forest. The present village was founded in the late 18th century by local landowner and magnate the Duke of Gordon who designated it the capital of Badenoch.

Badenoch is an ancient district lying at the heart of the Grampian mountains. It was once renowned as a wild upland place of few inhabitants where the conventions of more culturally sophisticated areas were unknown. It was here in the 18th century that the author James Macpherson of Ossian fame built a mansion on the proceeds of his literary works. Perhaps he felt Badenoch a suitably wild place for a man whose reputation was founded on myth.

On a natural earth mound outside Kingussie – and commanding a strategic position close to the meandering River Spey – are the striking ruins of the 18th-century Ruthven Barracks. They stand on the site of a medieval castle that was originally built in the 13th-century by the mighty Comyn lords of Badenoch, a powerful family who lost

Previous spread. Dawn mist over Abernethy Forest.

Above. Standing on the site of a medieval castle, Ruthven Barracks was built after the Jacobite rebellion of 1715.

out in the struggle against Robert the Bruce for power and influence in Scotland. In the 14th century the castle passed into the hands of Alexander Stewart, the infamous Wolf of Badenoch. It was here, and at Lochindorb Castle high above Grantown-on-Spey, that the Wolf had his lair.

Alexander Stewart, the bastard teenage son of King Robert II, arrived in Badenoch in 1370. His mission was to exercise royal authority on behalf of his father. But Alexander had 'youngest son syndrome'. He was quick to anger, oversensitive, and had a deep sense of natural injustice. He complained that all his brothers were earls, whereas he was merely a lord.

Much to the displeasure of his family, Alexander decided to rule his domain with the use of excessive force. He terrorised the local population and ran several protection rackets, extorting money with the threat of violence. To help him achieve dominance in Badenoch, he called upon the ancient fighting traditions of the cateran – the elite men at arms of the Highland kindreds who supported themselves by raiding their neighbours and by helping themselves to the produce of their own clans. Effectively, the cateran acted as Alexander's henchmen, helping him to establish control over the central Highlands.

When the Wolf of Badenoch turned his attention to the wealth of the church, he found a clever and resilient opponent in the person of the Bishop of Moray. Alexander tried to extort money from the bishop, but the bishop refused to pay.

The two men became implacable rivals in Badenoch. Effectively, a turf war broke out between them. It was about money and power and who had the right to raise revenue (i.e. rob the people). A showdown seemed inevitable.

To avoid a calamitous conflict, they agreed to meet at the Standing Stones of Easter Kingussie. For a long time I couldn't find the location of these ancient stones, then an old map revealed the site to be in Kingussie village. The stones have long since disappeared. In their place is the parish church and a burial ground. But in 1380, this is where the bishop and the Wolf met in a kind of open-air court to thrash out an agreement.

Both men arrived, accompanied by a heavily armed following: Alexander with his cateran, the bishop with his knights. Alexander had bribed the court to find in his favour. Too late, the bishop realised the event had been rigged. Humiliated, he returned to his cathedral at Elgin.

Alexander's rise seemed inexorable. The Wolf was at the top of his game, but there was something missing: he still hadn't been made an earl. Taking matters into his own hands Alexander proposed marriage to the widowed countess Euphemia of Ross. When she accepted, he finally achieved parity with his brothers by becoming an earl. But the marriage was purely one of convenience – a contract that allowed the Wolf to expand his territorial range. Besides, Alexander already had a meaningful relationship with his 'handfasted' or common-law wife Mariota, also known as Mairead inghean Eachainn – a Gaelic speaking woman with whom he'd fathered several children. Alexander refused to leave her. Euphemia felt outraged and humiliated and turned for help to the Bishop of Moray. The bishop used the threat of divorce, which would have resulted in the loss to Alexander of his newly acquired earldom, unless Alexander return to Euphemia. He also contacted Alexander's family. The king now put pressure on the Wolf to toe the line. Bullied into submission, Alexander surrendered to their terms and promised to be a good husband.

Of course, it didn't last. Alexander had been humiliated and desperately needed to reassert his authority in Badenoch. He spent the winter of 1389 licking his wounds and looking for an opportunity for revenge. He found it with an attack on Elgin Cathedral – the 'Lantern of the North' – one of Scotland's great centres of learning and scholarship.

Alexander and his 'wild, wicked heiland men' (as the bishop later described them to the king) descended from the Wolf's lair at Lochindorb and set fire to the cathedral, the ecclesiastical buildings and the parish church. The light of learning had indeed become a lantern in the north.

Alexander had gone too far. The church immediately excommunicated him. To save his mortal soul from the fires of damnation, Alexander answered a summons to Dunkeld Cathedral where he was forced to make a public apology. Dressed only in his underclothes, he stood before the king and the bishop and repented for a second time. If that wasn't humbling enough, he suffered further humiliation: Euphemia divorced him and he lost all the lands he'd gained in marriage.

There is a local legend in Kingussie that accounts for the final demise of the Wolf of Badenoch. As with most tales involving an element of the supernatural, this one starts on a dark and stormy night at Ruthven Castle. It's 1394. A tall stranger dressed in black arrives at the castle gates looking for shelter. He is ushered into the great hall where the stranger challenges the Wolf to a game of chess. The pair play through the night, accompanied by terrifying thunder and lightning. In the morning, when the clouds finally clear, the stranger has disappeared. Scattered about the castle are the charred remains of the Wolf's servants. They've been struck by lightning. Inside the great hall is a chess board. The Wolf's king has been checkmated. Slumped in his chair is the contorted body of the Wolf. His body is unmarked, but the iron nails of his boots have been torn out. Who was the mysterious stranger? None other than the Devil himself, come to claim his own.

Visitors to Ruthven today will see precious little of the original castle occupied by Alexander Stewart. Except for the well, it was completely demolished and rebuilt as a military barracks after the Jacobite rebellion of 1715. Seen from the A9, the ruins are very impressive. Originally, they consisted of two three-storey blocks, each capable of accommodating 60 soldiers. The whole complex was surrounded by a defensive curtain wall. Although designed as an infantry garrison, stables were added to accommodate the horses of a troop of dragoons. They were intended to act as a rapid response force in times of trouble, using General Wade's new road which ran past the barracks.

During the rebellion of 1745, Ruthven Barracks was attacked by a force of 300 Jacobites, but 12 plucky redcoat soldiers inside managed to hold them off. When the Jacobites returned after the Battle of Falkirk in 1746, they used cannons to pound the garrison into submission. The building was then set ablaze. Three months later the burnt-out shell became a rallying point for Jacobites after their defeat at Culloden. Several thousand clansmen expected the campaign to carry on. But the prince was already fleeing for his life. He sent his loyal followers a desperate message which crushed all their hopes: 'Let every man seek his own safety in the best way he can.' It was the bitter end of the high hopes of the '45. The barracks was never rebuilt and quickly became the stark ruin it is today.

Before moving on from Kingussie, I feel I

The traditional Highland game of shinty is particularly popular in the villages of Strathspey.

should say something about shinty – a game that's played throughout the Highlands, but perhaps with more gusto and with greater success in the villages of Strathspey than anywhere else. In 2005, the Kingussie club earned a mention in the *Guinness Book of Records* as the most successful sporting team of all time, having won 20 consecutive league titles, and for being unbeaten four years in a row. Their neighbours and rivals just a few kilometres down the road at Newtonmore have recently overtaken them, winning the prestigious Camanachd Cup – the sport's grand slam – a record 33 times.

Shinty is an ancient game and has been part of the social fabric of the Highlands for centuries. It closely resembles the Irish game of hurling, and is a bit like a game of free-for-all hockey played

on steroids, being fast, brutal and, frankly, dangerous. As a boy growing up in Argyll, I played shinty at school, so have first-hand experience of the injuries that can be inflicted by a player wielding a caman – the stick used to hit the ball. There were regular trips to the A&E department at the local hospital, I remember, by boys suffering broken noses, split heads, fractured shins and even a burst eye when a caman made contact with the wrong sort of ball. For my part, I was always a timid player and preferred to keep out of harm's way, which was difficult when the gym teacher was yelling at us to play with full commitment. To make matters worse, our playing field was a gravel pitch. Every time a boy swung his caman, a player nearby got a faceful of sharp stones. But as our gym

Insh Marshes, a wetland habitat that is owned by the RSPB.

teacher was fond of reminding us, 'If it hurts, boys, it's doing you good!' A phrase that's stayed with me all my life, even if it's patently untrue.

North of Kingussie, the River Spey slowly uncoils towards Loch Insh, passing through the flood plain of the Insh Marshes – a wonderful wetland habitat that is owned and managed by the RSPB. The area covers approximately 11 square kilometres and is a rarity in Great Britain, being largely undrained and unimproved by agriculture. This has allowed a range of native species to flourish. Depending on the season, visitors to this National Nature Reserve can expect to see a wealth of wildlife: whooper swans in winter that have migrated all the way from Iceland, lapwings in springtime, redshank and snipe. When these birds make their courtship flights they produce an eerie thrumming call, produced by their vibrating tail feathers, a sound that adds to the wild atmosphere of the marshes. On Loch Insh, which is filled by the River Spey, ospreys regularly nest and can sometimes be seen flying over the water in search of fish.

The area close to the western shores of Loch Insh is known as Dunachton, an ancient name that derives from Dun Neachdain, 'the fort of Nechtan'. Nechtan is thought to have been one of the early Pictish kings who reigned during the early medieval period. Recently, it has been argued that Dunechtan was the site of a decisive battle between the Picts and forces of the ambitious Northumbrian king Ecgfrith in AD 685.

The Anglo-Saxon chronicler Bede, writing some 50 years after the event, described the outcome of the battle as divine punishment for Ecgfrith's barbaric behaviour a year earlier in Ireland, when his army had subjected the country to wanton destruction: '. . . the very next year the king rashly took an army to ravage the land of the Picts, against the urgent advice of his friends and particularly of Cuthbert, of blessed memory, who had recently been made a bishop. The enemy feigned flight and lured the king into some narrow passes in the midst of inaccessible mountains; there he was killed with the greater part of his forces on the twentieth of May.'

Ecgfrith got his comeuppance, it seems. But his defeat was more than a punishment for his war crimes in Ireland. The victory at Dun Neachdain was a decisive turning point in the seemingly inexorable advance of the Northumbrian English into the land of the Picts. Henceforth, the Northumbrians abandoned their attempt to subjugate the Picts north of the River Forth.

The River Feshie joins the Spey just north of Loch Insh, having flowed through Glen Feshie, which to my mind is one of the loveliest glens in the Cairngorms. Its grandeur is said to have inspired one of the most iconic Victorian images to come out of the Highlands – Landseer's *Monarch of the Glen*, which depicts a majestic 12-pointer stag commanding all he surveys. Ironically, this regal beast has come to represent much of what went wrong across the Highlands, when the management of great sporting estates led to environmental degradation on a vast scale. In Victorian times, the Highlands became a fashionable destination for the super-rich of the day. Great swathes of the country were divided up and turned into sporting estates – playgrounds where the wealthy could indulge their love of shooting things, and the bigger, the better. The more points on a stag's antlers, the greater the prize it became when dead. To encourage the leisure pursuit of killing, the Duke of Gordon maintained artificially high numbers of deer in Glen Feshie. This was extremely detrimental to the ecology of the glen. The native forest of birch and Scots pine, which was already being exploited for timber, began to suffer as deer grazed beneath the tree canopy, eating all the young trees and seedlings. Very quickly, the forest stopped regenerating. This was a pattern that occurred throughout the Highlands. Where once there were trees and bountiful wildlife, now there is often a barren wilderness – beautiful perhaps, but greatly lacking in biodiversity.

Today, Glen Feshie can claim to be bucking this trend. Since the early 2000s, a rewilding programme has been underway to restore the wildlife riches of the glen. On a recent visit, I spoke to the conservation manager of the estate, Thomas MacDonell. Thomas originally trained as a mechanical engineer, then as a fencing contractor.

'That's when the penny dropped,' Thomas said. 'I realised that if deer were being fenced out of land, that meant that there were too many deer in the first place.'

The solution was a programme of deer culling, drastically reducing the numbers down to sustainable levels to allow for the natural regeneration of the forest cover, without the need for fencing. In Glen Feshie, this approach seems to be paying off.

'This corner of the Highlands was basically a desert caused by overgrazing which produced a monoculture and destroyed woodland. The glen lost the bulk of its wildlife, but this fresh approach

Glen Feshie, one of the loveliest glens in the Cairngorms.

– allowing the landscape to naturally achieve its ecological potential – will see wildlife returning. I want to see field voles, foxes, pine martens, black cock coming back. Woodland is their natural habitat.'

'What about deer?' I asked. Will there be a place for them at all in this new landscape?'

'Definitely,' said Thomas. 'It's just a matter of keeping the numbers at the right level. But because there are no apex predators left in Scotland, that will have to be achieved by regular culling.'

'That's a lot of death to promote just one view of what a natural landscape should look like,' I said.

Thomas thought for a moment. 'The reality is, nothing is really natural. Conservation is a compromise. The landscape is the product of management.'

This is undoubtedly true. The whole environment of the Highlands has been altered by the intervention of human beings. I have filmed Scottish wildlife programmes for the BBC featuring red squirrels, capercaillie and black grouse. At the time, I was amazed to discover that the red squirrels had been reintroduced from another part of Scotland. The capercaillie I'd recorded in the woods turned out to be a descendant of birds reintroduced from Scandinavia. The same was true of the black grouse I'd filmed lekking during the mating season. And so it goes on, right up to the reintroduction of beavers and white-tailed eagles – and the eradication of hedgehogs in the Hebrides.

On the high plateau above Glen Feshie.

Heading up Glen Feshie, I could see evidence of the regeneration that Thomas was so proud of. Young pines and birch trees danced in the breeze, adding a new feeling of freshness to the already lovely scene. About 6 kilometres south of the car park at the road end, the glen opens out to wide, grassy river flats where the River Feshie wanders among great banks of shingle. After a couple of kilometres, having flowed past glades of pine and juniper, the river turns in a more easterly direction, cutting through the high ground on either side, where it forms a gorge with broken crags, water-falls and clumps of ancient pine. The footpath continues climbing south and east to a wide open *bealach*. Crossing the watershed, it then drops down to Glen Geldie and eventually joins the Lairig Ghru and the path to the Linn of Dee. A grand walk of about 32 kilometres, but one that is best done if there's someone at the other end to pick you up!

In winter, Glen Feshie is transformed by snow into an arctic world where the isolated Scots pines of its upper reaches stand out bold and ink-black against the surrounding whiteness. The hills rising to the east are generally great whalebacks with few distinguishing features. This can make navigation in snow and low cloud a disorientating experience. A high-level Land Rover track climbs close to one of the Munros in the area, but in winter, it is usually obliterated by deep drifts.

A couple of years ago, I crossed the high plateau of the Glen Feshie hills with my pal Gus on a day of ever-changing visibility. Masses of snow-laden cumulus clouds scudded overhead as we struggled through deep drifts. In the showers, the visibility closed down to almost zero, with white-out conditions. Wind-whipped spindrift stung our faces, making progress north painfully slow. But when the showers passed and the wind dropped, the low sun dazzled us with a billion rainbow jewels of refracted light. On the summit of Sgòr Gaoith – 'the peak of the wind' – came a moment of brilliant clarity. Far below us, the frozen surface of Loch Einich shimmered white, surrounded by snow-plastered cliffs and the towering slopes of Braeriach, its summit catching the first pink rays of the setting sun. It was a long walk back to the car park, and even further to the pub. But it was worth it.

FROM LOCH INSH TO AVIEMORE

Skiing and bloomers – capercaillie and lekking – ospreys and the Shelter Stone

Kincraig, on the eastern shore of Loch Insh, marks the start and finish of the Speyside Way, a long-distance path that follows the River Spey to the Moray coast, and on to the fishing town of Buckie, a distance of about 115 kilometres. North of Kincraig the path runs close to the main railway line from Inverness to Edinburgh, passing the picturesque Loch Alvie and the wooded hill of Torr Alvie, which supports a huge monument on its summit. This landmark column, which can be seen for miles around, was erected to the memory of George Duncan Gordon, soldier, politician and the last Duke of Gordon, who died in 1836. Close to the duke's monument is another memorial. The more discreet Waterloo Cairn is dedicated to

the memory of the officers and soldiers of the Gordon Highlanders who were killed at the Battle of Waterloo in 1815. Both of these 19th-century structures lie within the boundaries of a large prehistoric fort which once dominated the landscape.

The Speyside Way shadows the original military road that my 18th-century travelling companion Sarah Murray would have taken when she first saw the Cairngorm mountains, which are named after one of its highest peaks Cairn Gorm, the 'blue mountain'. Glimpsed through the window of her chaise, Sarah admired the view: 'On the opposite side of the river I saw the district of Rothiemurchus beautifully situated, bounded by the Cairngorm mountains, whose hollow clefts are filled with never melting snow. The cap of winter upon these mountains was a contrast to the luxuriant smiling summer below, which I had never before beheld and I was delighted with it.'

A little while later, Sarah entered the village of Aviemore. Here, disappointment marred her experience – something which all travellers have to endure at some time or another, even in the Highlands: 'Aviemore Inn was within sight when I came down to the side of the Spey; and my heart jumped at the idea of passing the night in a spot so grateful to my sensations, because nature there shines in its natural garb, and in high beauty. But no sooner had I put my foot within the walls of that horrible house, than my heart sank; and I was glad to escape from its filth and smoke very early next morning.'

Aviemore has, of course, changed a great deal since Sarah's grim experience in the 1790s. Today, the village is the capital of the Cairngorm National Park, which was established by legislation in 1999. As a mountain resort, Aviemore caters for a great range of outdoor enthusiasts. Within a short distance there are opportunities for mountain biking, river rafting, kayaking, sailing, hill walking, rock climbing and bird watching. The list goes on and on. But the principal claim to Aviemore's fame lies 17 kilometres to the south-east – the Cairngorm Mountain snow sports centre.

Skiing in the Cairngorms has a long pedigree. Decades before the road was built to the modern ski centre, dedicated enthusiasts carried their skis, walking for miles along winding paths through the forest and up bare mountainsides, taking half a day just to find the snow. The first person on record to have taken up the challenge of skiing Scotland's mountains was the redoubtable William Wilson Naismith. In 1890 he made the very first ski tracks in the country. From then, skiing in Scotland snowballed. Some pioneers bought skis from Norway, others who were less well-off fashioned skis from wooden whisky barrel staves. Although the aspirations of these early enthusiasts were generally high, their skill levels left a lot to be desired. Despite this, and rather amazingly, Victorian Scots were actually skiing in the Highlands before the sport had been fully taken up in some parts of the Alps. Female skiers on Scotland's snowy slopes were discouraged from wearing trousers or 'trews', which were considered unladylike, so instead women obtained bloomers from select shops in Edinburgh and Glasgow. When leaving Aviemore for the snow slopes of the Cairngorms, the women wore their skirts, but once they had gained sufficient altitude they would change into bloomers. They would then tuck their skirts under handy boulders and strap on their skis. There is more than one story of the mist descending and a lady being unable to locate her skirt – then being forced to make a bloomer-clad descent into Aviemore. I'm sure the

redoubtable Sarah Murray would have carried off a similar wardrobe malfunction with splendid aplomb.

The real skiing revolution came with the outbreak of the Second World War. The British army was contemplating taking on the Italian Alpini, who were crack Olympic-standard skiers. In Scotland, training began in earnest to equip soldiers with the new skillsets required in arctic theatres of war. Estate houses in Strathspey were requisitioned to accommodate British servicemen, who were taught how to ski and survive in the snowbound Cairngorm mountains. After the war, many old soldiers retained their love for the sport, and passed their knowledge and expertise onto others who then arrived in Strathspey looking for winter fun.

In the 1960s an access road and a ski lift were built to take skiers to the snow. Ski instructors from mainland Europe were hired to give lessons. I met one of these men, who still lives in the area, in a bar just outside Aviemore. Hans Kuwall, from Austria, gave up his Alpine career to teach Scots how to ski. What, I wanted to know, was his first impression of Scotland?

'Where is the snow?' he said. 'Coming through the mountains and over the Drumochter Pass, all I could see were bare green hills. No snow! And I thought, "Oh dear, I've made a terrible mistake!" At first we drove around in a minibus looking for snow – little patches where we could take our beginners and teach them how to ski.'

At this time, Aviemore was developing rapidly, modelling itself on Alpine ski resorts like St Moritz. Movie star Omar Sharif was hired to appear in a casino, lending an air of international sophistication to the Speyside village. In the new bars and clubs, après ski had arrived.

The forest at Rothiemurchus contains more than 30 million trees.

'It actually worked quite well to begin with,' said Hans, 'Especially when continental instructors were in the bar. With their accents and their foreign language, you really could believe you were in an exclusive Alpine resort.'

Those were the highs. The lows were not long in coming. The Aviemore Centre, which became the focus for ski tourism in the village, was built by the controversial and corrupt businessman John Poulson. He was jailed in the 1970s for bribing political leaders for contracts, but not before his planning blight had scarred the village with substandard architecture. The Aviemore Centre, which had been going downhill ever since the BBC's *It's A Knock Out* had hosted a rain-soaked winter spectacular there, was demolished in the 1990s. Since then, Aviemore has used all kinds of creative means to win back tourists, with a menu of activities that now far outstrips the original

winter sports that were on offer. This is just as well. Global warming and climate change have made snow an increasingly scarce and unreliable commodity in the Cairngorms. Diversification is key to the future.

Aviemore lies between two great natural forests, Rothiemurchus and Abernethy, which together offer a glimpse of the ancient woods that once covered large swathes of the Highlands. Rothiemurchus, which is mostly owned by the Grant family, covers an area of over 30 square kilometres and contains upwards of 30 million trees. The principal species is the Scots pine, which can live for over 300 years. Interspersed among these 'granny pines' are aspen, birch, willow, holly and juniper on a carpet of heather and blaeberry bushes, which together provide a diverse wildlife habitat.

Several years ago, I worked with wildlife

cameraman John Aitchison on a BBC Scotland series called *Scotland the Wild*. For several days, we set up hides and filmed in both Rothiemurchus and Abernethy.

On the forest floor, usually in places where the sun penetrates the tree canopy, large ant hills can be found. These mounds of pine needles are constructed by hundreds of thousands of industrious wood ants, which John filmed in extreme close-up as they went about their busy lives collecting food for the colony, carrying in building material, or just sunning themselves before disappearing underground where their sun-warmed bodies heated up the interior of the nest. The Latin name for these wood ants is *Formica aquilonia* on account of their ability, when threatened, to eject a fine spay of formic acid towards an attacker. John demonstrated this by lowering his hand above the ants on the nest. They reacted immediately by waving their mandibles and squirting formic acid from their abdomens. Apprehensively, I lowered my hand over the teeming nest. Within seconds, there was a strong and unmistakable vinegar smell on the palm of my hand. John told me that formic acid was first extracted in the 17th century by the English naturalist John Ray, who distilled it from a very large number of wood ants.

Later during this wildlife expedition to the Cairngorms, John wanted to film a capercaillie in its native pine wood setting. Rothiemurchus was the ideal location for this enterprise. We woke well before dawn and drove to a secret location in the forest where we met a gamekeeper called Archie who was going to guide us to our location. Archie, dressed in his finest stalking tweeds, nipped his cigarette out, stuck it behind his ear and shook our hands vigorously.

'Do you think we'll see him this morning?' I asked.

'Oh aye. No problem. He was there yesterday about this time. He'll come and check us out alright. But he's a grumpy old bugger and likes to show how aggressive he can be.'

As the first grey light of dawn seeped through the network of branches overhead, we cautiously set off through the pine wood. I was looking forward to meeting the capercaillie. A male can weigh up to 7 kilograms and stands about 80 centimetres tall, but they are an increasingly rare sight and now face extinction in the Highlands for the second time around. Hunting, combined with the loss of their woodland habitat, caused them to die out in the 18th century. In 1837, a number of breeding pairs were reintroduced to Highland Perthshire and the population increased rapidly. By the 1970s there were around 20,000 of them, but since that high point, numbers have been declining rapidly.

'He's a lonely old soul,' said Archie as we neared the place where he recommended setting up the camera. 'He's the only one left in this part of Strathspey. Normally, this would be the mating season for him and he should be displaying, lekking, to all the females. But there are none left to impress.'

'That's sad,' I said.

'Aye. And it makes him angry.'

At that moment, Archie grabbed my arm. Emerging from the trees and into the dim light of dawn came a huge bird. It looked the size of a turkey, with dark, blue-black plumage and a red patch above its eye. This was the legendary capercaillie, which in Gaelic means the 'horse of the woods'. Maybe not quite that big, but big enough to impress.

John got the camera running. We all held our

The capercaillie – a bird which once made amorous advances towards me.

breath as the 'horse of the woods' came closer to inspect the intruders.

'He's very territorial and can give you a nasty nip with his beak,' whispered Archie. 'So keep your hands in your pockets and stay absolutely still.'

The capercaillie unfolded his fan-like tail, puffed out his chest and craned his neck forward to present himself in all his magnificence. He opened his yellow beak and began to make the weirdest collection of clicks, wheezes and croaking sounds I'd ever heard emanate from a bird. I stood rooted to the spot, hardly daring to breathe as he

came closer and closer towards me. I looked into his dark brown eye. He looked into mine. There seemed to be a connection. He was close now, just inches way. Then suddenly, he backed off and disappeared through the blaeberry bushes and into the undergrowth. Archie grinned at me.

'I don't think he was aggressive and territorial this time. He was making love to you. That was his mating display! Do you always have that effect on birds?'

Having been humiliated by a capercaillie, it was a relief to turn my attention to a smaller feathered subject. I helped John set up his hide, where

With naturalist Rob Lambert at Loch Eilien.

he spent three or four days in patient solitude waiting to get enough shots of Scottish crossbills to make up a sequence about these rare birds, which are the UK's only endemic bird species. It was a difficult task. The birds feed on pine cones and spend almost all their time in the tree canopy, feeding acrobatically and fluttering from cone to cone. Given the height of the trees, the few cross-bills that were feeding, and the swarms of midges in the forest, John's task wasn't an easy one. But he never complained and always had a beatific smile on his face at the end of each long day.

The most famous avian resident of the Cale-donian forests of Strathspey is the osprey. Ospreys and the Cairngorms have a long association. In recent years the birds have come to symbolise the fortunes of the area and especially the National Park, being emblematic of a phoenix-like rise from the brink of extinction and a triumph for

conservation. I was interested to learn that Victo-rian visitors had enjoyed seeing Scottish ospreys and came to regard them as an integral part of the authentic Highland experience. But even then, people were concerned about their fate. As osprey numbers declined, early 'twitchers' visited Loch an Eilein in the Rothiemurchus forest to see the birds nesting on the ruins of the castle, built on an island in the loch by the Wolf of Badenoch in the 14th century. My Victorian copy of *Black's Picturesque Guide to Scotland* describes Loch an Eilein as 'the last remaining haunt of the osprey in Scotland'. By 1899 there was just one nesting pair of ospreys in the whole of Britain.

On an unusually cold morning in early June, I met writer and naturalist Dr Rob Lambert at Loch an Eilein. A chill wind was blowing across the grey loch. The ruined castle, overgrown with trees, looked gaunt and stricken on its island. In her celebrated *Memoirs of a Highland Lady*, Elizabeth Grant of Rothiemurchus, who grew up nearby on the family estate, The Doune, in the 19th century, describes how her family restored the ruins at Loch an Eilein.

'People were very worried about osprey numbers in Scotland, and they came here to see them before they became extinct in Great Britain,' Rob explained. 'The landowners at Rothiemurchus – the Grant family who had owned much of Strath-spey for centuries – were very keen to do what they could to save the species. They were the early pioneers in osprey conservation and guarded the birds at Loch an Eilein.'

Unfortunately, such enlightened estate management was to no avail. By 1916 the osprey was declared extinct in Britain. The last bird was allegedly shot by a clergyman, but ospreys had been persecuted for generations, killed for sport

Ospreys returned to the Cairngorms in 1954. There are now over 200 nesting pairs.

and taxidermy, destroyed as vermin by game-keepers, and their eggs stolen by collectors.

'Then something amazing happened,' said Rob. 'The big return happened in 1954 when a pair of birds – probably from Scandinavia – started nesting at Loch Garten in the Cairngorms. Immediately the RSPB, the Grant family and other conservation bodies set up a watch. But even then, the nest was disturbed by egg collectors. George Waterston, the director of the RSPB in Scotland, made a visionary decision. He decided to open up the nest site to the public. He wanted people to see the birds and to be enthused by them. He wanted them to feel as passionately about their future as he did. He realised that to save the osprey, public attitudes towards birds of prey had to change.'

The gamble paid off. There are now over 200 nesting pairs of ospreys across the country. Every year, over 300,000 visitors come to the Cairn-gorms to see them, pumping more than £3.5 million into the local economy. Is it any wonder that the osprey has become a symbol of good fortune for the area?

The woods of Rothiemurchus and Abernethy were once part of the domains of Clan Grant. They became a powerful force in this part of the Highlands after the demise of Alexander Stewart, the Wolf of Badenoch. By the 1600s, the Grant chiefs began to realise that their wealth was not measured in the numbers of their extended clan, but in the land they possessed. The forests of Strathspey became a prized asset to exploit and to nurture.

Maintaining the forests was a serious business, and actions that threatened their value were not tolerated. According to old clan records, in 1696 a young man was caught burning heather close to the woods. He was apprehended, charged and found guilty. His punishment was one that he never forgot. He was nailed by the ear to the gallows.

The trees that the young man had been accused of endangering were Scots pine, an important building material for houses and for ships. Cutting down the trees was a simple enough task, but transporting the felled timber from the remote forests of Strathspey was a real problem. The River Spey provided a solution. Trees were cut into manageable logs, tied together to make a raft, and then floated downstream. This was a highly skilled and potentially dangerous occupation. The men who guided the logs were known by the unglamorous name of 'floaters'. To discover more about this forgotten slice of Rothiemurchus history, I spoke to a modern forester and keen kayaker, Phil Whitfield.

'At the height of the industry there were between 80 and 100 men involved in floating the logs all the way from Nethy Bridge to Kingston at the mouth of the Spey,' Phil explained, as we carried two tiny kayaks to the banks of the river. 'It took between 12 and 16 hours to complete the journey, which is pretty fast when you think of it. The Spey flows quickly here, and you have to remember that they had very little control over their rafts of logs, and there were plenty of obstacles in the way.'

A few years ago, Phil and some friends re-enacted a log raft journey for themselves. By a miracle, the logs held together and they reached journey's end safely. The experience made a strong impression on Phil, who has nothing but respect for the men who were the floaters.

'The man charged with overseeing the safe arrival of logs to Kingston had the unenviable name of "chief floater",' Phil chuckled. 'The most famous chief floater was a man called Alasdair

Mor. He was the Clan Grant champion and a fierce warrior. Not a man to cross!'

Although Phil didn't have a raft to float down-river, he wanted me to experience part of the journey in a kayak. The one he lent me was small (I would say laughably small). I had never been in such a tiny craft before. Within seconds, it had turned turtle and I was upside down in the fast-flowing Spey, with my helmeted head bumping off the bottom. Phil came to my rescue. I apologised for my ineptitude and tried again – with the same hapless results. I was at the point of giving up when Phil suggested we make a raft of our two kayaks to increase stability. And so it was that I became a floater on the Spey.

As we navigated our way to Kingston at the mouth of the river, Phil told me that the town had once been an important ship-building centre. For almost 200 years, from the 18th century onwards, about 500 ships were built there with wood from the forests of Rothiemuchus and Abernethy. Today, there is nothing to be seen of the once active shipyards that launched ships into the Spey.

From Aviemore, the broad shoulders of the Cairngorm mountains rise like a breaking wave above the pine trees of Rothiemurchus. Unlike the mountains of the west coast, these rounded summits form a high-level granite plateau that was created about 400 million years ago when a huge magma plume rose from deep beneath the earth's crust. As it slowly cooled, a dome of crystalline granite formed. Millions of years of erosion have since exposed the underlying rock. Successive ice ages have exploited geological weaknesses, cutting corries and creating glaciated valleys. Today the high plateau of the Cairngorms is a unique habitat in the UK. Its elevation at around 1,000 metres produces a subarctic environment. Up

The Cairngorm plateau was created over 400 million years ago. Winter reveals its true majesty.

here, there are places where the winter snows never entirely melt away.

This is the haunt of rare alpine and subarctic plants, a place with a tundra-like appearance where subarctic animal species survive, like the ptarmigan and the mountain hare, which both adopt white winter coats for camouflage in the snow. In the northern corries, the snow bunting – a rare breeding bird in Britain – can sometimes be seen in summer feeding on windblown seeds caught on the ridges of the melting snow pack. When I was filming with wildlife cameraman John Aitchison, we climbed all the way into Corrie an t-Sneachda – 'the corrie of the snow' – with our heavy equipment. After an entire day spent chasing the buntings' call, clambering over boulder fields and sliding on old snowfields, we only managed to record a six-second shot of the bird we had come to film. Amazingly, it was enough,

and the full six seconds appeared in the final programme.

I was reminiscing about this one January morning as I plodded alongside Greg Wise, an actor friend and climbing companion, as we headed towards the cliffs and gullies of Corrie an t-Sneachda. Our plan was to scale the rocky and serrated Fiacaill Ridge before crossing the plateau and dropping down to Loch Avon and the Shelter Stone. From there we intended to climb the snow-filled Pinnacle Gully before returning to the car park at the Cairngorm Mountain ski centre.

We had been up long before dawn, and the sun was only just beginning to reveal itself as a halo of light radiating behind the cliffs ahead of us. A strong breeze was blowing, sending snakes of spindrift coiling across the hard-packed snow. We were both invigorated at the prospect of a day in the mountains. I have walked and climbed in

Greg Wise above the Shelter Stone.

the Cairngorms many times, but rarely in summer. Winter, I feel, reveals their true majesty. There is something intoxicating about the cold, when frost polishes skin, and nostrils momentarily stick together with each lungful of freezing air. The light, too, is ever-changing: the snow reflecting, dazzling and creating its own subtle shades and colours, from turquoise to purple, from lilac to pink, depending on the height of the sun and the depth of the shadows.

In front of us were a couple of other parties – early birds wanting to catch the moment and be ahead of the game. They were looking for the adrenaline rush of ice climbing on the various routes that Corrie an t-Sneachda has to offer. Our route was less demanding, but still involved an element of danger on the narrow ridge, which climbed sinuously between two dramatic corries. Once on the plateau, we made our way across an unbroken expanse of hard-packed snow to the summit of Stob Coire an t-Sneachda, before heading down to the blue eye of Loch Avon. I was amazed to see that it hadn't frozen over, although ice fringed its shores.

As we descended steep snow slopes, I was aware of the solitude of our location. Although I knew there were dozens of other climbers and winter walkers taking advantage of the superb weather, we seemed to be entirely alone in the landscape. This is often the case in the mountains. Highland spaces seem big enough to absorb a lot of people. Despite the number of cars parked at the bottom of a mountain, it's still possible to spend an entire day without seeing a soul.

After reaching the lochside, we made our way towards the towering cliffs and the huge castle-like buttress of Shelter Stone Crag, where our objective, Pinnacle Gully, breached its northern defences. Before we tackled the climb, Greg was keen to explore the legendary Shelter Stone, or Clach Dhion as it is called in Gaelic. This huge block of granite weighs an estimated 1,361 tons and sits on several small boulders, elevating it sufficiently to allow access to the space beneath it. Clach Dhion has been used as a refuge for centuries. In the *Statistical Account* of 1794, the minister described it as 'a retreat for freebooters' and was capable of holding 'eighteen armed men'. Early climbers used the shelter both as a place to camp and as an emergency refuge in bad weather. The first climbing club in Scotland was founded at Clach Dhion 'on the morning of the night of Queen Victoria's Golden Jubilee on the 24th of June 1887'. When we arrived, it looked fairly uninviting, being in the deep shadow of the cliffs that surround it. The entrance was also partly filled in with snow. We didn't go inside to investigate, but I've been told there is space enough for five people to sleep comfortably. Personally, being prone to claustrophobia, I don't really fancy it. The thought of that huge weight of granite just inches above my head would keep me awake all night.

After contemplating grim thoughts of entombment, we finished our packed lunch, roped up and spent an hour or so climbing Pinnacle Gully. A celebratory photograph after topping out was followed by the long return trek towards the headwall of Corrie an t-Sneachda. The light was already fading, and by the time we reached the corrie floor, darkness had engulfed the mountains. Winter expeditions in the Highlands are often marked by a long walk at the end of the day. Following the beam of a head torch, the only sounds are the crunch of crampons on hard-packed snow, the jingle of carabiners and the occasional grunt when you or your companion miss your footing. Memories of the day's adventure fade with distance, displaced by all-consuming thoughts of a warm pub and a well-deserved pint of beer – or maybe two.

AVIEMORE TO CORGARFF CASTLE

Clan betrayal and slavery – the Laird of Tomintoul – whisky smuggling

From Aviemore, the Speyside Way runs alongside the Strathspey Railway, which is operated and staffed by a dedicated group of volunteers. The railway was brought back to life in 1978. A 16-kilometre section of the original Highland Railway Line, which once ran all the way from Aviemore to Forres, has been restored to working order. Currently, the Strathspey Railway runs a steam train service from Aviemore to the village of Broomhill. There are plans to continue the line all the way to Grantown-on-Spey. As a fan of steam engines, I thoroughly applaud this initiative, although in my opinion, one of the best ways of seeing and appreciating steam trains is not to be in a carriage, but to be standing close to the line and watching them puff past in a plume of steam and black coal-smoke.

The railway and the long-distance path both pass through the village of Boat of Garten. According to early maps, the village was simply called Garten. The 'Boat' was later affixed as a reference to a ferry which once crossed the River Spey close to the modern village.

Grantown-on-Spey is the largest settlement in Strathspey and was originally built as a Highland new town, conceived by the big landowner in the area, Sir James Grant. Sir James, the 8th baronet, was the first Grant clan chief to be educated in England. Graduating from the University of Cambridge, he embarked on a grand tour of Europe. As a cultivated man of the world, he returned to Scotland to change and improve his estates, and in 1765 announced the establishment of his new capital of Strathspey, which he naturally

The Strathspey Railway Line is a short section of the original Highland Railway Line which ran from Forres to Aviemore.

named after himself. Grantown was then populated with tenants (most of them Grants) who had earlier lost their homes because of Sir James's agricultural reforms.

With its neat granite houses and elegant town square, Grantown was considered a success story and earned for its founder the title of 'the good Sir James Grant' – a benevolent laird doing his best to improve the lot of the people. As ever, the truth is more complicated. Grant took advice from a man who had seen the 'civilising' effect on native Americans of the new colonial settlements in North America and hoped that his Grantown would have a similar influence on the unruly native Scottish Highlanders. This fitted neatly with the aims of the British government post 1745 to subdue and pacify the 'barbarous' Highland population, reducing the likelihood of further rebellion in 'North Britain'. Grantown has a quiet charm, which appeals to visitors looking for a

slower pace of life. The same was true in Victorian times. With the coming of the railways, tourists began to arrive looking for clean air and beautiful scenery. Grantown seized the opportunity and began to develop as a dignified resort. About this time, the suffix 'on-Spey' was added to enhance the town's prestige.

A couple of kilometres north of Grantown-on-Spey is Castle Grant, once the ancestral seat of Clan Grant. This was home to Sir James Grant when he planned his Grantown. Over several generations, rebuilding, restoration and adaptation have greatly altered the appearance of the original castle, so that today it looks more like a mansion than a fortified dwelling. Although the castle's origins are said to date back to the 11th century, it was substantially rebuilt in the early 15th century. At that time it was known as Freuchie Castle, Freuchie being derived from the Gaelic for a 'heathery place'. In 1694 it was renamed Castle

Castle Grant, which dates back to the 11th century.

Grant by the aggrandising Ludovic Grant, the Laird of Freuchie. He had obtained a crown charter that combined all his lands into a regality – something which amounted to a big step up the social ladder. To project his new-found status Ludovic made a number of improvements to the castle and commissioned several portraits. These depict family members, servants and other clansfolk, including his piper William Cumming, and the Grant champion Alasdair Mor, who was also the 'chief floater' of logs on the Spey.

Heading south-east from Grantown, the A939 follows the course of an old military road built under the direction of Major Caulfield in 1752. From Strathspey, the road climbs over high moorland hills that mark the north-eastern fringes of the Cairngorm massif. The only settlement of any size in the area is Tomintoul. The village, which claims to be the highest in the Highlands, was founded by Alexander, the 4th Duke of Gordon.

Copying Sir James Grant, the duke attempted to bring order to a lawless and impoverished region by building Tomintoul. In this 'model' village, he tried to introduce productive industry in the form of linen manufacture.

The experiment failed, and the local population reverted to subsistence farming, cattle rustling and illegal whisky distilling. The local minister writing in 1797 claimed that there were 37 families living in Tomintoul, 'without industry. All of them sell whisky and all of them drink it. When disengaged from this business, the women spin yarn, kiss their inamoratos or dance to the discordant sounds of an old fiddle.' The same old story told by those occupying the moral high ground – how dare the poor have fun!

Morality wasn't foremost in the mind of a later resident of Tomintoul. Dubbed by the press the 'Laird of Tomintoul', Tony Williams passed himself off as a wealthy English aristocrat. During the

Corgarff Castle, which was at various times the home of the Forbes family and a military fort.

1990s he became involved in various business ventures in the area, and was admired locally for his affability, good manners and deep pockets. Quietly spoken, and often wearing a kilt, this tweed-clad, self-styled laird turned out to be a fraud living out a Walter Mitty fantasy. In real life Williams was an accountant with over 50 years' service with the Metropolitan Police. The money he spent locally around Tomintoul, including a million-pound refurbishment of the Gordon Arms Hotel, was embezzled from his employers. Over the course of eight years, he siphoned off £4.5 million from the police force to fund his life of make-believe. Williams was eventually unmasked, arrested and sentenced to seven years in prison. But many residents mourned his departure. He'd poured several million pounds into reviving the fortunes of the village, and his ill-gotten money had created over 40 local jobs.

From Tomintoul, the A939 climbs towards the Lecht at 645 metres where a ski centre has been operating since 1977. From the roadside centre, ski tows and a chairlift take skiers to over 750 metres to enjoy the snow slopes on the surrounding hills. From the Lecht, it's downhill all the way, whether you're on skis or not, to the famous Cock Bridge. The original bridge was built in the 18th century to carry Caulfield's military road. It was called the Cock Bridge by the soldiers who were building it. They erected a weathervane on a pole with a cockerel on the top beside the bridge, and the name stuck. In later years, a pub close to the bridge hung the image of a red muircock – a red grouse – over the door as an inn sign. This high-level hostelry was sadly demolished along with the old bridge when the road was widened in the 1980s.

From the Cock Bridge there's a view of a striking white building standing alone on a bare hill-side. This is Corgarff Castle. Owned by Historic Environment Scotland and opened to the public, Corgarff has a fascinating history, first as a private castle, and then as a military fort.

The castle was originally built in the 16th century the Forbes family of Corgarff. At the time, they were in conflict with their neighbour, Sir Adam Gordon of Auchindoun in Glen Fiddich. In November 1571 Sir Adam Gordon and his men came to Corgarff when the laird and his men were away. When the lady of the castle, Margaret Forbes, saw the men approach, she closed the doors against them. The Gordons then laid siege to the castle and set it alight. Inside Margaret, her children, and all their servants were burned to death. In total, 27 perished that night, a massacre that was commemorated in the old Scots ballad 'Edom o' Gordon'.

'But yonder stands a castle faire,
Is made of lyme and stone;
Yonder is in it a fayre lady,
Her lord is ridden and gone.'
The lady stood on her castle wall,
She looked upp and downe;
She was ware of an host of men,
Came rydinge towards the towne.

The castle was both rebuilt and razed to the ground twice during the turbulent years of the Jacobite rebellions. In the mid 18th century, at about the time the military road was under construction, Corgarff was fortified by the British army and became a barracks, from where soldiers regularly patrolled the neighbouring glens in search of fugitive Jacobites. After the final collapse of Jacobite hopes, the soldiers were redeployed to combat the illegal distilling and smuggling of whisky.

Illegal whisky production was long the main economic activity for many people in this part of the Highlands. Although small-scale distilling had always been carried out, it became really profitable after the union of the parliaments in 1707. The new government in Westminster introduced an English customs and excise system which put a tax on whisky, or more specifically a tax on the malt used to produce whisky. In addition, whisky producers now had to purchase an expensive licence to authorise their distilling activities. All this was regarded by many Scots as an unjustified imposition and only encouraged the boom in both illegal distilling and whisky smuggling. To give a sense of the scale of this black market, by the early 19th century, over 14,000 illicit stills were being seized from secret locations in Highland glens every year.

Whisky was king. *Uisge beatha*, the 'water of life', helped maintain the population of the Highland glens. A minister writing in the *Statistical Account* commented, 'While this infamous and demoralizing practice prevailed, population increased through the facilities by which families were maintained in the hills and valleys by its profits.'

In 1823 the Excise Act was introduced to tackle the problem. It now became cheaper to purchase a distilling licence and therefore easier to make a profit legally. Gradually, the illegal trade began to die out. In 1831 the last soldiers left Corgarff Castle.

Whisky is still a hugely important part of the economic life of this corner of the Highlands. Just to the north of Corgarff are a multitude of world-famous distilleries which employ a large percentage of the local workforce to produce the 'water of life' we love today.

PART EIGHT

**FROM BALLATER TO BRAEMAR AND THE CAIRNWELL, THEN ON TO
THE LAIRIG GHRU, WITH A DETOUR ALONG JOCK'S ROAD TO GLEN DOLL**

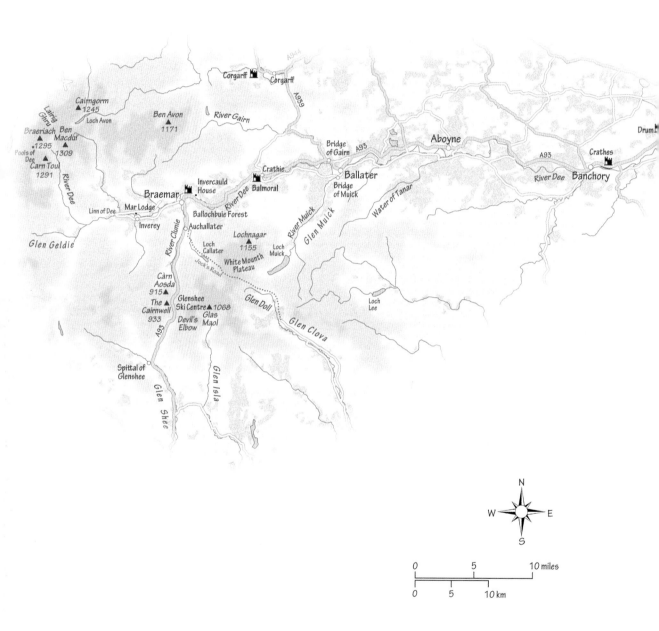

BALLATER TO BALMORAL

Tsars and spas – Dark Lochnagar – Mrs Brown's Highland paradise

Ballater is an attractive small town on the banks of the Dee, situated where the river takes a meandering detour around a wooded hill called Craigendarroch, which in Gaelic means the 'hill of the oaks'. With its neat, granite houses and grey-slated roofs, Ballater has a quiet gentility that is appropriate for a place that has come to be known as the capital of Royal Deeside. In Victorian times, the new Deeside railway, which sadly closed in the 1960s, brought Queen Victoria and her family to their Highland home at nearby Balmoral Castle. Over the years, a long succession of royals from across Europe and beyond stepped onto the platform at the old Ballater station. Kaiser Wilhelm II came with his father, both dressed for the occasion in kilts; Tsar Nicholas arrived with Tsarina Alexandra; in fact, nearly all the royals who would later go on to plunge Europe into the cataclysm of the First World War were at one time familiar with the streets of Ballater.

By the late 19th century, the original village had been spruced up and redeveloped by the local landowner, with streets and squares laid out on a grid system. My *Black's Guide* from 1886 informs the traveller: 'Great improvements have been effected in recent years, many of the old thatched houses having been replaced by neat slated cottages and an Albert Square erected.'

Previous spread. Glen Doll.

Above. Ballater, the capital of Royal Deeside.

The presence of so much royalty in the vicinity added a regal gloss to Victorian Ballater – and still does. Tourists arrive from far and wide hoping for a glimpse of the Queen, or perhaps a prince or a princess – even a duke would do. Failing that, at least they can breathe the same air as royalty. Interestingly, the quality of the air is also something mentioned by my Victorian guide: 'The village is a favourite resort in the summer months; and, on account of its elevated position (660 feet above the sea) the air is bracing.'

The air, combined with water from the natural mineral springs at Pannanich across the Dee, made Ballater a health resort long before the royals and the railways came. According to a local story, in 1760 a woman who was suffering from scrofula – a type of tuberculosis that affects the lymph nodes in the neck – began to bathe in the waters of the well. Her neighbours thought she was mad at first, until her regular bathing seemed to cure her. News of her recovery spread, and from then on the Wells of Pannanich became the focus of an early spa where people 'took the waters'. Visitors included some early celebrities: Queen Victoria came frequently with royal guests from Balmoral, Sir Walter Scott came, so did the 'mad, bad and dangerous to know' Lord Byron.

When I arrived in town for the first time, I was sitting on the back of my friend Jan's motorbike – a 1,000 cc two-cylinder BMW. We'd escaped classes at the University of Aberdeen for the day after I'd persuaded Jan, who was from the Netherlands, to drag his bike out of storage so we could go for a jaunt. Jan, who was doing a master's degree in Scottish history, had seen very little of the country he'd come to study. Before he returned to his family home on the Frisian island of Texel I thought he should at least do a tour of the neighbouring hills and glens. So with education in mind we set off on a bright but very cold day in late March. Just outside Ballater, Jan pulled over. He was excited. Lifting his visor, he pointed to a vision of sparkling white rising above the trees on the other side of the River Dee.

'Now that's what I call a mountain!' he almost shouted. 'From here it looks like Everest.' For a man more used to the flatlands and polders of Holland, even Scotland's smallest hills held a certain grandeur, but on this occasion the object of Jan's attention was the mighty Lochnagar. Draped in its winter finery, it was indeed a vision to behold.

Lochnagar is a majestic mountain, especially in winter when snow and blue ice plaster the cliffs of the great northern corrie. It dominates the entire district and has been depicted in art, literature and song, perhaps most notably by the poet Lord Byron. He grew up in its shadow and was inspired to verse by his childhood memories of the mountain:

Ah! there my young footsteps in infancy
    wander'd,
My cap was the bonnet, my cloak was the
    plaid.
On chieftains long perish'd my memory
    ponder'd
As daily I strode through the pine-cover'd
    glade.
I sought not my home till the day's dying
    glory
Gave place to the rays of the bright polar
    star,
For fancy was cheer'd by traditional story
Disclos'd by the natives of dark Loch na
    Garr!
[. . .]

Lochnagar, the mountain which inspired both Lord Byron and Prince Charles.

Years have rolled on, Loch na Garr, since I
    left you,
Years must elapse ere I tread you again:
Nature of verdure and flowers has bereft
    you,
Yet still are you dearer than Albion's plain.
England! thy beauties are tame and
    domestic,
To one who has roved o'er the mountains
    afar:
Oh for the crags that are wild and
    majestic!
The steep frowning glories of dark Loch
    na Garr.

Byron was the champion of the Romantic movement and helped to change the way people in
polite society came to regard the wild places in
Scotland. Perhaps inspired by his poem, Queen
Victoria made the trek up Lochnagar on a pony
in 1848, accompanied by her husband Prince
Albert. She wrote about the experience in her journal, but her account doesn't have quite the same

heroic ring as Byron's description. The summit
brought only disappointment: 'But alas! Nothing
whatever was to be seen, and it was cold and wet
and cheerless. At about twenty minutes after two
we set off on our way downwards, the wind blowing like a hurricane and the mist like rain.'

The experience doesn't seem to have deterred
the queen from revisiting the summit, which she
climbed on horseback several times throughout
her life. There is a magnificent painting by the
Bavarian artist Carl Haag in the Royal Collection
that depicts one of these royal outings. The young
family is on horseback; Albert leads the way.
Queen Victoria and four of their children follow
behind on ponies, led by several kilted ghillies and
retainers.

Lochnagar has continued to make an impression on successive royals. In the 1980s Prince
Charles was inspired to write the children's book
The Old Man of Lochnagar, which later became an
animated BBC film, narrated by the prince himself.
He even recorded a Gaelic version, which is pretty
impressive.

My first expedition to the summit of Lochnagar took place one summer when I was a student in Aberdeen. It was during the holidays, and at that time I was working as a labourer on a building site. Desperate to find some relief from the tedium, I contacted my pal Gus one weekend, and together we headed out of the city. Gus was on his CZ 250 cc motorbike. I was on my Honda 90 with L-plates. We headed west, not exactly channelling *The Wild Bunch* or *Easy Rider*, me putt-putting in Gus's wake to Ballater and then down Glen Muick – a bone-rattling experience that left me feeling exhausted before I'd even begun the climb.

I was grateful to leave my Honda and set off on foot along a mountain track. High on the eastern shoulder of Lochnagar, where the path winds over the *bealach* close to a top called the Meikle Pap – 'the big breast' – we stopped for a spot of lunch. The view of the great northern corrie was stupendous. Far below, the dark waters of the lochan of Lochnagar shimmered in the summer heat. Lying on a patch of exposed gravel close to the path, an adder uncoiled itself warily as we rose to leave. It slithered off through the heather while we dropped into the corrie and made our way to the bottom of The Black Spout – a dark and uninviting gash in the cliffs to the west.

As a name, 'The Black Spout' says just about all you need to know about the route. It's a long, steep and sunless scramble over a jumble of slippery boulders, and really has very little to commend it. We emerged like grimy moles into the sunlight of the summit plateau close to the highest point of Lochnagar, a place with a curious Gaelic name: Cac Càrn Beag, which I've been unreliably informed by my Gaelic speaking chums means, 'the cairn of the faeces' – although most Gaels would translate it as 'a pile of crap'. This, I feel, is an entirely inappropriate name for a summit that offers such magnificent and commanding views – unless of course you happened to have been Queen Victoria on her misty, drenching climb to the top. Unamused, 'Cac Càrn Beag' might have been muttered under her breath if she'd had command of the Gaelic at the time.

To the west and south of Lochnagar, the plateau of the White Mounth stretches for several kilometres. It runs up to the edge of the great granite walls above Dubh Loch and extends to the snowy Coire Loch nan Eun, which overlooks the ancient pines of Ballochbuie forest. Snow can sometimes linger all year round on parts of the White Mounth but it rarely lasts long these days. Interestingly, an old rhyme suggests a colder climate in the past:

When ye White Mounth frae snow is clear
Ye day of doom is drawing near.

It sounds like something Private Frazer of *Dad's Army* might say. Who knows? Perhaps there is truth in those lines.

From the summit of Lochnagar, Gus and I descended almost due south, following the course of a burn called the Glas Allt down towards Loch Muick – an ugly-sounding name for a spectacular stretch of water. Muick comes from the Gaelic *muice*, which means 'pig', although what the connection is, I have no idea. Whatever the etymology, this is a spectacular location, and one that was enjoyed by Queen Victoria, who built a lodge at Glas Allt Shiel, known to locals as 'the widow's house', where she planted sheltering pines. Victoria loved to spend a night or two out there, especially in October when the tops of the hills were dusted white with the first snows of winter.

To the east of Loch Muick, a path climbs up to the even more spectacular Dubh Loch – 'black loch'. It lies at over 600 metres above sea level and is surrounded by high cliffs and steep, treeless mountainsides. In my opinion, it's one of the grandest locations in the Cairngorms. Had Sarah Murray ever visited, I'm sure she would have found a plethora of adjectives to describe the sublime spectacle of Eagle's Rock and the dark wall of cliffs known as Creag an Dubh-loch, which cast an almost permanent shadow across the water. This deep shade gives the whole place a sombre atmosphere, even on the brightest day. It was in this dramatic setting that Queen Victoria's son Albert, the Duke of Edinburgh, once swam across the cold waters in pursuit of a wounded stag. He eventually caught it and killed the beast with his bare hands.

Albert would no doubt have returned with tales of his heroic encounter to the family holiday home at Balmoral Castle. The Balmoral estate, which covers a huge tract of mountain, moor, forest and river is the place that came to symbolise the love Queen Victoria had for both Scotland and her adored husband Prince Albert.

The real-life royal romance did much to enhance Scotland's reputation as a place to visit. Touring Scotland for the first time in 1842, the young newlyweds discovered a shared passion for Scotland and all things Scottish. Albert saw a reflection of his own German homeland in both the landscape and the culture. In Victoria's mind, Scotland gave her the space to be herself.

On their second Scottish tour, Victoria and Albert visited the west coast and the Hebrides. Although they enjoyed their time there, it was

Queen Victoria's lodge at Glas Allt Shiel sits in the most spectacular location.

Victoria's son Albert, Duke of Edinburgh, once swam across Dubh Loch – 'the black loch' – in chase of a wounded stag.

somewhat spoiled by typical west-coast weather. It rained nearly every day, but their enthusiasm for Scotland wasn't dimmed. When Albert received a letter from the son of his doctor, who was staying on Deeside and who wrote that the weather there had been glorious for weeks, Albert commissioned a report on the climate of the eastern Highlands. This concluded that the weather was indeed much sunnier and drier in the east. When the lease on the Balmoral estate became available, Albert bought it without ever having seem the property.

In 1848, the royal couple made their first visit. At that time, the old castle stood in the grounds. This was demolished and the new castle erected in its place. Designed by an Aberdonian architect, the grey granite edifice expressed Albert's own romantic vision of what a Highland castle should be. The very fabric of the building came to represent the consummation of the love Victoria and Albert had for each other and for Scotland. On the exterior walls are allegorical friezes that depict romantic scenes from legend. At ground level, cut into the foundation stone laid by the queen herself are the entwined initials V and A.

This was a place to be happy. Right from the start, Victoria felt that Balmoral was set apart from real life. She wrote: 'All seemed to breathe freedom and peace, and to make one forget the world and its turmoils.'

Victoria referred to Balmoral as, 'My dear paradise in the Highlands.' In 1852, a large cairn was built to commemorate her taking possession of 'this dear place'. In her journal, she describes how the whole family and their servants helped in its construction. On that joyous day, whisky was drunk, reels were danced and Albert climbed to the top of the cairn where he ceremoniously placed the last stone.

The young queen and her German prince loved being at Balmoral with their children. Scotland gave them the time and space to be a family. Secluded in their Highland hideaway the royal couple acted out their own version of Highland life. She wore tartan dresses; he studied Gaelic. They ate bannock, oatcakes and haggis. Guests often remarked that the family behaved less like royalty and more like country gentry. Inadvertently, Victoria and Albert made holidaying in the Highlands an aspiration of the rising middle classes, who began to flock to Deeside. *Black's* speaks reverentially about the royal Deeside abode, although noting that admittance is rarely granted to members of the public, and hardly ever when the queen is in residence. 'The castle at a distance looks as if it had been hewn out of one of the huge granite rocks which abound in this part of Scotland.'

The lucky *Black's* correspondent reports on the decor of the inner sanctum. 'All the furnishings give evidence of that simplicity and purity of taste for which the Royal family are distinguished. The carpets are of clan tartan and the cabinet work of African Ash.'

For Victoria and Albert, the Highland idyll was sadly not to last. In 1861, five years after the completion of Balmoral Castle, Albert died of typhoid, which he'd caught from the medieval drainage system at Windsor Castle. In deep mourning, Victoria returned to Balmoral, intending to spend as much of her life as possible on her Highland estate. Here she began to turn the grounds into a sort of memorial to Albert. More cairns were erected to mark the places where they had been happy together, others to celebrate the marriages of each of their nine children. The biggest monument of all, a ten-metre-high stone pyramid on a wooded knoll, is dedicated to the memory of Albert.

As is now well known, there was another significant man in Victoria's life – the kilted ghillie and faithful retainer John Brown. In the woods of Balmoral stands his life-sized statue, commissioned by the queen shortly after his death at the age of 56. On the pedestal is the inscription: 'Friend more than Servant: Loyal. Truthful. Brave. Selfless than Duty, even to the grave.'

After Albert's death, John Brown, who had been her husband's favourite ghillie on the hill, became Victoria's personal attendant. He had joined the staff as a 16-year-old stable lad and served the queen for a further 18 years until his death. The depth of their relationship was explored in the 1997 film *Mrs Brown*, starring Judi Dench and Billy Connolly. Whether the queen and her favourite were ever lovers is still a subject of speculation. It has been suggested Victoria was buried with a lock of John Brown's hair, his photograph and his mother's wedding ring, which the dead queen wore on the third finger of her right hand. Whatever the truth, their close friendship caused friction within the royal household. Victoria's eldest son Edward was particularly disapproving of Brown's influence. When his mother died, he had all Brown's letters destroyed and his statue at Balmoral removed to an inconspicuous position amongst the trees.

Perhaps the last word should go to Victoria. The following comes from a letter she wrote shortly after Brown's death: 'Perhaps never in history was there so strong and true an attachment, so warm and loving a friendship between the sovereign and servant … Strength of character as well as power of frame – the most fearless uprightness, kindness, sense of justice, honesty,

Balmoral Castle, which Queen Victoria described as 'my paradise in the Highlands'.

independence and unselfishness combined with a tender, warm heart . . . made him one of the most remarkable men. The Queen feels that life for the second time is become most trying and sad to bear deprived of all she so needs . . . the blow has fallen too heavily not to be very heavily felt . . .'

BRAEMAR TO GLEN DOLL

Bobbing John and Jacobites – Glen Shee and the Spittal – Jock's Road and the right to roam

Balmoral may be the only royal castle on Deeside, but there are many others with varying degrees of status. To the east, there's Crathes Castle and Drum Castle, closer to Balmoral there's Abergeldie Castle which was nearly swept into the swollen

River Dee during the winter of ceaseless storms in 2016, Invercauld House is close by, and, finally, Braemar Castle – an extraordinary, forbidding 17th-century tower house overlooking the River Dee.

Braemar Castle was first built by the powerful earls of Mar in 1628, for use as both a hunting lodge and as a fortress against the neighbouring Farquharson clan of Inverey, who were the belligerent vassals of the earl. In 1689, Jacobite forces led by the Farquharson 'Black Colonel' burnt Braemar Castle to the ground. In 1717, John Erskine, the new Earl of Mar, changed his allegiance from the government side to the Jacobite cause. On a small hill near the castle, he raised his standard and began a new rising in support of the exiled Stuart kings. The earl, known to song as 'Bobbing John' on account of his habit of changing sides, marched an army of 12,000 Jacobites south.

Braemar Castle, one of the most impressive of the Deeside castles.

Hey for Sandy Don!
Hey for Cockolorum!
Hey for Bobbing John,
And his Highland Quorum!

After taking the city of Perth, Mar encountered a government force of about 4,000 men led by the Duke of Argyll at Sheriffmuir near Dunblane. The ensuing battle should have been won by the superior Jacobite numbers, but Mar was reluctant to commit his whole army to the fight and retired from the field. This was a strategic disaster. Demoralised by Mar's ineffective and indecisive leadership, the rising fizzled out and Mar fled into French exile. In 1732, the Farquharson family seized their chance and bought the property. But it was once again torched by Jacobites in the rebellion of 1745. To this day, the chiefs of Clan Farquharson continue to own the now restored castle.

Braemar Castle lies a kilometre or so to the north-east of the village of Braemar, which straddles the banks of the turbulent River Clunie just before it enters the Dee. Originally there were two distinct settlements at Braemar, each facing the other across the river, Auchendryne and Castleton, the latter being described by *Black's Guide* in rather unflattering terms as a 'straggling collection of huts and houses on a piece of irregular broken ground.' In the 1870s, when Queen Victoria was sprinkling the fairy dust of royal association from Balmoral across the whole of Deeside, the two villages amalgamated to become a Victorian tourist resort. In many ways it has changed very little since.

For me, Braemar is forever associated with the bitterest of bitter winters. I have stood on the bridge over the Clunie and looked down on its frozen waters, and then marvelled at the length of icicles hanging from the roofs of houses. A hard Highland winter can transform an otherwise unremarkable place into a glistening wonderland. Braemar is justly proud of its wintry credentials and for a long time was the location of the coldest-ever-recorded temperature in the UK, a chilly –27.2°, recorded first in 1895 and then again in 1982. In 1995 this was equalled by the weather station at Altnaharra in Sutherland. Since then, nowhere has sunk lower.

Braemar continues to be a tourist village with visitors crowding the streets for the annual Braemar gathering – the traditional Highland Games that are always attended by members of the royal family. They dutifully arrive to watch the competitions from their pavilion, politely applauding pipers and dancers, hammer throwers and shot-putters, runners and caber tossers, handing out prizes to the lucky winners.

Two roads run south from Braemar through Glen Clunie and up to the Cairnwell: the main A93 follows the right bank of the River Clunie, while the old military road follows the left bank to just beyond Auchallater, where it crosses the river by a fine old bridge before merging with the main road. Glen Clunie comes from the Gaelic Gleann Cluanaidh and means 'the glen of the green plain'. Before the 19th century its fertile soils held a large farming community. The ruins of these townships can still be seen at places such as Coireyaltie, where low stone walls and raised patches of ground mark the outlines of houses and outbuildings. Higher up the glen are the fragile remains of dozens of old shielings – the mountain huts that were occupied by herders during the summer months when cattle and other grazing animals were taken to the high pastures. The road eventually crosses a pass that takes its name from

the Munro peak to the immediate west: the Cairnwell, which is pronounced 'Cairnwal'. The name derives from the Gaelic An Càrn Bhalg, which means 'the hill of the blisters'. I'm not sure if this is because the rounded hills in the vicinity resemble blisters, or whether the long road to reach the pass encourages blisters to form on walkers' feet. I know that the last time I made my own way up to the Cairnwell without the help of motorised transport I was tired enough. I had been cycling my Rudge Lever Tricycle. When I say cycling, I should more accurately say pushing, having given up the lung-busting, sweat-inducing exertion required to pedal my Victorian contraption up the legendary Devil's Elbow – a double hairpin bend on the old road to the summit.

Interestingly, close to the Devil's Elbow are several unsightly concrete blocks arranged on the hillside. These are remains of a Second World War defensive anti-tank barrier called the Cowie Line. Built in 1940, it was designed to hold back invading German forces if they ever landed in the north of Scotland and then tried to push south. Eighty years on, the concrete blocks and occasional decaying pillbox make a forlorn sight. I'm guessing, but I seriously doubt that the Cowie Line could have resisted the might of the Wehrmacht. More of a token gesture at defence, its obvious weakness seems to demonstrate today just how desperate the situation was for Britain in the early years of the war.

In the 1970s, the Devil's Elbow was straightened out when the A93 was widened. The Cairnwell Pass is now reached from the south with less drama, allowing easier access to the extensive ski developments that have grown up on both sides of the road. Skiing began in the 1930s when enthusiasts who'd learnt to ski in Europe came to practise

Glen Shee in the snow. The ski centre here is the biggest in Scotland.

their parallel turns in the hills between the head of Glen Clunie and the head of Glen Shee (from the Gaelic meaning the 'glen of the fairies'). After the Second World War, the Dundee Ski Club installed a tractor-powered ski tow. From then on, skiing became increasingly popular at the Cairnwell. Today, it is by far the biggest of Scotland's ski centres, with 21 lifts and tows sprawling across a range of four mountains and three glens. When the snow conditions are right the skiing on offer at the Glenshee centre can be superb, with excellent sport at all levels, from beginners wobbling on nursery slopes to show-offs tackling the difficult black run called The Tiger. The views are spectacular. From the summits of Glas Maol or Càrn Aosda the Cairngorm massif rises in all its white, arctic splendour, giving an impression of wintry desolation and vast empty spaces despite the crowds of happy skiers flying past.

During the summer, when only a few small patches of snow cling to the upper reaches of the mountains, the scene is very different, but the car park is often full of tourists and visitors. The chairlift up to the Cairnwell still operates, taking walkers to the easiest Munro summit in Scotland. Many years ago, my brother, The Professor, and I took this lift, encumbered by a four-metre-long furled-up hang-glider which we balanced across our knees. The Professor was taking part in a national hang-gliding competition, and the Cairnwell summit was the designated launch site. The day was beautiful, without a cloud in the sky. My brother rigged his hang-glider and watched as another pilot took off ahead of him, circling to catch a thermal to carry him higher. Once he was clear, the competition marshal gave my brother the signal. The Professor gave me a nod and then stepped effortlessly into the air. A moment later he had swung forward into a prone position and begun his search for lift, making wide circles of the mountain summit. Within minutes, he and his kite became a small dot amongst others, wheeling like vultures above the heather-clad hills of Glen Shee.

My job in this enterprise was to locate my brother when he landed. Precisely where and when this would be, neither he nor I could know. Finding him was therefore going to be a tricky business, especially back then when mobile phone signals in the Highlands were weak or non-existent. By the time I had travelled back down the chairlift and found the car, The Professor was miles away. I drove down Glen Shee at some speed, peering skywards, hoping to make him out from the other hang-gliders suspended in the vault of heaven, but I couldn't see him.

After a couple of hours I was growing anxious. Had he crashed somewhere? I then saw some nonchalant aviator types hanging around the Spittal of Glenshee Hotel car park. Incidentally, 'Spittal' has nothing to do with expectorating, slavering, spitting or groggling. It derives from 'hospitality' and indicates a place that offers accommodation and the comforts of home. As I approached the building, hospitality was being enjoyed by several hang-glider pilots, sitting together in the sun, enjoying a beer and discussing the highs and lows of their flying adventures. Among them was my brother. He'd apparently been picked up by someone else, which is why I hadn't been able to find him. While I'd been scouring the countryside thinking he might have crashed, he'd been in the beer garden quaffing ale. Typical!

To the east of the A93 as it passes through Glen Clunie is an ancient right of way called Jock's Road. Also known as the Tolmount, it starts at Auchallater and links Braemar and upper Deeside to Glen Doll and the Angus Glens. Over the generations, this historic path has been used by a motley collection of travelling folk; rogues and vagabonds, clansmen and reivers, Jacobites, whisky smugglers, pedlars and cattle drovers have all used Jock's Road

to traverse the high hills of the East Mounth to reach the fertile plain of the east coast. But because it's a high-level route, climbing to over 900 metres above sea level, it can be blocked by winter snow for weeks on end. This no doubt explains why it never developed as a road for motorised traffic.

In the 19th century the right to use the footpath was challenged by a local landowner who attempted to block public access. In the 1880s the Scottish Rights of Way and Recreation Society successfully took the landowner to court. In what became a landmark case for the campaign for the right to roam, the Society successfully argued that it had been the long-standing practice of drovers to take cattle and sheep over the Tolmount to markets in the Angus Glens. This historic precedent established a prior right of way along the route.

It has often been claimed that one of the campaigners in the case was a man called Jock Winter, and that the name Jock's Road honours his participation in the legal campaign. But apparently, the name Jock's Road is older than the court case, so exactly why the Tolmount route is called Jock's Road, and who the original Jock might have been, is something of a mystery.

It has been a long time since Jock's Road was used by cattle drovers or Jacobites. Today it is frequented by hillwalkers, many of whom use it to gain access to the Munro summits that rise above the plateau of the desolate East Mounth. From the car park at Auchallater on the A93 a Land Rover track heads south to an old shooting lodge at the foot of Loch Callater. The path skirts the loch before entering the narrow defile of Allt an Loch, where steep-sided hills and crags rise up on either side. Having climbed the headwall of the glen, which is dominated by the Munro summit

Davy's Bourach, the emergency shelter on Jock's Road.

of Tolmount, Jock's Road heads south-east across the exposed plateau. It was somewhere up here in the winter of 1959 that a party of five experienced walkers lost their lives in a January blizzard, when temperatures fell to −20°. Their bodies weren't recovered until the spring four months later. This tragedy served as a reminder of the dangers of the exposed high plateau of the Mounth. Spurred on by this thought, the legendary hill-goer Davy Glen built an emergency shelter on Jock's Road, close to where it descends to beautiful Glen Doll. Over the years, Davy's Bourach, as the stone, turf and corrugated iron howf is called, has provided a welcome refuge for walkers caught out in extreme weather conditions. It goes without saying that you'd have to be desperate to use it. The cramped, dark and decidedly damp interior is an uninviting place with an unnerving tomb-like atmosphere.

MAR LODGE TO THE WELLS OF DEE

Trophy hunting – the Lairig Ghru and the Big Grey Man – Braeriach and the source of the Dee

Returning to Braemar, the road west continues towards the ornate ironwork of the Victoria Bridge that spans the River Dee. From here an unmade estate road leads to the grounds of Mar Lodge, a building which, perhaps more than any other location I've visited, represents the apotheosis of the Victorian idea of a 'sporting life'. When I arrived, I was on board my Rudge Lever Tricycle, so came with an authentic period flourish. The Swiss-style hunting lodge was built in 1895 for Princess Louise, the Duchess of Fife, granddaughter of Queen Victoria. The principal reason for the Duke and Duchess of Fife to spend time at Mar Lodge, apart from dropping in on family members at Balmoral, was to participate in aristocratic pastimes such as hunting, shooting and fishing.

Although the sporting life on Deeside was all the rage in the late 19th century, its origins go back to at least the early Middle Ages. According to legend, King Malcolm Canmore came to Braemar in the 11th century to hunt for deer. In those pre-gunpowder days lines of men would beat the heather with sticks to flush the deer from cover. Once a stag was cornered, he was baited by the deerhounds and finished off. After the hunt, the local clan chiefs entertained the king with athletic games and music. Malcolm Canmore's après-hunt revels were the first Highland Games to be recorded in this part of Scotland.

Much later, when the joys of shooting with a gun were discovered, Scotland's potential as a hunting playground was quickly realised. There were just so many targets to choose from – wood cock, black cock, snipe, capercaillie, ptarmigan, mountain hare, roe deer, red deer – anything that moved became 'fair game'. In the 19th century, there seemed an inexhaustible array of targets for southern aristocrats, sporting gentlemen, princes and princesses to have a pop at.

In the early 1800s the formidable sportsman Colonel Thornton arrived in the Highlands and blasted his way around Scotland. He published his adventures in a book titled *A Sporting Tour*. His account became something of a bestseller, encouraging others to follow his trailblazing example; I doubt many were able to match the sheer scale of his military-style campaign.

The list of Colonel Thornton's equipment is impressive: three boats, extensive tents, six falcons, four setters, six pointers and a deerhound, 80 pounds of gunpowder, four servants and a housekeeper, porter ale and small beer, 'the latter being

a necessity I had great need of,' writes the good colonel.

By the end of the 19th century, hunting had developed into a sophisticated leisure-time pursuit, and few gentlemen were prepared to rough it as Thornton had done. All across the Highlands, sporting estates developed. These vast deer forests were centred on the shooting lodge. By the end of the 19th century, lodges offered owners and guests every modern convenience.

Mar Lodge set the standard in Victorian sporting luxury. In the entrance hall I met Chris Hewitt, the estate factor, who gave me a quick tour. As we wandered from room to room, under the glassy gaze of numerous stuffed stag heads mounted on the walls, Chris explained that Mar Lodge had been the last word in luxury when it was built. It had all the mod cons – running hot water, en suite bedrooms, central heating and discreet servants. Coming to the Highlands for the shooting season was considered a great event in the aristocratic social calendar and Mar Lodge celebrated this fact in the most luxurious way.

'The cream of European society were guests in the early days,' said Chris. 'Kings and queens, princes and dukes from across Europe came to enjoy the sport on offer. For most of the year, the lodge was shut up, but when it opened for the season – which ran from August to late September – the Duke and Duchess of Fife would arrive by train with their London staff, an entourage that included butlers, footmen, cooks and maids. This generally antagonised the permanent staff, who were mostly local. They felt that they weren't good enough for this metropolitan crowd.'

Chris led me to the Ballroom where he showed me an astonishing visual reminder of the insatiable Victorian appetite for killing. From floor to rafters,

The ballroom at Mar Lodge contains thousands of deer antlers and skulls.

the entire space is filled with a grizzly display of thousands of stag skulls and antlers, hung, I suppose, as an adornment, a monument in bone and horn to thousands of days spent in the most manly of pursuits – shooting deer. The National Trust for Scotland, which owns and runs the Mar Estate, advertises the Ballroom as a perfect wedding venue. It wouldn't be to my taste. Who would want to celebrate their nuptials in a charnel house?

To try to understand the lust for hunting, I met up with the chief stalker on the estate. Stuart Cumming seemed a cheery, practical-minded man with a wickedly dry sense of humour. He looked at me balefully when I explained my unwillingness to shoot a living animal. I wanted to shoot with my camera and not with a gun. I asked if he got many requests like mine.

'Not many. But we're getting more and more nowadays,' Stuart replied.

'I understand that deer stalking is an expensive business – is that right?' I asked.

'It depends on what you call expensive.'

'And what does that depend on?'

'How much money you've got in your bank account, I should have thought.'

'So how much for a day spent stalking on the hill?'

Stuart smiled. 'You won't get much change from £350. Plus VAT. Would you call that expensive?'

'Would a client get to keep the kill?' I rejoined.

'No. The kill belongs to the estate. But you can have a trophy. You get to keep the antlers.'

My mind returned to the skulls in the Ballroom at Mar Lodge. 'Well, I'm not interested in antlers or bits of deer. I want a photograph, so I think I deserve a discount.'

'I'm sure we can work something out for you. But let's see if we can find a deer first,' Stuart said, as we climbed into his Land Rover.

We did indeed find deer – a herd of hinds and

a single stag in a high corrie. To get within range, Stuart's tactical approach was to stay below the skyline at all times. This meant we were forced to do a lot of crawling and rolling around in the heather to get into position. I lined up the big stag with my camera lens and fired the shutter.

'Bullseye! If I'd had a gun, I'd have got him,' I said, demonstrating an innate killer instinct after all.

Stuart smiled wryly and shook my hand. 'Well done, sir. Good shot!'

When it was time to leave the Mar Estate, I remounted my tricycle and set off along the single-track road to the famous Linn of Dee. A picturesque bridge spans the river at this point. Here the Dee has cut a deep cleft in the bedrock, forming a narrow, slit-like gorge. Through this dark channel, water rushes and swirls in a white, hypnotic blur.

Beyond the Linn, I left my trike and exchanged it for a bike and a guide. Lee Craigie is a champion Scottish mountain biker and she'd agreed to lead me through an ancient right of way called the Lairig Ghru – a great, ice-worn glaciated trench that slices through the heart of the Cairngorms. Although it forms a natural pass, the top of the Lairig Ghru is too high and snowbound to have ever developed as a road link, although history records its use by thieves and cattle drovers in the summer months.

I was 18 years old the first time I attempted to walk the route from the Linn of Dee to Rothiemurchus near Aviemore. Back then, a twisted ankle had forced me to abandon the expedition. Later I'd used the Lairig Ghru to access the high mountains on either side, the Devil's Point and

The racing waters of the Linn of Dee.

Ben Macdui, but I had never walked the route in its entirety. Today I was attempting to cycle through.

Lee soon put me right about the nature of the challenge: 'It's a long way, Paul. It's well over 30 kilometres of rough track. It's rocky, rooty. Steep up and steep down. If anything goes wrong, you are a long way from civilisation.'

With this caveat, we set off at a cracking pace, although I quickly realised that the term 'cycling' had to be used loosely here. There was as much carrying of the bike – uphill and over streams and burns – as pedalling it. Keeping up with the Scottish champion was an exhausting business. Then I got my first puncture, which gave me a welcome break and time to catch my breath as Lee repaired the gaping hole in my inner tube.

Looking across the great glaciated valley, my eye was drawn to the rocky pyramid of the Devil's Point guarding the entrance to the Lairig Ghru. The English name for the mountain is a polite anglicisation of the Gaelic Bod an Deamhain which translates as 'the Devil's penis'. Map-makers obviously didn't want to offend their clientele with distasteful topographical annotations.

Puncture repaired, we were off again. The deeply scalloped corries of Cairn Toul still held the old snows of winter. Ahead of us, the slopes of Ben Macdui rose steeply to the east of the pass. Ben Macdui is Scotland's second highest peak, although for a long time it was thought to be the highest. The first attempt to settle the matter came in 1810 when the Rev. Dr G. S. Keith set out to measure the Deeside hills by carrying a barometer to the summit of each and reading the atmospheric pressure. A simple calculation converted this reading into altitude, an exercise that produced a height for Ben Macdui of 4,300 feet. When the reverend

gentleman dispatched his son to Fort William to measure the pressure on the summit of Ben Nevis, he returned with a number that gave a height 50 feet greater than Ben Macdui. Over the years, the methods of measuring mountains have changed, along with the values obtained. But the stark fact remains: Ben Nevis is still the higher of the two.

Ben Macdui, which has been described as the most arctic environment in the whole of the UK, is also synonymous in popular culture with the mysterious Big Grey Man – or *Am Fear Liath Mòr* in Gaelic, a supernatural being who is supposed to haunt the summit plateau. Although this now legendary figure has all the charisma of the Loch Ness Monster, and seems to have a folklore pedigree conferred by his Gaelic name, his true origins are obscure. It's claimed that one of the first references to the Big Grey Man was made by the Borders poet James Hogg, who toured the Highlands in the first decade of the 19th century. After a brief excursion to Ben Macdui, Hogg wrote in verse that he knew a man who 'Beheld the *fahm* glide o're the fell.' Apparently, *fahm* might either refer to a giant (*famhair*), or bizarrely to a supernatural mole (*famh*), as big as a dog, which supposedly haunts the high Cairngorm plateau. Whatever Hogg meant, he does seem to have been alluding to a mysterious creature in the mist on Ben Macdui.

The experience of Professor Norman Collie is perhaps closer to the image of the Big Grey Man. Norman Collie was a scientist and a pioneer of Scottish mountaineering. In 1925, at the general meeting of The Cairngorm Club in Aberdeen, he gave an account of a strange and terrifying encounter on Ben Macdui.

I was returning from the cairn on the summit in a mist when I began to think I

A supernatural being is said to haunt the summit of Ben Macdui.

heard something else than merely the noise of my own footsteps. For every few steps I took I heard a crunch, and then another crunch as if someone was walking after me but taking steps three or four times the length of my own. I said to myself, 'This is all nonsense'. I listened and heard it again, but could see nothing in the mist. As I walked on and the eerie crunch, crunch, sounded behind me, I was seized with terror and took to my heels, staggering blindly among the boulders for four or five miles nearly down to Rothiemurchus Forest. Whatever you make of it, I do not know, but there is something very queer about the top of Ben MacDhui and I will not go back there again by myself I know.

Professor Collie was the last man anyone expected to have had a supernatural experience. He was a rationalist and scientist of great distinction. His work in chemistry had produced the first ever medical X-ray photograph. Now this same man, whose forensic mind had lifted the veil on the previously 'unseen' of the medical world, was seeing things of a different kind entirely. His description of what had happened on Ben Macdui caused a sensation and attracted a good deal of press coverage. His surprising candour prompted other people to speak out about similar experiences on Ben Macdui. The legend of the Big Grey Man began to have a life of its own.

So what is going on here? Is there a such a thing as a Caledonian Yeti or Bigfoot up on the Cairngorm plateau? I remember reading a chapter in W. H. Murray's excellent *Mountaineering in Scotland* called 'The Evidence of Things not Seen' – a useful title when discussing our perceptions of the mountain environment and how they change with our own inner state of being. Here's an example of what I mean.

I was a teenager when I first climbed Ben

On the Lairig Ghru with Lee Craigie.

Macdui. My friend Gus and I were crossing the summit plateau when the mist came down. It was early winter and there was snow on the ground. Consequently, we could see absolutely nothing and were forced to walk on a compass bearing. This laborious process involves walkers taking turns to follow the bearing, pacing out the distance until the point they disappear into white cloud. The other partner then walks up and past, continuing on the bearing until he too almost disappears. Using this navigation method, I passed Gus in the mist and was crunching my way forward when I stopped. Although I could see nothing in the white-out conditions, I was convinced I was standing close to the edge of a huge drop – an unseen precipice that wasn't marked on my map. I called Gus over. Together we peered into the white void. Occasional snowflakes landed on my cheek, blown there by the updraft coming from the depths of the corrie below. Then the wind shifted and the mist lifted a little. To our amazement, we found we weren't standing on a cliff edge above a huge drop. In front of us was nothing more than a shallow depression in the snow. The mist and our perception of danger had transformed the entire landscape.

As we laughed at our mistake, I heard the sound of approaching footsteps. They seemed to be getting closer. I turned and looked into the blank wall of mist but there was no one and nothing there that I could make out. Still I heard the sound of heavy boots crunching across the wind-packed snow.

'Do you hear that?' I said, half under my breath.

'No. What?'

'Footsteps.'

Now we were both listening. Then I laughed for a second time with the realisation that the sound wasn't out there at all. It was coming from inside my head. In the mist-muffled white-out world, my auditory senses had turned inwards. The sound that had disturbed me was my own beating heart.

Fast-forward a quarter of a century and I'm making painfully slow progress through the Lairig Ghru following in Lee Craigie's athletic wake. I have fallen off my bike several times and have had two more punctures. Lee, perhaps understandably, is losing patience with me. We stop for a breather.

'Do you think we'll make it through?' I ask.

Lee wrinkles her nose. 'To be honest, we should be much further along. Our pace is definitely too slow.'

She pauses for a moment and then hits me with a killer blow.

'It would have been better if you'd done a bit more training, Paul.'

I wasn't going to get through the Lairig Ghru this time. Another failed attempt. Ah well!

To the west of us was the hollowed-out summit of Braeriach and the shimmering white of An Garbh Choire, which holds the snows of winter longer than anywhere else in the Highlands. Above the melting snow pack a long stream of water dropped vertically against the dark rocks of the cliff face. It was the infant River Dee, born close to Braeriach's highest point.

I'd been up there before, on an October day five years previously when the fragrant warm air felt deliciously smooth against my skin. I had spent the morning toiling along the path in summer-like heat, through the pine trees of Rothiemurchus. When I left the forest, I was dismayed to see low cloud clinging to the summits on either side of the Lairig Ghru. But as I progressed, the clouds began to dissolve, making giddying patterns as they unfurled themselves from the flanks of the mountains.

The path ahead continued to wind upwards and I entered a world of mist again. Scattered across the hillside were metal fragments – mostly warped pieces of aluminium. These were the remains of a Second World War aircraft that had crashed in October 1943. There were four men on board – a pilot, a pupil and two passengers. They were on a planned route across the Cairngorms, flying at a height of 6,000 feet. The pilot pupil was flying when the instructor noticed that the aircraft was being buffeted by strong winds blowing off the mountains. Suddenly they lost height. The instructor took over the controls and opened up the throttle to full power. But the plane kept descending, finally dropping into a bank of low cloud. Moments later it crashed into the summit of Braeriach. Amazingly, all four men survived. Despite suffering injuries that included a broken arm, concussion, cuts and bruises, they were able to walk down the mountain to a farmhouse near Aviemore.

As I continued my upward slog towards the summit of Braeriach, the mist began to thin again, unveiling a dazzling world. I had climbed out of the cloud and into the blue. Below me, the cloud extended towards the horizon like a vaporous ice sheet. In this sea of white were a few dark islands. These were the tops of the highest mountains: Cairngorm, Ben Macdui, Cairn Toul, the Devil's Peak, and away in the distance – and looking as lonely as a desert atoll, dark Lochnagar. But even as I watched, the cloud filling the Lairig Ghru began to sink slowly – as if draining away – revealing more of the surrounding landscape.

Under a brilliant sun, I dropped off the summit towards a patch of ground marked on my map by small blue circles. These were the Wells of Dee – the ultimate source of the great River Dee and a place I'd wanted to visit ever since reading Nan Shepherd's wonderfully poetic book *The Living Mountain*. This is how she described the sight of the embryonic Dee: 'This is the river . . . Like all profound mysteries, it is so simple that it frightens me. It wells from the rock and flows away. For unnumbered years it has welled from the rock, and flowed away. It does nothing, absolutely nothing, but be itself.'

I dipped in my hand, scooped out some of this infant river water and savoured its chill, fresh mountain taste. From the Wells, the crystal-clear water gathers into rivulets and becomes a stream. I followed its progress across the high plateau for about 500 metres and watched as it tumbled over the cliff edge and disappeared into the cloud-filled hollow of An Garbh Choire. A rainbow hung above the ethereal mist below. It was a visionary experience, putting me in touch with something primal and out of this world.

FURTHER READING

Baker, Patrick, *The Cairngorms: A Secret History*, Birlinn, new edn. 2021

Baker, Patrick, *The Unremembered Places: Exploring Scotland's Wild Histories*, Birlinn, 2020

Black, Adam and Charles, *Black's Picturesque Guide to Scotland*, 1840

Boardman, Stephen, *The Wolf of Badenoch*, John Donald 2012

Borthwick, Alastair, *Always a Little Further*, Faber & Faber 1939

Burt, Edmund, *Burt's Letters from the North of Scotland*, Birlinn 1998

Douglas, Hugh, *The Private Passions of Bonnie Prince Charlie*, Sutton Publishing 1998

Gordon, Seton, *Highways and Byways in the Central Highlands*, Macmillan 1948

Gordon, Seton, *The Cairngorm Hills of Scotland*, Cassell 1925

Gray, Affleck, *The Big Grey Man of Ben Macdhui*, Birlinn, 2013

Haldane, A.R.B., *The Drove Roads of Scotland*, Birlinn 2015

Hunter, James, *The Last of the Free: A Millennial History of the Highlands and Islands of Scotland*, Mainstream 2000

Jones, Bill, *Black Camp 21*, Polygon 2018

Keay, John, *Highland Drove*, John Murray 1984

Leaves from the Journal of Our Life in the Highlands Queen Victoria 1848 to 1861, Kessinger 2010

Linklater, Eric, *The Prince in the Heather: The Story of Bonnie Prince Charlie's Escape*, Hodder and Stoughton 1965

MacGill, Patrick, *Children of the Dead End*, Leopold Classic Library 2016

McGregor, John, *The New Railway: The Earliest Years of the West Highland Line*, Amberley 2105

McHardy, Stuart, *The School of the Moon: The Highland Cattle-raiding Tradition* Birlinn 2004

McKirdy, Alan, *Set in Stone – The Geology and Landscapes of Scotland*, Birlinn 2015

Miller, Joyce, *Magic and Witchcraft in Scotland*, Goblinshead 2004

Mitchell, Ian, *Mountain Outlaw: Encounters with Ewan Macphee*, Luath Press 2003

Mitchell, Ian, *Scotland's Mountains before the Mountaineers*, Luath Press 2004

Mountain Moor and Loch, Causton and Sons 1894

Munro, Neil, *The New Road*, William Blackwood & Sons 1928

Murray, Sarah, *A Companion and Useful Guide to the Beauties of Scotland*, Byway Books 1982

Murray, W.H., *Undiscovered Scotland*, J.M. Dent & Sons 1951

Murray, W.H., *Mountaineering in Scotland*, J.M. Dent & Sons 1947

Pennant, Thomas, *A Tour in Scotland and Voyage to the Hebrides*, Birlinn 2019

Pennell, Elizabeth Robins and Joseph, *Our Journey to the Hebrides*, Franklin Classics 2018

Prebble, John, *Culloden*, Penguin 1969

Prebble, John, *Glencoe*, Penguin 1973

Prebble, John, *Mutiny*, Penguin 1977

Riding, Jacqueline, *Jacobites: A New History of the '45 Rebellion*, Bloomsbury 2017

Robertson, James Irvine, *The Poet Chief*, Alexander Robertson 13th of Struan, 1670–1749, Librario Publishing, 2011

Scott, Sir Walter, *Rob Roy*, Archibald Constable 1817

Scott, Sir Walter, *The Lady of the Lake*, John Ballantyne & Co. 1810

Seward, Desmond, *The Jacobites: A Complete History*, Birlinn, 2019

Shepherd, Nan, *The Living Mountain*, Canongate 2011

Smith, Jess, *The Way of the Wanderers*, Birlinn 2015

Stevenson, David, *Highland Warrior: Alasdair MacColla and the Civil Wars*, John Donald 2003

Stevenson, David, *The Hunt for Rob Roy: The Man and the Myths*, Birlinn 2016

Stevenson, Robert Louis, *Kidnapped*, Cassell and Co. Ltd 1886

Thompson, Francis, *The Supernatural Highlands*, Luath Press 1997

Tranter, Nigel, *Rob Roy MacGregor*, Neil Wilson Publishing 2021

Wordsworth, Dorothy *Recollections of a Tour Made in Scotland*, Yale University Press 1997

INDEX

PICTURE CREDITS